Brian Hart
with Herbert Puchta & Jeff Stranks

English in Mind

Second edition

Teacher's Resource
Book 2

CAMBRIDGE UNIVERSITY PRESS
Cambridge, New York, Melbourne, Madrid, Cape Town,
Singapore, São Paulo, Delhi, Mexico City

Cambridge University Press
The Edinburgh Building, Cambridge CB2 8RU, UK

www.cambridge.org
Information on this title: www.cambridge.org/9780521170369

© Cambridge University Press 2010

It is normally necessary for written permission for copying to be obtained *in advance* from a publisher. The worksheets, role playcards, tests and tapescripts at the back of this book are designed to be copied and distributed in class. The normal requirements are waived here and it is not necessary to write to Cambridge University Press for permission for an individual teacher to make copies for use within his or her own classroom. Only those pages which carry the wording 'PHOTOCOPIABLE © Cambridge University Press' may be copied.

First published 2004
Second edition 2010
6th printing 2013

Printed in Poland by Opolgraf

A catalogue record for this publication is available from the British Library

ISBN 978-0-521-17036-9 Teacher's Resource Book
ISBN 978-0-521-15609-7 Student's Book with DVD-ROM
ISBN 978-0-521-12300-6 Workbook
ISBN 978-0-521-18336-9 Audio CDs (3)
ISBN 978-0-521-13684-9 Testmaker Audio CD/CD-ROM
ISBN 978-0-521-15932-6 DVD (PAL)
ISBN 978-0-521-18448-7 DVD (NTSC)
ISBN 978-0-521-12353-4 Classware DVD-ROM

Cambridge University Press has no responsibility for the persistence or accuracy of URLs for external or third-party internet websites referred to in this publication, and does not guarantee that any content on such websites is, or will remain, accurate or appropriate. Information regarding prices, travel timetables and other factual information given in this work is correct at the time of first printing but Cambridge University Press does not guarantee the accuracy of such information thereafter.

Contents

Map of Student's Book	4
Introduction	6

Teacher's notes and keys

Welcome section		10
1	Great idea!	16
2	He ran faster	22
	Check your progress	28
3	Our world	30
4	Holiday or vacation?	37
	Check your progress	43
5	Growing up	45
6	Have fun!	52
	Check your progress	57
7	Disaster!	59
8	Ways of living	65
	Check your progress	71
9	Your mind	73
10	Music makers	79
	Check your progress	85
11	A visit to the doctor's	87
12	If I had …	94
	Check your progress	100
13	Lost worlds	102
14	A stroke of luck	108
	Check your progress	114

Pronunciation	116
Get it right! key	120
Projects	121
Workbook key	123
Entry Test A	136
Entry Test B	137
Entry Test C	138
Entry Test D	139
Entry Tests key	140
Teaching notes for communication activities and grammar practice	141
Communication and grammar 1–14	149

3

	Welcome section	A Present simple; present continuous; *have to / don't have to*; hobbies and interests; jobs	B Past simple; *much/many*; *some/any*; comparative and superlative adjectives; food; multi-word verbs	

Unit	Grammar	Vocabulary	Pronunciation
1 Great idea!	Past continuous Past continuous vs. past simple; *when* and *while*	Phrases with *get* Vocabulary bank: phrases with *get*	*was* and *were*
2 He ran faster	Comparative and superlative adjectives Intensifiers with comparatives *(not) as … as* Adverbs / comparative adverbs	Antonyms Sport Vocabulary bank: sport	*than* and *as*
CHECK YOUR PROGRESS			
3 Our world	*will/won't* *might/may (not)* *if/unless* + first conditional	The environment	/əʊ/ *won't*
4 Holiday or vacation?	Question tags Present perfect simple, *just / already / yet*	British vs. North American English Vocabulary bank: North American and British English	Intonation in question tags
CHECK YOUR PROGRESS			
5 Growing up	Present simple passive *let / be allowed to*	Describing a person's age Vocabulary bank: talking about people's ages	/aʊ/ *allowed*
6 Have fun!	Present perfect simple *for* vs. *since*	Verb and noun pairs Vocabulary bank: verb and noun pairs	*have*, *has* and *for*
CHECK YOUR PROGRESS			
7 Disaster!	Past simple passive *a*, *an*, *the* or zero article	Disasters Vocabulary bank: disasters	'Silent' letters
8 Ways of living	*too much/many* + *not enough* *will* vs. *be going to*	Homes Vocabulary bank: houses/homes	Sound and spelling: *-ou-*
CHECK YOUR PROGRESS			
9 Your mind	Determiners (*everyone / no one / someone* etc.) *must/mustn't* vs. *don't have to*	Thinking Vocabulary bank: thinking	*must*
10 Music makers	Present perfect continuous Present perfect simple and continuous	Music and musical instruments Vocabulary bank: music and musical instruments	Sentence stress: rhythm
CHECK YOUR PROGRESS			
11 A visit to the doctor's	Defining relative clauses *used to*	Medicine Vocabulary bank: medicine	/z/ or /s/ in *used*
12 If I had …	Second conditional	Information technology and computers Vocabulary bank: electrical matters	*'d*
CHECK YOUR PROGRESS			
13 Lost worlds	Past perfect	Noun suffixes, *-r*, *-er*, *-or* and *-ist*	*had* and *'d*
14 A stroke of luck	Reported statements Third conditional	Noun suffixes, *-ation* and *-ment* Vocabulary bank: luck	*would* (*'d*) *have / wouldn't have*
CHECK YOUR PROGRESS			

Pronunciation • Vocabulary bank • Get it right! • Projects • Speaking B • Irregular verbs and phonetics

C will/won't; too + adjective; adverbs; be going to; expressions to talk about the future; future time expressions; the weather

D First conditional; should/shouldn't; present perfect with ever/never; adjectives for feelings and opinions; personality adjectives

Speaking & Functions	Listening	Reading	Writing
Describing past activities Discussion: music	Science fiction story	Article: What did they invent? Article: Be an inventor! Culture in mind: The history of listening to music	Story about an invention
Making comparisons Apologising Last but not least: talking about sport	Talk: Olympic medallists	Article: Australia almost the champions Photostory: A marathon	Report about a sports event
Discussing environmental problems Predicting future events Discussion: using water responsibly	Interview: water as a natural resource Song: Big Yellow Taxi	Article: Bicycle revolution? Culture in mind: Water as a natural resource	Website article about your town
Checking information Asking about habits, routines, likes and dislikes Last but not least: exchanging information about Canada and the USA	Answering a quiz about Canada & the USA Conversation about things recently done	Quiz: Canada & the USA Opinion postings: Is free wireless internet a good idea for Vancouver? Photostory: New girl	Email about a holiday
Describing a ceremony Retelling a story Talking about permission	Story from Papua New Guinea Dialogue about minimum ages Quiz about minimum ages	Article: Where boys become crocodile men Quiz: How old do you have to be? Culture in mind: Coming of age in Japan	Magazine article about a special day
Talking about unfinished situations Expressing different points of view Last but not least: talking about having fun and laughing	Song: Don't Worry, Be Happy	Article: The power of humour Questionnaire: Are you fun to be with? Photostory: Very funny!	Email about how you have fun
Exchanging information about past events Describing a dream Talking about natural disasters and environmental issues	Interview: a famous hurricane	Informative text: A flying disaster Culture in mind: Tuvalu	Newspaper story about a forest fire
Describing quantity Talking about your town, country and home Last but not least: talking about future plans	Descriptions of homes	Brochure: A holiday in a cave Email about a holiday Photostory: All over the place	Email about a plan for a holiday
Talking about how you learn best Discussion: talent and intelligences	Interview: 'multiple intelligences'	Article: Your brain is like a muscle Culture in mind: Girl genius, university student at 15!	Competition entry
Describing recently completed and unfinished actions Giving advice Last but not least: talking about music and becoming a pop star	Identifying different types of music People talking about music and musical instruments	Article: Music that changes lives Photostory: Talent? Me?	Letter about your favourite type of music
Expressing past habits Discussing medical problems	Dialogues at the doctor's Dialogue about Joseph Lister Song: Run That Body Down	Article: Medicine in the past Culture in mind: Médecins Sans Frontières: Doctors without Borders	Article about a famous scientist
Giving advice Talking about unreal situations and problems Last but not least: discussing computers and the internet	Descriptions of problems caused by computers	Survey on the internet Article: On the internet, it's girl time! Photostory: Don't judge a book ...	Competition entry
Describing events in the past and earlier past Telling a picture story Talking about 'mythical cities'	Radio programme: the paintings of Lascaux	Article: A city in the jungle Culture in mind: Mythical cities	Short story
Reporting past events Last but not least: discussing popular sayings	Conversation: an unlucky day Song: Lucky Day	Article: The man with seven lives Photostory: Nervous about the exams	Email to apologise

MAP 5

Introduction

> *'If you can teach teenagers, you can teach anyone.'* Michael Grinder

Teaching teenagers is an interesting and challenging task. A group of adolescents can be highly motivated, cooperative and fun to teach on one day, and the next day the whole group or individual students might turn out to be truly 'difficult' – the teacher might, for example, be faced with discipline problems, disruptive or provocative behaviour, a lack of motivation, or unwillingness on the students' part to do homework assigned to them.

The roots of these problems frequently lie in the fact that adolescents are going through a period of significant changes in their lives. The key challenge in the transition period between being a child and becoming an adult is the adolescent's struggle for identity – a process that requires the development of a distinct sense of who they are. A consequence of this process is that adolescents can feel threatened, and at the same time experience overwhelming emotions. They frequently try to compensate for the perceived threats with extremely rude behaviour, and try to 'hide' their emotions behind a wall of extreme outward conformity. The more individual students manage to look, talk, act and behave like the other members of their peer group, the less threatened and insecure they feel.

Insights into the causes underlying the problems might help us to understand better the complex situation our students are in. However, such insights do not automatically lead to more success in teaching. We need to react to the challenges in a professional way[1]. This includes the need to:

- select content and organise the students' learning according to their psychological needs;
- create a positive learning atmosphere;
- cater for differences in students' learning styles and intelligence(s), and facilitate the development of our students' study skills.

English in Mind second edition has been written taking all these points into account. They have significantly influenced the choice of texts, artwork and design, the structure of the units, the typology of exercises, and the means by which students' study skills are facilitated and extended.

The importance of the content for success

There are a number of reasons why the choice of the right content has a crucial influence over success or failure in the teaching of adolescents. Teachers frequently observe that teenagers are reluctant to 'talk about themselves'. This has to do with the adolescent's need for psychological security. Consequently, the 'further away' from their own world the content of the teaching is, the more motivating and stimulating it will be for the students. The preference for psychologically remote content goes hand in hand with a fascination with extremes and realistic details. Furthermore, students love identifying with heroes and heroines, because these idols are perceived to embody the qualities needed in order to survive in a threatening world: qualities such as courage, genius, creativity and love. In the foreign language class, students can become fascinated with stories about heroes and heroines to which they can ascribe such qualities. *English in Mind* treats students as young adults, offering them a range of interesting topics and a balance between educational value and teenage interest and fun.

As Kieran Egan[1] stresses, learning in the adolescent classroom can be successfully organised by starting with something far from the students' experience, but also connected to it by some quality with which they can associate. This process of starting far from the students makes it easier for the students to become interested in the topic, and also enables the teacher finally to relate the content to the students' own world.

A positive learning atmosphere

The creation of a positive learning atmosphere largely depends on the rapport between teacher and students, and the one which students have among themselves. It requires the teacher to be a genuine, empathetic listener, and to have a number of other psychological skills. *English in Mind* supports the teacher's task of creating positive learning experiences through: clear tasks; a large number of carefully designed exercises; regular opportunities for the students to check their own work; and a learning process designed to guarantee that the students will learn to express themselves both in speaking and in writing.

Learning styles and multiple intelligences

There is significant evidence that students will be better motivated, and learn more successfully, if differences in learning styles and intelligences are taken into account in the teaching-learning process.[2] The development of a number of activities in *English in Mind* has been influenced by such insights, and students find frequent study tips that show them how they can better utilise their own resources.[3]

---

[1] An excellent analysis of teenage development and consequences for our teaching in general can be found in Kieran Egan: *Romantic Understanding*, Routledge and Kegan Paul, New York and London, 1990. This book has had a significant influence on the thinking behind *English in Mind*, and the development of the concept of the course.

[2] See for example Eric Jensen: *Brain-Based Learning and Teaching*, Turning Point Publishing, Del Mar, CA, USA, 1995, on learning styles. An overview of the theory of multiple intelligences can be found in Howard Gardner: *Multiple Intelligences: The Theory in Practice*, Basic Books, New York 1993.

[3] See Marion Williams and Robert L. Burden: *Psychology for Language Teachers*, Cambridge University Press, 1997 (pp. 143–162), on how the learner deals with the process of learning.

The methodology used in English in Mind

Skills: *English in Mind* uses a communicative, multi-skills approach to develop the students' foreign language abilities in an interesting and motivational way. A wide range of interesting text types is used to present authentic use of language, including magazine and newspaper clippings, interviews, narratives, songs and engaging photostories.

Grammar: *English in Mind* is based on a strong grammatical syllabus and takes into account students' mixed abilities by dealing with grammar in a carefully graded way, and offering additional teaching support (see below).

Vocabulary: *English in Mind* offers a systematic vocabulary syllabus, including important lexical chunks for conversation and extension of the vocabulary in a bank at the back of the book.

Culture: *English in Mind* gives students insights into a number of important cross-cultural and intercultural themes. Significant cultural features of English-speaking countries are presented, and students are involved in actively reflecting on the similarities and differences between other cultures and their own.

Consolidation: Seven **Check your progress** revision pages per level will give teachers a clear picture of their students' progress and make students aware of what they have learned. Four **projects** give students the opportunity to use new language in a less controlled context and allows for learner independence.

Teacher support: *English in Mind* is clearly structured and easy to teach. The Teacher's Resource Book offers step-by-step lesson notes, background information on content, culture and language, additional teaching ideas and the tapescripts, photocopiable materials for further practice and extra lessons, taking into consideration the needs of mixed-ability groups by providing extra material for fast finishers or students who need more support, as well as entry tests.

Student support: *English in Mind* offers systematic support to students through: Study help sections and Skills tips; classroom language; guidance in units to help with the development of classroom discourse and the students' writing; lists of irregular verbs and phonetics (at the back of the Student's Book); and a Grammar reference (at the back of the Workbook).

English in Mind: components

Each level of the *English in Mind* series contains the following components:

- Student's Book with accompanying DVD Rom
- Audio CDs
- Workbook
- Teacher's Resource Book
- Testmaker Audio CD / CD-ROM
- DVD
- Classware DVD-ROM
- Website resources

The Student's Book

Student's Book 2 has a **Welcome section** at the beginning. This is to allow teachers to revise, reasonably quickly, some of the key areas of language which students covered in level 1 of *English in Mind* or in their previous learning. An alternative use of the Welcome section might be as diagnostic exercises, allowing teachers to gauge the strengths and weaknesses of their particular group of students before embarking on the level 2 material.

The units have the following basic structure, although with occasional minor variations depending on the flow of an individual unit:

- an opening **reading** text
- a **grammar** page, often including pronunciation
- two pages of **vocabulary** and **skills** work
- either a **photostory** or a **Culture in mind** text, followed by writing skills work and extra speaking

The **reading texts** aim to engage and motivate the students with interesting and relevant content, and to provide contextualised examples of target grammar and lexis. The texts have 'lead-in' tasks and are followed by comprehension tasks of various kinds. All the opening texts are also recorded on the Audio CDs, which allows teachers to follow the initial reading with a 'read and listen' phase, giving the students the invaluable opportunity of connecting the written word with the spoken version, which is especially useful for auditory learners. Alternatively, with stronger classes, teachers may decide to do one of the exercises as a listening task, with books closed.

Grammar follows the initial reading. The emphasis is on active involvement in the learning process. Examples from the texts are isolated and used as a basis for tasks, which focus on both concept and form of the target grammar area. Students are encouraged to find other examples and work out rules for themselves. Occasionally there are also Look! boxes which highlight an important connected issue concerning the grammar area, for example, in Unit 2, work on adverbs and comparative adverbs has a Look! box showing when and how to use them. This is followed by a number of graded exercises, both receptive and productive, which allow students to begin to employ the target language in different contexts and to produce realistic language. Next, there is usually a speaking activity, aiming at further personalisation of the language.

Each unit has at least one **Vocabulary** section, with specific word fields. Again, examples from the initial text are focused on, and a lexical set is developed, with exercises for students to put the vocabulary into use. Vocabulary is frequently recycled in later texts in the unit (e.g. photostories or Culture in mind texts), and also in later units.

Pronunciation is included in every unit. There are exercises on common phoneme problems as well as aspects of stress (within words, and across sentences) and elision.

Language skills are present in every unit. There is always at least one **listening** skills activity, with listening texts of various genres; at least one (but usually several) **speaking** skills activity

INTRODUCTION 7

for fluency development. **Reading skills** are taught through the opening texts and also later texts in some units, as well as the Culture in mind sections. There is always a **writing skills** task, towards the end of each unit.

The final two pages of each unit have either a **photostory** (even-numbered units) or a **Culture in mind** text (odd-numbered units). The **photostories** are conversations between teenagers in everyday situations, allowing students to read and listen for interest and also to experience the use of common everyday language expressions. These Everyday English expressions are worked on in exercises following the dialogue. The photostories are expanded with videostories on the DVD, where students can follow the progress of the characters through a term at school. The **Culture in mind** texts are reading texts which provide further reading practice, and an opportunity for students to develop their knowledge and understanding of the world at large and in particular the English-speaking world. They include a wide variety of stimulating topics: the history of listening to music, the importance of water, coming of age, Tuvalu, a disaster waiting to happen, girl genius, doctors without borders and mythical cities.

Towards the end of each unit there is a **writing skills** task. These are an opportunity for students to further their control of language and to experiment in the production of tasks in a variety of genres (e.g. letters, emails, reports, etc.). There are model texts for the students to aid their own writing, and exercises providing guidance in terms of content and organisation. Through the completion of the writing tasks, students, if they wish, can also build up a bank of materials, or 'portfolio', during their period of learning: this can be very useful to them as the source of a sense of clear progress and as a means of self-assessment. A 'portfolio' of work can also be shown to other people (exam bodies, parents, even future employers) as evidence of achievement in language learning. Many of the writing tasks also provide useful and relevant practice for examinations such as Cambridge ESOL PET or Trinity Integrated Skills Examinations.

At the end of every even unit there is an extra speaking section, titled, 'Last but not least' where students are given the opportunity for freer practice of the grammar and vocabulary that they have learned in the unit.

There is a **Check your progress** section after every two units. Here the teacher will find exercises in the Grammar and Vocabulary that were presented in the previous two units. The purpose of these (as opposed to the more formal tests offered on the Testmaker CD-ROM) is for teachers and students alike to check quickly the learning and progress made during the two units just covered; they can be done in class or at home. Every exercise has a marking scheme, and students can use the marks they gain to do some simple self-assessment (a light 'task' is offered for this).

Beyond the units themselves, *English in Mind* offers at the **end of the Student's Book** a further set of materials for teachers and students. These consist of:

- **Vocabulary Bank:** extension of vocabulary from the units in the main body of the Student's Book for students to build on their vocabulary. This section is attractively illustrated and the words are taught either through definitions or pictures. This section is particularly useful for those students who want to learn more.

- **Get it right!** This section is based on the **Cambridge Learner Corpus** and concentrates on typical errors that students often make at this level. These errors are dealt with through a variety of exercises and activities which allow students to focus on the errors they make and give them the opportunity to correct them.

- **Projects:** activities which students can do in pairs or groups (or even individually if desired), for students to put the language they have so far learned into practical and enjoyable use. They are especially useful for mixed-ability classes, as they allow students to work at their own pace. The projects produced could also be part of the 'portfolio' of material mentioned earlier. You can use the four projects at appropriate points as you work through level 2.

- An **irregular verb** list for students to refer to when they need.

- A listing of **phonetic symbols**, again for student reference.

The DVD-ROM

The Student's Book includes a DVD-ROM which contains the listening material for the Workbook (listening texts and pronunciation exercises) in MP3 format and a range of carefully graded grammar and vocabulary exercises to provide further practice of the language presented in each unit. It also contains the 'Team Spirit' videostories corresponding to the seven photostories in the Student's Book. These complement the photostories by dealing with the same themes and reflecting the same values, but they contain separate stories and scenes to them. They may take place before, at the same time as or after the photostories. There are four exercises for each videostory on the DVD-ROM, including a 'videoke' one in which students record their voices onto a short section of the videostory and can then play it back, either solo or as a pair with a friend. This provides a fun, sociable element, but also good practice of spoken English. The DVD-ROM also includes games for students to practise in an enjoyable and motivating way.

The Workbook

The Workbook is a resource for both teachers and students, providing further practice in the language and skills covered in the Student's Book. It is organised unit by unit, following the Student's Book. Each Workbook unit has six pages, and the following contents:

Remember and check: this initial exercise encourages students to remember the content of the initial reading text in the Student's Book unit.

Exercises: an extensive range of supporting exercises in the grammatical, lexical and phonological areas of the Student's Book unit, following the progression of the unit, so that teachers can use the exercises either during or at the end of the Student's Book unit.

Everyday English and **Culture in mind**: extra exercises on these sections in alternating units, as in the Student's Book.

Study help: these sections follow a syllabus of study skills areas, to develop the students' capacities as independent and successful learners. After a brief description of the skill, there are exercises for the students to begin to practise it.

Skills in mind page: these pages contain a separate skills development syllabus, which normally focuses on two main skill areas in each unit. There is also a skill tip relating to the main skill area, which the students can immediately put into action when doing the skills task(s).

Unit check page: this is a one-page check of knowledge of the key language of the unit, integrating both grammar and vocabulary in the three exercise types. The exercise types are: a) a cloze text to be completed using items given in a box; b) a sentence-level multiple choice exercise; c) sentences to be completed with given vocabulary items.

At the end of the Workbook, there is a **Grammar reference** section. Here, there are explanations of the main grammar topics of each unit, with examples. It can be used for reference by students at home, or the teacher might wish to refer to it in class if the students appreciate grammatical explanations.

The audio for the Workbook is available on the Audio CDs as well as on the Student's Book DVD-ROM in MP3 format.

The Teacher's Resource Book

The Teacher's Resource Book contains:

- clear, simple, practical teaching **notes** on each unit and how to implement the exercises as effectively as possible
- complete **tapescripts** for all listening and pronunciation activities
- complete **answers** to all exercises (grammar, vocabulary, comprehension questions, etc.)
- **optional further activities**, for stronger or weaker classes, to facilitate the use of the material in mixed-ability classes
- **background notes** relating to the information content (where appropriate) of reading texts and Culture in mind pages
- **language notes** relating to grammatical areas, to assist less-experienced teachers who might have concerns about the target language and how it operates (these can also be used to refer to the Workbook Grammar reference section)
- a complete **answer key** and **tapescripts** for the **Workbook**
- 'Memo from Mario': a page per unit of teaching notes and ideas for further exploitation of the material in the Student's Book written by the well-known Mario Rinvolucri
- four **entry tests** which have been designed with two purposes. They can be used purely as diagnostic entry tests, or teachers can also use them for remedial work before beginning the Welcome section
- **photocopiable communication activities**: one page for each unit reflecting the core grammar and/or vocabulary of the unit. The Communication Activities recycle the key grammar and/or vocabulary in each unit. They are designed to activate the new language in a communicative context. They cover a range of fun and motivating activity types: board games; quizzes; information gap activities; descriptions, etc.
- **photocopiable extra grammar exercises**: one page of four exercises for each unit, reflecting the key grammar areas of the unit. The Grammar Practice Exercises cover specific areas of the key grammar from each unit. They are intended for fast finishers or students who need extra practice
- **teaching notes** for the Photocopiable Communication Activities which contain clear step-by-step instructions for all the activities. In addition, there are **answers** for the Communication Activities, where relevant, and answers for all of the Grammar Practice Exercises.

Other resources

Testmaker Audio CD / CD-ROM: This allows you to create and edit your own texts, choosing from unit tests, which can be combined in unit pairs to match the course syllabus, or end-of-year tests. The tests offer 'standard' and 'more challenging' levels of testing, and can be created in A and B versions to avoid the sharing of answers. The listening test recordings are provided in audio CD format.

DVD: This contains both the 'Team Spirit' videostories and the complete 'EiMTV' material from the original edition.

Classware DVD-ROM: This contains the Student's Book in digital format to project on a whiteboard or via a computer with projector. You can enlarge parts of the page for a clearer focus. The 'Team Spirit' videostories and class listenings are also included, together with scripts.

Web resources: In addition to information about the series, the *English in Mind* website contains downloadable pages of further activities and exercises for students as well as interactive activities for students and wordlists with multiple translations. It can be found at this part of the Cambridge University Press website:

www.cambridge.org/elt/englishinmind *extra material*

Introductory note from Mario Rinvolucri

As you read through the Teacher's Resource Book you will, at the end of each unit, find small contributions of mine that offer you alternative ways of practising a structure, of dealing with a text or of revising words.

- I want to stress that the ideas presented are simply alternatives to the ways of working proposed to you by the authors. I strongly recommend that you try the authors' way first.
- When you teach the book through for the second or third time you may be ready then to try something a bit different. The authors and I believe that options are important but options are not useful if they confuse you.
- Maybe you could think of my contributions as a sort of sauce with a slightly different flavour to be tried for variety's sake.

Mario Rinvolucri, Pilgrims, UK, guest methodologist.

Welcome section

A

This section is designed to serve as a review, giving students the opportunity to revise and practise language they already know, and it is also a tool for teachers to find out how much students know already and which areas students may need to do more work on before continuing with the course.

1 Read and listen

a ▶ CD1 T1 As an introduction, ask students what job they would like to do when they are older. Play the recording while students read and answer the question. Check the answer (He is worried about his future). If necessary, play the recording again pausing to check for understanding.

b Ask students to read through the questions and check understanding. Students answer the questions. Encourage them to answer the questions without looking back at the text, but let them look back if necessary. Allow them to discuss their answers with a partner before open class feedback.

> **Answers**
> 1 It's almost midnight.
> 2 Because he has to think about his future.
> 3 Because he has to study for a long, long time.
> 4 Because he hates flying.
> 5 Because you don't have to be very clever and he likes listening to music.
> 6 Because he's getting tired and his fingers are hurting.

2 Present simple

For a quick review of the present simple, ask students to think of five things they do before coming to school in the morning. Listen to some of their ideas in open class, paying attention to accuracy. When students have given you some examples, check usage of the third person *s* by asking other students to remember what was said, e.g. *What does Juan do in the morning? He has breakfast*, etc. Read through the example with students and ask them to complete the rest of the exercise. Check answers.

> **Answers**
> 2 gives   3 don't know   4 doesn't like
> 5 Do, go   6 does, live

3 Present continuous

To introduce the present continuous, mime some actions and ask the class to describe what you are doing. Write an example on the board and draw attention to the use of *to be* and the *-ing* form to describe actions happening now. Students complete the exercise and check answers with a partner before open class feedback.

> **Answers**
> 2 're staying   3 'm having   4 's shining
> 5 are playing   6 'm sitting   7 'm not doing
> 8 are, doing

4 Present simple vs. present continuous

Write the following on the board:
I write a letter to my brother every week.
I am writing a letter to my brother.

In open class, ask students to explain the difference between the two sentences (the first sentence is present simple and refers to a habitual, repeated action; the second is present continuous and refers to an action taking place at or around the time of speaking). Listen to their ideas and clarify any misunderstanding. Read through the example with students and ask them to complete the rest of the exercise. Check answers.

> **Answers**
> 2 go   3 have   4 is cooking   5 is listening
> 6 plays

5 Hobbies and interests

Ask students what they like doing in their free time. Encourage students to explain when they do their hobbies and why they enjoy them. Write any interesting vocabulary on the board. Read through the instructions with students and check understanding. Students complete the exercise. During feedback, draw students' attention to the use of the *-ing* form after the verbs like, love, enjoy, go and prefer.

> **Answers**
> 1 dancing   2 going   3 swimming   4 playing
> 5 running   6 painting   7 listening   8 reading
> 9 computer

> ⭐ **OPTIONAL ACTIVITY**
>
> In small groups, students can discuss how they feel about the hobbies mentioned in the text. Circulate and help with vocabulary as required. Encourage open class discussion during feedback.

6 have to / don't have to

Read the examples with students. Make sure they understand that *have to* is used when somebody tells you to do something and *don't have to* is used when something is not necessary. Point out the use of *don't have to* rather than *haven't to*.

Students read through sentences 3–6. Go through the first item with them as an example. Remind students of the third person form *does/doesn't*. Students complete the exercise. Check answers. During feedback, ask students questions based on the exercise to clarify understanding, e.g. *Do you have to study for a test tomorrow?*

> **Answers**
> 3 You have to study for the test tomorrow.
> 4 My older sister doesn't have to go to bed before 11 o'clock.
> 5 My brother has to go to school on Saturday.
> 6 I don't have to get up early on Sunday.

7 Jobs

As an introduction, divide the class into pairs and give students two minutes to list as many jobs as possible. Listen to some of their ideas in open class. Read through the instructions with students and ask them to write the names of the jobs next to the pictures.

> **Answers**
> 2 architect   3 lawyer   4 vet
> 5 flight attendant   6 teacher   7 dentist
> 8 firefighter   9 pilot   10 shop assistant

> ⭐ **OPTIONAL ACTIVITY**
>
> Ask students to work in small groups and create a list of jobs. Groups then take it in turns to write a jumbled-up job on the board and the other teams have a ten-second time limit to name the job. Give a point each time a group gets the correct answer.

B

1 Read and listen

a As an introduction, ask students how often they eat out in a restaurant and which types of restaurants they like going to most. Ask students to read the text and answer the question. Check answer (It was the most awful meal he'd ever had).

> ⭐ **OPTIONAL ACTIVITY**
>
> Read through the text with the class, pausing each time you read a verb in the past simple. Ask students to tell you the base form of the verb and if it is regular or irregular.

b ▶ **CD1 T2**   Read through items 1–6 with students and do the first one as an example if necessary. Play the recording while students listen and answer the questions. Check answers. If necessary, play the recording again pausing to check for understanding. Students can also correct the false statements.

> **Answers**
> 1 F – there was a waiter   2 T   3 F – the ham came with salad   4 T   5 F – he asked her if she wasn't hungry   6 T

2 Past simple: regular and irregular verbs

Read through the example with students and check understanding of the formation of questions in the past simple. Elicit possible answers to the question (Yes I did. / Yes, I watched the film. / No I didn't. / No, I didn't watch the film.). Students complete the exercise and check answers with a partner before open class feedback.

To check students' understanding at this point, you can call out a few base forms of regular and irregular past simple verbs and ask students to call out the past simple form.

> **Answers**
> 1 wanted   2 called   3 went   4 Was
> 5 were   6 fell   7 woke   8 saw   9 didn't stay
> 10 did, enjoy   11 started   12 lost   13 missed
> 14 did, get   15 did, phone   16 took   17 paid

3 Food (countable and uncountable nouns)

a To introduce the topic, write the words *vegetables, fruit, starters, main meals, desserts, drinks* at the top of six columns on the board. Divide the class into pairs and ask them to discuss what they ate and drank last time they went to a restaurant. Circulate and help with vocabulary as necessary. Listen to some of their ideas in open class and write any interesting vocabulary on the board under one of the six headings. In the same pairs, give students a five-minute time limit to think of as many words as possible in each of the six groups. During feedback, give students one point for each word they write and two points if they are the only pair to write a word. As students give their answers, write various words on the board in preparation for Exercise 3b.

WELCOME SECTION   11

Sample answers
Vegetables: potatoes, cabbage, cucumber, lettuce, courgettes
Fruit: oranges, lemons, bananas, pineapples, grapefruits
Starters: prawn cocktail, salad, smoked salmon
Main meals: fish and chips, spaghetti bolognaise, lasagne, steak pie, pork chops
Desserts: apple pie, cheesecake, profiteroles, caramel pudding
Drinks: water, lemonade, beer, wine

b Write several food and drink items on the board and ask students if they are countable or uncountable nouns. Check students understand that uncountable nouns do not have an article or a plural. Ask students to decide if the words in their lists are countable or uncountable. Circulate and help with any questions. Check answers in open class.

c Divide the class into small groups. Students work together to create a dialogue in a restaurant. If necessary, spend some time eliciting some possible language before students create their dialogues. Listen to some of the dialogues in open class and hold a class vote to decide on the best one.

4 Much/many

To check understanding, write *much* and *many* on the board and ask students which is used with countable nouns (much) and which with uncountable (many). Students complete the exercise. Check answers.

Answers
2 much   3 many   4 much   5 many

5 Some/any

To introduce this topic, write some countable and uncountable nouns on the board and write the article before the countable nouns. Ask students which word we put before uncountable nouns (some) and ask them to make some sentences. Ask them to make a question and negative sentence and elicit the use of *any*. Read through the example. Students complete the exercise and check their answers with a partner before feedback in open class.

Answers
2 some   3 some, any   4 some, any
5 some, any   6 any, some

6 Comparative and superlative adjectives

As a review of this area, write the adjectives *tall*, *intelligent*, *old* and *young* on the board. Invite three students to come to stand at the front of the class. Ask the other students to compare the three students and write some of their examples on the board. Draw their attention to the use of *-er* or *more* + adjective with comparatives, and *-est* or *most* + adjective with superlatives. Students complete the exercise. Check answers.

Answers
2 biggest, bigger   3 best, better
4 most interesting, more interesting
5 worst, worse

7 Multi-word verbs

Write the sentence *I get up at seven o'clock* and ask students to find the verb. Point out that the verb is *get up* and consists of a verb + preposition. Divide the class into pairs and give them two minutes to think of some more examples of multi-word verbs. Listen to some of their ideas in open class. Read through the words in the box with students and check understanding. Go through the first item with students as an example if necessary. Students now complete the exercise and compare answers with a partner before a whole class check.

Answers
2 tell off   3 given up   4 look up   5 work out   6 check out

C

1 Read and listen

Warm up

Ask students if they have a mobile phone and if so, how often they text their friends. If they do not have a mobile phone, ask them why not. Is it because their parents do not allow it? Listen to some of their ideas in open class.

a Students read through the texts quickly and answer the question. Check any problems. If necessary, go through the first text message with them as an example. Check answer.

Answer
Their mums won't let them play volleyball.

b ▶ CD1 T3   Read through the questions and check understanding. Play the recording while students read the texts and answer the questions. You could pause as necessary to check understanding and clarify any difficulties. Students answer the questions and compare answers with a partner before feedback.

> **Answers**
> 1 Tony and Jane
> 2 Tony and Jane
> 3 Tony
> 4 Jane
> 5 Saturday

2 will/won't

Read the example sentence with the class. Remind them that *won't* is the contracted form of *will not* and is the negative form of *will*. Explain that *will/won't* is used to refer to possible or predicted future actions. Students complete the exercise. Check answers.

> **Answers**
> 2 'll know   3 won't win   4 'll send
> 5 won't be   6 'll go

✱ OPTIONAL ACTIVITY

Divide the class into pairs and ask students to create short dialogues that include one of the sentences from the exercise. Circulate and help with vocabulary as necessary. Listen to some of the best dialogues in open class as feedback. If possible encourage students to perform their dialogues without looking at their notes.

3 too + adjective

As an introduction to this topic, write the following sentences on the board:

Can you drive a car? Why not?
Did you buy your mother a diamond ring for her birthday? Why not?

Elicit the answers: *Because I am too young* and *Because it is too expensive*.

Go through the first item as an example. Students complete the exercise and check answers with a partner before feedback in open class.

> **Answers**
> 2 too big   3 too cold   4 too fast
> 5 too expensive   6 too late

4 Adverbs

To introduce this area, ask students if they walk to school quickly or slowly. Remind them that *quickly* and *slowly* are adverbs and are used to describe a verb. Ask them which adjectives they come from (quick and slow) and how adverbs are formed (They are usually formed by the addition of *-ly* to an adjective). You may like to give them further practice by reading out a list of adjectives and asking them to form the adverb.

Read through the sentences with students to check understanding. Students complete the exercise. Check answers.

> **Answers**
> 2 played, loud   3 ran, fast   4 cooks well

5 Expressions to talk about the future

Refer back to Welcome section C, Exercise 2 and draw students' attention to some of the expressions used with *will* (I'm sure, maybe, probably, I'm sure, I think). Explain that we use these words to describe how possible we think the future action is. Read through the words in the box and check understanding. Students complete the exercise and check answers with a partner before open class feedback.

> **Answers**
> 2 hope   3 doubt   4 probably

✱ OPTIONAL ACTIVITY

Students can write sentences that are true for them using the words in the box and *will/won't*. Listen to some examples as feedback.

6 be going to

To introduce the language in this exercise, mime an action, e.g. throwing a pen, but stop before you complete the action. Ask students: *what am I going to do?* Repeat the procedure with different actions and make a note of their answers on the board. Remind students that we use *going to* for a future action or intention for which there is present evidence. Look at the pictures with students and ask them to complete the sentences. Go through the first item as an example if necessary. Check answers.

> **Answers**
> 2 are going to   3 're going to   4 's going to

7 Future time expressions

To review this language, write the day of the week on the board and write today next to it, e.g. *Monday – today*. Then write *Tuesday – tomorrow* and follow this with the other days of the week.

WELCOME SECTION 13

Ask students how we can describe these days and elicit *the day after tomorrow*, *in three days' time*, etc. You may like to do a similar exercise with hours, months and years. Students complete the exercise. Check answers.

Answers
2 the day after tomorrow 3 next month
4 in two weeks' time 5 in four years' time

✱ OPTIONAL ACTIVITY

For further practice of future time expressions, write the following on the board:
The day after tomorrow ...
In three months' time ...
In five years' time ...
In ten years' time ...
In twenty years' time ...

Ask students to write sentences making predictions about their futures. They can also write sentences about other people in the class or famous people using the same phrases. Listen to some of their ideas in open class as feedback.

8 The weather

To introduce the topic, ask students to tell you what the weather is like today. You could also ask them to describe the weather at different times of year and write any weather-related vocabulary on the board.

Divide the class into pairs and ask students to complete the crossword. Check answers.

Answers
2 lightning 3 sun 4 weather 5 thunder
6 shower 7 hot 8 wind 9 warm

D

1 Read and listen

Warm up
Write the word *impress* on the board and ask students what things they might do if they wanted to impress their friends. Encourage students to try to impress each other. You may like to give them some examples of your own to get them started.

 ▶ CD1 T4 Tell students that they are going to read and listen to a dialogue between two teenagers. Play the recording while students listen and read to answer the question. Tell them not to worry if they do not understand every word at this stage. Check answer.

Answers
He's going to start diving lessons because Emily Jones said he was boring.

b Students read through the list of questions and check any vocabulary problems. Go through the first item as an example, if necessary. Play the recording for students to listen and read the text at the same time. Students complete the exercise and compare answers in pairs. Play the recording again, pausing as necessary for students to check or change their answers.

Answers
1 He thinks he is really boring.
2 He thinks she is attractive, but unkind.
3 He thinks you shouldn't do things just to impress other people.
4 Because he has never taken a risk before.
5 Because he can't swim.
6 Be himself.

2 First conditional

To introduce this topic, write the following jumbled sentence on the board.

good buy if will cake you a I are you.

Tell students that they should reorder the words in two different ways.

If you are good, I will buy you a cake.
I will buy you a cake if you are good.

Remind students these are first conditional sentences and they refer to possible future actions. Read through the first item in the dialogue as an example. Students complete the dialogue and check answers with a partner before open class feedback. For practice of the intonation of first conditional sentences, divide the class into pairs for them to practise the dialogue. Circulate and correct intonation as required.

Answers
2 don't finish, won't give 3 don't give, will be
4 'll be, don't come 5 come, will, help

3 Adjectives for feelings and opinions

In open class, ask students how they feel when their team wins a football match/at the end of a long day at school/during a TV programme/ if they fail an exam. Listen to some of their ideas in open class and write any adjectives for feelings and opinions on the board. Students complete the exercise. Check answers.

14 WELCOME SECTION

> **Answers**
> 2 dull 3 ugly 4 cool 5 excited
> 6 interested

> **Language note**
> Check that students are aware of the difference between -ed and -ing adjectives. -ed adjectives like bored, interested, excited, etc. refer to the feeling somebody has when a person or a thing is boring, interesting, exciting, etc.

 ## should/shouldn't

Check understanding of the words in the box. Read through the first item with students and remind them that we use *should/shouldn't* to give advice to somebody or to express mild obligation. Divide the class into pairs and ask students to complete dialogues 2–6. Check answers. You may like to ask students to practise the dialogues with their partners.

> **Answers**
> 2 should eat more breakfast
> 3 should be more relaxed
> 4 shouldn't go this evening
> 5 shouldn't go to school
> 6 should be more polite

★ OPTIONAL ACTIVITY

For further practice of *should/shouldn't*, give students two minutes to think of some problems that they have (these can be invented). Divide the class into small groups and ask students to take it in turns to read out their problems for the other students to give them advice using *should/shouldn't*.

 ## Present perfect with ever/never

To review this language, write on the board:

In your life, ... Paris?
In your life, ... a famous person?

Ask students to add the missing words to the sentences and to answer the questions. Elicit from students that these are examples of the present perfect and that we use this tense to describe past actions or experiences which occurred at a non-specified time. If necessary, go through the first item as an example. Students complete the exercise and check answers with a partner before open class feedback.

> **Answers**
> 2 Have, ever tried; 've never swum
> 3 Have, ever stayed; 've never slept
> 4 've never eaten; 've never tried

6 Personality adjectives

a As an introduction, ask students to write down the names of five friends or members of their family and to think of a different adjective to describe each of them. Listen to some of their answers in open class and write any interesting adjectives on the board. Check understanding of the adjectives in the two lists. Divide the class into pairs and ask students to complete the two lists. During feedback, check students can pronounce the words correctly.

> **Answers**
> disorganised unkind honest hardworking
> impolite happy stressed

b Read through the first item as an example. Ask students to complete the exercise with an adjective from Exercise 6a. With stronger classes, students may be able to complete this exercise without referring to the lists. Check answers.

> **Answers**
> 2 relaxed 3 lazy 4 polite 5 miserable
> 6 dishonest 7 disorganised 8 friendly

WELCOME SECTION 15

1 Great idea!

Unit overview

TOPIC: Inventions; stories in the past

TEXTS

Reading and listening: a magazine article about famous inventions
Listening: a science fiction story
Reading: an article about inventors
Reading: an article about listening to music
Writing: a text about an inventor and his/her invention

SPEAKING AND FUNCTIONS

Describing past activities
Discussing different ways of listening to music

LANGUAGE

Grammar: Past continuous; Past continuous vs. past simple; *when* and *while*
Vocabulary: Phrases with *get*

1 Read and listen

If you set the background information as a homework research task, ask students to tell the class what they found out.

BACKGROUND INFORMATION

Mary Anderson (1866–1953) was a real estate developer, rancher and inventor of the windscreen wiper blade.

Thomas Adams (1818–1905) was an American photographer, glass maker and inventor. In February 1871, Adams New York Gum went on sale.

James Henry Atkinson (1849–1942) was a British ironmonger from Leeds, Yorkshire who invented the mousetrap.

Josephine Garis Cochran (1839–1913) made the first practical mechanical dishwasher in 1886, in Shelbyville, Illinois.

Warm up

Ask students (in L1 if appropriate) what they think people did before the following inventions, e.g. the telephone, TV, computer, fridge, etc. Ask them if they know when these things were invented and who they think invented them.

a Ask students to read through the words in the box. Check any problems with meaning or pronunciation. Go through the first item as an example, explaining that they must write the relevant number in the boxes. Students complete the exercise. Check answers.

Answers
1 G 2 F 3 H 4 B 5 C 6 E 7 D 8 A

b **Weaker classes:** Encourage students to read the texts, trying to guess any unknown vocabulary from context. If students are still having problems, check the meaning of e.g. *rubber, nipper, frozen*. Go through the first text with students as an example, encouraging them to think about the inventions from Exercise 1a and choose the appropriate one. Students complete the exercise.

Do not check answers at this point, as this will be done in Exercise 1c.

c ▶ **CD1 T5** Play the recording while students listen and check their answers. Play the recording again, pausing as necessary to clarify any problems.

TAPESCRIPT

Narrator: What did they invent?

Speaker 1: In 1903, Mary Anderson and a friend were driving to New York. It was raining heavily and they had to open the windows of their car and put their heads out to see better. Suddenly, Mary had an idea. She invented a moving arm made of metal with a piece of rubber on it. The driver could operate it from inside the car without opening the window. People liked her invention because it helped them to drive safely when it was snowing or raining. Mary Anderson invented the windscreen wiper.

Speaker 2: In 1869, Thomas Adams was trying to produce rubber out of the juice he got from Mexican sapodilla trees. He wanted to produce toys, rain boots and bicycle tyres. The experiment didn't work. While he was thinking about this, he took a piece of the rubber he was working on and put it in his mouth. He liked the taste of it and decided to add something to the rubber to give it a nice taste. Not long after that, he opened the world's first chewing gum factory.

Speaker 1: In 1897, British inventor, James Henry Atkinson, was looking at the family's supply of potatoes, which they kept in a room under their house. He noticed that mice had eaten some of the potatoes, so he invented something that he called 'Little Nipper' to stop them. He sold his mouse trap idea to a big company. They still produce mouse traps called 'Little Nippers', and they even have a mouse trap museum.

Speaker 2: In 1886, Josephine Cochran was standing in her kitchen in Illinois, USA. The family lunch was finished, there was a mountain of dishes in front of Mrs Cochran and she got quite angry, thinking that she had to do this job every day. 'If nobody else is going to invent a machine for this, I'll do it myself,' she thought. And then suddenly she had an idea. Josephine Cochran invented the first dishwasher. First, only hotels and large restaurants bought her invention. It was not until the 1950s that dishwashers also became popular with families.

Speaker 1: In the early years of the eighteenth century, in the middle of the summer, an unknown Dutchman was looking at one of the many canals in Holland. He was thinking that he often travelled along the frozen canals on ice skates in the winter. He got a little impatient. 'I don't want to wait for winter!' he thought. The unknown inventor made wooden wheels and fixed them to his shoes. He invented the first roller skates.

> **Answers**
> Text 1: windscreen wipers
> Text 2: chewing gum
> Text 3: mouse trap
> Text 4: dishwasher
> Text 5: roller skates

d ▶ CD1 T5 Ask students to read through questions 1 to 4. Check any problems. If necessary, go through the first item as an example, pausing the recording after text 1. Play the recording again while students complete the exercise. Remind students to listen for the key words they will need to answer each question. Students can compare answers in pairs before a whole class check.

> **Answers**
> 1 He liked the taste and added something to it to make it even nicer.
> 2 He sold it to a big company.
> 3 Hotels and large restaurants bought it.
> 4 Because the canals weren't frozen and he couldn't travel along them on ice skates.

2 Grammar

✱ Past continuous

a **Stronger classes:** Students read through the example sentences. Ask them what they notice about how the past continuous tense is formed (*was/were* + *–ing* form of main verb).

Weaker classes: Books closed. Elicit a present continuous singular and plural example from students and write them on the board. Remind them of the form of the present continuous (present tense of *be* + *–ing* form of main verb). Now ask students what the past tense of *be* is and elicit *was/were*. In your example sentence, write *Yesterday at six o'clock* at the beginning of the sentence and replace *is/are* with *was/were*. Explain to students that they have just formed the past continuous. Students now open their books at page 13 and look at the example sentences from the text.

b Read the instructions with the class. Go through the first text with them as an example and underline the first past continuous verb they come across. Give them a few minutes to re-read the texts and find further examples of the past continuous. Students can compare answers in pairs before a whole class check.

> **Answers**
> Text 1: was raining
> Text 2: was trying; was thinking; was working
> Text 3: Atkinson was looking at
> Text 5: was looking at; was thinking

Students now complete the table with the correct form of the past continuous. Do the first item with them as an example, if necessary. Check answers and then read through the rule as a class. Make sure students understand when to use the past continuous. It may be useful to remind students when we use the present continuous (an action happening now / at the moment of speaking).

> **Answers**
> Positive: was; were
> Negative: wasn't
> Question: Was; Were
> Short answer: was; wasn't; were; weren't

To check understanding of the form at this point, call out a few verbs in the present continuous and ask students to put them into the past continuous.

c Read the instructions and the verbs in the box with students and go through the example as a class, focusing on the picture. Make sure students can explain why *was* is used. Students complete the exercise. Remind them to look at the picture and each sentence carefully and remind them to think about the spelling rules for *–ing* forms. Students can compare answers in pairs before a whole class check. If students are still having problems with the spelling of *–ing* forms, you may want to revise this area.

> **Answers**
> 2 were playing   3 was sitting   4 was writing
> 5 was dreaming

UNIT 1   17

d This exercise can be set for homework. Students read through dialogues 1 to 7. Go through the example with them, eliciting the verbs for B's part. Remind students of the question form. Students complete the exercise. In pairs, students compare answers. Ask a few pairs to read out their completed dialogues to the class to check answers.

> **Answers**
> 1 B: was waiting; was buying
> 2 A: were you talking
>   B: was telling
> 3 A: Were his parents living
>   B: were living; was working
> 4 A: Were you watching
>   B: was reading
> 5 A: were you having
>   B: were talking
> 6 A: Were you playing
>   B: wasn't playing; was doing
> 7 A: were they wearing
>   B: weren't wearing; were wearing

Grammar notebook
Encourage students to note down the completed table and the rule from Exercise 2b.

 Speak

Divide the class into small groups. Each student thinks of a famous personality and spends some time thinking about how they spend their days. Each student should choose a different personality. Read through the example dialogue as a class. Pay attention to intonation in the questions. In groups, students ask and answer questions using the past continuous. Give students a few minutes to ask and answer. Then ask for some groups to feed back to the rest of the class. If anyone was doing anything interesting, discuss this further as a class.

 Listen

Warm up
Ask students to look at the picture and to predict what happened.

a Ask students to read the questions and the beginning of the story to check their predictions.

Ask for some ideas about what happened next. Do not give answers at this point.

b ▶ CD1 T8 Play the recording while students listen to see if any of their ideas from Exercise 5a were correct. Check answers.

TAPESCRIPT
Narrator: Olivia was sitting at her desk, writing one of her stories. It was a story about a faraway planet, XR017. Lots of people were living on the planet and there wasn't enough space for everyone, so the President of XR017 sent five spaceships to find out more about the Earth. As they were getting near the Earth, four of the spaceships caught fire. Only one of them got to the Earth and landed safely. In it was Commander Q5. He was a tall alien with a dark green face, and red eyes that shone like volcanoes. Q5 was a creature who almost never smiled. But when he opened the door of the spaceship, and saw how beautiful the Earth was, he smiled.

Commander Q5: This is the right place for my people, but there's not enough space. First I must fight the humans. Hahahahahahaha!

Narrator: Q5 knew that he had to be careful. For days, he sat in one of the trees near a little village and watched the humans. With the help of his brain reader, he was quickly learning to move, to think and to talk like a human. And he knew he also had to change his looks. That was easy. One of his special look-alike pills was enough.

Three months later Q5 was living in a small town in England, and nobody knew who he was. Every night, while all the humans were sleeping, he worked in his garage, building a very powerful brain machine.

Commander Q5: I'll hypnotise all the humans. Hahahahahaha! And nobody, nobody will know who I am!

Narrator: Q5 knew that he was safe. While he was working on his plan, his brain machine was checking people's brains to find out what they were thinking. Every now and then, Q5 looked at the huge screen. Everything was going well. All the human brains were thinking of other things, and none of them knew about his terrible plans. None of them. Once again, Q5 smiled, but while he was smiling, he got a shock.

Commander Q5: What's that? Oh, noooooooo!

Narrator: Olivia was writing the last sentence of her story, when suddenly she heard a noise behind her. She turned round, and saw their new neighbour. He was usually a very friendly man, but tonight his face was cold.

Commander Q5: Listen. I know what you were thinking a minute ago.

Narrator: Olivia was shocked.

Commander Q5: You know who I am!

Narrator: When Olivia looked at her neighbour, she saw that he was holding something in his hand. It looked like a mobile phone. He started to laugh out loud, and pressed a button on the phone. There was a strange noise, and Olivia started to feel very tired. She looked at her neighbour again.

Olivia: His eyes. They were burning like volcanoes!

Narrator: Then Olivia fell to the floor.

18 UNIT 1

c In open class, students discuss how they think the story ended. Help with difficult vocabulary and write any interesting new words on the board.

6 Grammar

★ Past continuous vs. past simple

a Write the sentence on the board and ask a stronger student to come out and underline the past continuous and circle the past simple verb in it. Leave it on the board for Exercise 6b.

b Copy the diagram onto the board above the sentence you wrote up in Exercise 6a. Explain how the first action is going on and the other action interrupts it. Ask them the questions and elicit the answers (*past continuous tells us the background action and past simple tells us what happened at one moment*). Students now read through the rule box and complete it. Check answers.

> **Answers**
> past continuous; past simple

c ▶ CD1 T8 Students read through sentences 1 to 3. Go through the first item as an example, if necessary. Students complete the exercise. At this point, you could play the recording in Exercise 5b again for students to listen and check their answers. Check answers as a class.

> **Answers**
> 1 was working; was checking; were thinking
> 2 looked; was going; were thinking; knew
> 3 looked; saw; was holding

★ *when* and *while*

d Ask students to read through the two examples. Ask them which actions are the background action (*writing/smiling*) and which actions interrupt the background actions at one particular moment (*heard a noise / got a shock*). Now ask them to read through the rule box and complete it using the examples to help them. Check answers.

> **Answers**
> simple; continuous

e Ask students to read through sentences 1 to 4. Check any problems. Go through the example with students and ask them to explain why each tense is used. Students complete the exercise and compare answers in pairs before a whole class check.

> **Answers**
> 2 was running; fell
> 3 were playing; arrived
> 4 was having; had

f Refer back to the rule in Exercise 6d. Students write sentences with *while* and *when*. Circulate and help with any difficulties. Check answers.

Grammar notebook

Encourage students to note down the rules from Exercise 6 and some example sentences. They may find it useful to translate some of the sentences.

7 Read

a In open class, ask students to guess the answers to the two questions. Ask students to read the text quickly and check their answers. Remind them that they should only be looking for the information to answer the questions and they don't need to understand every word in the text.

> **Answers**
> 1 A flying machine.
> 2 No, young people invent things too.

b Students read through items 1 to 4 and a to d. Check any problems. Students continue reading the text silently, or you can read it aloud to the class yourself. Go through the example, making sure students understand what they have to do.

Students complete the exercise and compare answers in pairs before a whole class check.

> **Answers**
> 2 d 3 a 4 b

c Students discuss the questions as a whole class or in small groups. Ask for feedback. Find out if anyone has an idea for an invention of their own.

8 Vocabulary

★ *get*

a Read the instructions with the class. Go through the example, making sure students understand why *became* is the answer. Students write the meaning of *got* in the other sentences. Check answers.

> **Answers**
> 2 received 3 arrived 4 received

LOOK!

Read through the examples in the Look! box. Make it clear that we use *get to* when we arrive somewhere, except in certain situations such as when we get home. You could introduce other phrases such as *get back*, *get in* and *get there*.

b This exercise can be set for homework. Ask students to read the phrases in the box and make sure they understand them all. Go through the example, eliciting why this is the only possibility.

UNIT 1   19

Students complete the exercise. Remind them to look carefully at the tenses they need to use and to choose the past simple or the past continuous. Check answers.

Answers
2 got to school   3 was getting wet
4 got angry

Vocabulary notebook

Encourage students to note down the various meanings of *get* from Exercise 8 and to write some example sentences of their own.

9 Read and listen

a Divide the class into pairs and ask them to discuss the questions. Also ask them to talk about the types of music they listen to and whether they prefer different types of music in different situations. Listen to some of their opinions in open class and encourage discussion.

b Students look at the question. Ask them to read the text quickly to decide on the best title. Remind them they don't need to understand every word.

Answer
2 The history of listening to music

c ▶ CD1 T9   Ask students to read through questions 1 to 4. Check any problems. If necessary, go through the first item as an example, locating the point in the text. Students listen, read and complete the exercise. Students can compare answer in pairs before a whole class check.

Answers
1 In the mid 1920s because the radio became more popular.
2 They were made of aluminium foil and people could listen to them only a few times before the foil broke.
3 Gramophones used flat vinyl disks to hold music, phonographs used cylinders.
4 They could listen to music while they were travelling, doing sports or going for walks.

d Read through the definitions with students. Tell students that they may be looking for more than one word (numbers 3 and 5).

Weaker classes: Ask them to read the text again and find words to fit the definitions.
Stronger classes: Let them try the exercise without looking back and then read the text again quickly to check answers.

Answers
1 popular   2 disappear   3 a few times
4 similar   5 a disc jockey

10 Speak

Stronger classes: In pairs or small groups, students go though the questions and discuss them.

Weaker classes: They can choose one question only to discuss. If necessary, elicit a few prompts for the question they have chosen to help them.

Monitor and help as necessary, encouraging students to express themselves in English.

Ask pairs or groups to feed back to the class and discuss any interesting points further.

11 Write

The preparation for this can be done in class and the story written for homework.

a Ask students to read through questions 1 to 3. Check any problems. Pre-teach any vocabulary (*burrs, tape*). Go through the first item as an example, if necessary. Students then read through the story and answer the questions. Check answers.

rough coverage prickly coverage

Answers
1 Velcro, George de Mestral
2 Because it helps fasten clothes, shoes, etc. and it's quick and easy to use.
3 He was walking in the woods and he got lots of burrs stuck on his clothes.

b Students now match the questions with the paragraphs in the text. If necessary, do the first one with them as an example. Check answers.

Answers
1 A   2 C   3 B

c Students underline the expressions in the text. Check understanding and explain to students that these expressions will form the core of their story in Exercise 12d.

d Students now choose an invention from this unit or they could think of one of their own. If they can't think of a real invention, they can make one up. Remind students of the structure of Alex's story.

Memo from Mario

Great idea!

Five four-minute warmers for lessons

1 Month tennis

▶ Demonstrate the activity with a student:

You: July + 1
Student: August ... December minus 2
You: October ... March plus 11

▶ Tell the students to work in pairs and play month tennis.
▶ Play for three minutes.

> **RATIONALE**
> If the students have come from home, from Maths, from lunch, from History, etc. they need a buffer zone in which they can adjust to your weird demand: *Please speak English!*
> A brief, undemanding game like the one above offers such an adjustment zone.

2 Counting backwards and forwards

▶ Demonstrate with a student:

You: one two three four five
Student: five four three two one
You: two three four five six
Student: six five four three two
You: three four five six seven

▶ Tell the students to work in pairs and stop when they get to twelve.
▶ Play for three minutes.

> **RATIONALE**
> Maybe some of your weaker students do not like working in a foreign language.
> Some may find it really hard to get their heads around it all. However some will be really good at arithmetical things. Why not offer them four minutes happiness out of the 45 or so minutes the lesson lasts?

3 Measure a minute

▶ Tell the students you want them to measure a minute in any way they want, apart from looking at a timepiece.
▶ Explain that you will tell them when to start measuring their minute and that they must shout out END when they finish.
▶ Ask them to close their eyes and give them the signal START!
▶ Round off the activity by asking half a dozen students how exactly they measured their minute.

> **RATIONALE**
> This warmer, that comes from the work of the late nineteenth century Maria Montessori, is more a calmer than a warmer. It is useful on windy days or when the students have just been doing sport or have just come from a long break. Measuring a minute with eyes closed slows down breathing and calms down over-excitement.

4 Counting by twos

▶ Demonstrate with a student:

You: zero
Student: one hundred
You: two
Student: ninety eight
You: four
Student: ninety six.......

▶ Tell the students to work in pairs and count towards each other by two. Tell them to stop when they reach 50.

> **RATIONALE**
> The counting allows students who are deft with numbers to shine.

5 Remembering words from last time

▶ Write up on the board six to eight words from the last class that you suspect some people may have forgotten.
▶ Suppose you are teaching in Slovenia and suppose one of the words to be revised is *butterfly*, have a dialogue with a volunteer student using <u>only</u> the words *metul* and *butterfly* (*metul* is the Slovene equivalent of *butterfly*).

You: Metul ... metul ... butterfly?
Student: Butterfly! Butterfly! Butterfly!
You: Butterfly ... butterfly, metul!   etc

▶ Tell the students to stand up and have energized dialogues using the English words to be revised and their mother tongue equivalents. They only have one pair of words in play at any one time.
▶ If you have an international class, pair people of the same mother tongue. Pair any language isolates: they use the English word and the equivalent word in <u>one</u> of their languages.

> **RATIONALE**
> This is a useful exercise in contrastive phonology and fixes the meaning of the words being revised once and for all. It is particularly effective with very auditorily gifted learners.

UNIT 1   21

...e ran faster

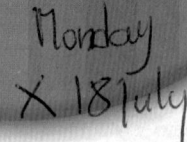
Monday
✗ 18 July

Overview

TOPIC: Olympic and Paralympic sportspersons; sporting events

TEXTS
Listening: a talk about the Paralympics
Reading: a text about a wheelchair basketball team
Writing: a magazine report of a sports event

SPEAKING AND FUNCTIONS
Making comparisons
Describing a sports event
Comparing yourself with others
Asking questions about sport

LANGUAGE
Grammar: Comparative and superlative adjectives; Intensifiers with comparatives; (not) as ... as; Adverbs/comparative adverbs
Vocabulary: Antonyms; sport
Everyday English: *Guess what?*; *that sort of thing*; *We're talking about*; *an awful lot of*; *That's not the point*; *At the end of the day*

1 Listen

If you set the background information as a homework research task, ask students to tell the class what they found out.

> **BACKGROUND INFORMATION**
>
> **Jason Smyth** (born 1986) is a visually impaired sprinter from County Londonderry in Ireland.
>
> **Stefanie Brown Trafton** (born 1979) is an American shot putter and discus thrower.
>
> **Usain Bolt** (born 1986) is a Jamaican sprinter.
>
> **Marianne Buggenhagen** (born 1953) is a German Paralympic discus thrower.
>
> **Natalie Du Toit** (born 1984) is a South African Paralympic swimmer.
>
> **The Paralympic Games** are for athletes with physical and visual disabilities. They are held every four years, following the Olympic Games.

Warm up

Ask students if they have any sporting heroes/heroines. If so, in which sports do they compete? Ask them to give reasons why they like these people. Ask them to look at the photos and see if anyone has ever done any of the sports in the photos. Discuss this as a class, in L1 if appropriate.

a Ask students to read through the list of sports and look at the photos. Do the first item with them as an example, if necessary. Students complete the exercise. Check answers.

> **Answers**
> 2 D   3 B   4 F   5 C   6 E

b ▶ **CD1 T10**   Divide the class into pairs. Ask students to read the instructions and the profiles of the athletes. Check any problems. Give students a few minutes to predict the type of missing information, e.g. word or number. Ask them to guess the answers and listen to some of their predictions in open class. Do not give answers at this stage. Play the recording. Check answers, reminding students to focus on the information needed to fill the gaps. Pause and play the recording again as necessary.

TAPESCRIPT

The 2008 Olympic Games in Beijing produced some wonderful sporting performances. In athletics, for example, the Irish sprinter Jason Smyth won a gold medal in the 100 metres sprint event for men. His time was 10 point 62 seconds, and he set a new world record.

Another great performance was by Usain Bolt from Jamaica. He's a sprinter too, and he also ran in the men's 100 metres sprint event. He was the fastest runner — his time was 9 point 69 seconds. So he won the gold medal, and he set a new world record.

Hmm! Something strange there? How can two people win the gold medal for the same event? And Jason Smyth was slower than Bolt, but he won the gold. So: two people won the gold medal for the same event. And one was faster than the other? Yes, you've understood correctly. But before we tell you how this is possible, let's look at another example.

In the women's discus throwing event, the best throw was by Stefanie Brown Trafton from the USA — she threw the discus 64 point 74 metres and won the gold medal. But Marianne Buggenhagen from Germany also won the gold medal for throwing the discus — she threw it 27 point eight metres. So — Marianne Buggenhagen's throw was shorter, but she also came first.

How is this possible?

22   UNIT 2

> **Answers**
> Jason Smyth: 100 metres sprint; 10.62 seconds
> Stefanie Brown Trafton: USA; 64.74 metres
> Usain Bolt: Jamaica; Gold
> Marianne Buggenhagen: Germany; throwing the discus; Gold

c ▶ CD1 T11 In pairs or small groups, students discuss the questions and give reasons for their answers. Ask some pairs or a spokesperson from each group to give their views to the rest of the class. Does everyone agree? If there are any interesting opinions, encourage students to talk about them further and see what the rest of the class think. Play part 2 of the recording for students to check their predictions.

TAPESCRIPT

How is this possible? Well, the answer is this: Jason Smyth and Marianne Buggenhagen are disabled – Jason is blind and Marianne is in a wheelchair. They took part in a different Olympic Games, one called the Paralympics – an Olympic Games for disabled people.

The Paralympics started in 1960 in Rome – there were 400 sportspeople there. In 2008 in Beijing, there were more than 4,000 athletes.

The athletes in the Paralympics produce wonderful performances. Are they as good as ordinary athletes? Usually they're not as fast or as strong, but some disabled runners and swimmers are only a little slower than regular athletes. Not many people in the world, for example, are able to run as fast as Jason Smyth! Another remarkable example is Natalie Du Toit, a swimmer from South Africa, who in 2008 took part in both the Olympic games and the Paralympics. In the Paralympics, she won five gold medals for swimming. In the regular Olympics, Du Toit swam in the ten kilometre race. She swam most of the race with her hair in her eyes because her swimming cap came off. But she still finished sixteenth! Du Toit has only one leg – she lost her left leg above the knee in a motorcycle crash in 2001.

d ▶ CD1 T11 Read the questions with students. Play the recording. Allow students to compare answers with a partner before checking in open class.

> **Answers**
> 1 An Olympic Games for disabled people.
> 2 In 1960
> 3 More than 4,000
> 4 Sixteenth
> 5 She has only one leg.

e Students think of other famous disabled people and tell the class about them. Ask students to describe them without saying the name and ask the rest of the class to guess who is being described.

2 Grammar
★ Comparative and superlative adjectives

a Books closed. To introduce this grammar point, write the following examples on the board: *I am younger than my brother.* Or, *I am the youngest in my family.* Ask students to identify the comparative and superlative form and elicit or explain how to form comparatives and superlatives.

Ask a student to come out and underline each form on the board. Students now open their books at page 19 and complete the exercise.

Check answers, asking students to tell you which are the comparatives and which the superlatives.

> **Answers**
> 2 slower 3 best 4 shorter

b Ask students to read through the adjectives in the box and the table. Go through the examples with them, making sure they remember which are comparatives and which are superlatives. Students complete the exercise. Check answers.

> **Answers**
> -er/-est: fast; quiet; high; new
> -ier/-iest: tidy
> more/most: interesting; expensive
> Irregular comparatives: bad

> **Language notes**
> 1 Students may produce incorrect comparatives, e.g. ~~more interesting that~~. Remind them we use *more ... than* in English.
> 2 It may be useful to remind students of the spelling rules for comparatives and superlatives:
> - one syllable adjectives: add *-er/-est*, e.g. *fast – faster – fastest*
> - one syllable adjectives which end consonant + vowel + consonant: double the final consonant + *-er/-est*, e.g. *big – bigger – biggest*
> - two syllable adjectives ending in consonant + *-y*, delete the *-y* and add *-ier/-iest*, e.g. *tidy – tidier – tidiest*
> - two or more syllable adjectives: add *more/most* in front of the adjective, e.g. *more/most successful*
> - irregular adjectives: learn them! E.g. *far – further – furthest*

UNIT 2   23

✱ Intensifiers with comparative adjectives

Stronger classes: Students look at the pictures and the example sentences. Ask them to identify the comparative adjectives in each sentence and then elicit or explain what difference the intensifiers make (*much / far / a lot* are used with comparative adjectives to show a big difference; *a bit / a little* are used with comparative adjectives to show a small difference). To check understanding at this point, ask students to give you an example of their own for one or both of the intensifiers.

Weaker classes: Books closed. Write two example sentences of your own on the board, e.g. *I'm much younger than my brother. / I'm a bit older than you.* Ask students to identify the comparative adjectives (*younger/older*). Ask them to look at the words before each adjective and explain the purpose of each (*much* is used with comparative adjectives to show a big difference; *a bit* or *a little* are used with comparative adjectives to show a small difference). Students now open their books at page 19 and look at the picture and example sentences.

[c] Students read through prompts 1 to 6. Go through the example and then ask students to produce another example sentence using *easy*. Students complete the exercise. Remind them to use the correct comparative forms and to start each sentence with *I think* ... . Monitor and check students are using the forms correctly, noting down any repeated errors. Students compare answers in pairs before a whole class check.

> **Example answers**
> 2 I think an MP4 player is much more expensive than a mobile phone.
> 3 I think girls are much tidier than boys.
> 4 I think Maths is much more difficult than History.
> 5 My best friend is far taller than me.
> 6 My country is a lot bigger than Britain.

Grammar notebook
Students should note down the table and rules from Exercise 2 and write some examples and translations of their own.

Vocabulary and grammar
✱ Antonyms

[a] Ask students to read through the adjectives 1–10 and the adjectives in Exercise 2b and check understanding. Go through the example with them. Students complete the exercise. Check answers.

Students now read the second part of the instruction. Go through the first item with them, eliciting the first comparative. Students complete the exercise. Allow them to compare answers with a partner before a whole class check.

> **Answers**
> 1 bad – worse – worst
>   good – better – best
> 2 difficult – more difficult – most difficult
>   easy – easier – easiest
> 3 fast – faster – fastest
>   slow – slower – slowest
> 4 interesting – more interesting – most interesting
>   boring – more boring – most boring
> 5 cheap – cheaper – cheapest
>   expensive – more expensive – most expensive
> 6 high – higher – highest
>   low – lower – lowest
> 7 quiet – quieter – quietest
>   noisy – noisier – noisiest
> 8 messy – messier – messiest
> 9 ugly – uglier – ugliest
>   beautiful – more beautiful – most beautiful
> 10 young – younger – youngest
>   new – newer – newest
>   old – older – oldest

> **Language note**
> Remind students that some adjectives can have more than one opposite, e.g. *old/young; old/new; tidy/messy; tidy/untidy*, etc.

✱ (not) as ... as comparatives

[b] Ask students to read through the two examples. Explain that we use *as ... as* to say two nouns are the same and *not as ... as* to say that the first noun is less than the second. Elicit what is being compared in the first example sentence (*Smyth and Bolt*) and in the second (*Smyth and an ordinary athlete*).

Students answer the questions. Check answers. To check understanding at this point, it may be useful to ask students to produce some sentences of their own using the construction (*not*) *as ... as*.

> **Answers**
> a Bolt   b No, they are the same.

[c] Ask students to read through sentences 1 to 4. Go through the example, asking students to explain why *not as ... as* is used. Students complete the exercise. Remind them to use adjectives they have seen already in this unit and to think about how the two sentences will mean the same using the construction (*not*) *as ... as*. Check answers.

24 UNIT 2

> **Answers**
> 2 as messy as 3 as slow as 4 as quiet as

> **Answers**
> 2 Our team beat the other team / won 2–1.
> 3 It was a draw.
> 4 The referee sent a player off.

5 Read

Warm up
Ask students which sports are at the Paralympic Games. Make a list on the board and ask them which ones they think are the most difficult for disabled people to do and why. Discuss this as a class, in L1 if appropriate.

a Students look at the picture and the title of the text and read the questions. Elicit some ideas. Students read the text quickly to check their ideas. Remind them that they don't need to understand every word at this stage. Check answers.

> **Answers**
> 1 The sport is wheelchair basketball.
> 2 Australia and Canada.
> 3 Canada won.

b Students read through questions 1 to 4. Check any problems. Go through the first one as an example, showing students how to locate the answer in the text. Students complete the exercise. Check answers.

Weaker classes: You may want to pre-teach the following words: *beat, period, came back, took the lead, draw, blew, whistle*.

> **Answers**
> 1 49:47
> 2 Australia was winning by eight points.
> 3 He said that Australia played very well, but Canada played hard and fast and better than Australia.
> 4 He feels that Australia will do very well.

6 Vocabulary

★ Sport

a Read through the sentences with students and check understanding. Students match the sentences and the pictures. Allow them to check answers with a partner before open class feedback.

> **Answers**
> 1 G 2 C 3 F 4 A 5 H 6 B 7 E 8 D

b Look at pictures 1–4 with students. Elicit sentences to describe what they can see. Ask students to write sentences. With stronger classes ask them to cover Exercise 6a while they do this exercise.

7 Grammar

★ Adverbs/comparative adverbs

a **Stronger classes:** Students read the example. Elicit the formation of regular adverbs (adjective + -ly).

Students now go through the text on page 20 and underline other examples of adverbs. If necessary, find the first one as a class. Check answers.

Weaker classes: Books closed. Write the following sentences on the board:
1 I am very nervous before exams.
2 I waited nervously before the results arrived.

Ask students which sentence contains an adjective (1) and which an adverb (2). Elicit the formation of regular adverbs (adjective + -ly). Students open their books at page 21 and look at the example sentence. Students now go through the text on page 20 and underline other examples of adverbs. Tell them there are nine in total. If necessary, find the first one as a class. Check answers.

> **Answers**
> Para 2: brilliantly
> Para 3: badly; well; hard; fast; better
> Para 4: regularly; harder; well

b **Stronger classes:** Ask students to read the questions and elicit the form of each type of adverb.

Weaker classes: It may be useful to put an example of each type on the board for them and then elicit the formation rules, e.g. *quick, easy, fast*.

> **Answers**
> • Regular adverbs: add *-ly* to the adjective, e.g. *quick – quickly*
> • Adjectives ending in *-y*: change the *-y* to *-i* and add *-ly*, e.g. *easy – easily*
> • Irregular adverbs: learn them! e.g. *hard, fast, well*

To check understanding at this point, call out several adjectives of your choice, e.g. *nervous, bad, easy, slow, hard* and ask students to give you the adverbs.

c Ask students to read through the diary entry. Go through the example with them, making sure they are clear that they have to circle the correct option. Students complete the exercise. They can then compare answers in pairs before a whole class check.

UNIT 2   25

> **Answers**
> 1 well   2 quickly   3 terrible   4 fluently
> 5 badly   6 easy   7 quickly   8 good
> 9 happily

d **Stronger classes:** Students read the example sentence. Explain that comparative adverbs are used when two actions are compared. Ask students what the action is in the example sentence (*practising*). Students then read and complete the rule box.

Weaker classes: Books closed. Put two examples on the board, e.g. *I can speak L1 more quickly than English. / I understand French more easily than Spanish*. Ask a student to come out and underline the comparative adverbs. Point out that we use *more ... than* with adverbs as well as adjectives for comparison and explain that comparative adverbs are used when two actions are compared. Students open their book at page 21 and read the example sentence and complete the rule box.

> **Answer**
> more

e **Stronger classes:** Ask students to look at the two examples and complete the exercise. Check answers.

> **Answers**
> 3 better   4 harder   5 faster   6 worse

Weaker classes: Write the headings: *Regular / Adjectives ending in -y / Irregular* on the board. Ask a student to come out and write *soon/sooner* under the correct column (*Regular*). Do the same with all the other examples.

> **Answers**
> Regular: fast – faster; hard – harder
> Adjectives ending in -*y*: early – earlier
> Irregular: good – better; bad – worse

f This exercise can be set for homework. Students read through sentences 1 to 8. Check any problems. Go through the example with them, if necessary. Students complete the exercise. Remind them to look carefully at each adjective and decide if it is regular or irregular. Check answers.

> **Answers**
> 2 more clearly   3 more fluently
> 4 more slowly   5 better   6 more quickly
> 7 harder   8 earlier

Grammar notebook

Remind students to note down the examples and rules for comparative adjectives and adverbs from this exercise.

 Speak

Divide the class into pairs. Students read through the verbs in the box. Check any problems. Ask a stronger pair to read out the examples to the rest of the class. Students now take turns to compare themselves with famous people or people in the class. Monitor and check students are using the forms correctly and note down any repeated errors to go through as a class after the exercise. Ask for some feedback and follow up any interesting comparisons as a class.

A marathon

 Read and Listen

Warm up

Introduce the characters to students. They are two boys, Joel and Pete, and two girls, Jess and Debbie, from the same school. If students have studied *English in Mind 1*, ask them if they can remember the characters' names. Tell students the characters will appear regularly later in the book.

Look at the first picture with students. Ask students where the children are (in the street) and what they might be talking about (a marathon). Ask students if they have ever run a long distance. How far did they run? Were they tired?

a ▶ CD1 T13   Read the questions with students and ask them to look at the photos. Play the recording for students to read and listen to find the answers.

TAPESCRIPT
See the text on page 22 of the Student's Book.

> **Answers**
> Joel's father was running in a marathon. Joel is laughing because his father took 7 hours and 12 minutes.

b Pre-teach difficult vocabulary: *enthusiastic, impressed*. Go through the first item with students as an example. Ask students to find the wrong information in each sentence and to correct it. Allow students to go back through the dialogue if they can't remember what happened.

26   UNIT 2

Answers
1 Joel doesn't think his dad is enthusiastic about sports.
2 Joel's dad finished the marathon, and Joel wasn't impressed with his time.
3 Some other runners were slower than Joel's dad.
4 Pete doesn't think he is a better runner than Joel's dad.
5 Debbie and Pete don't think it's ridiculous to run a marathon in seven hours.

OPTIONAL ACTIVITY

In groups, students can act out the dialogue from the photo story.

10 Everyday English

a Read through the expressions from the dialogue with students. Do the first item as an example. Ask students if they can remember (without looking back) who said this (Joel). Students complete the exercise, only looking back at the dialogue if they need to. Check answers.

Answers
1 Joel 2 Joel 3 Pete 4 Pete 5 Joel 6 Jess

b Ask students to read through the dialogues and check they understand them. Check any vocabulary problems. Go through the first item as an example. Students complete the exercise and compare answers in pairs before a whole class check.

Answers
2 We're talking about 3 that's not the point
4 that sort of thing 5 At the end of the day
6 an awful lot of

Vocabulary notebook
Students should start a section called *Everyday English* in their vocabulary notebooks and note down these expressions.

Discussion box

Weaker classes: Students can choose one question to discuss.

Stronger classes: In pairs or small groups, students go through the questions in the box and discuss them.

Monitor and help as necessary, encouraging students to express themselves in English and to use any vocabulary they have learned from the text. Ask pairs or groups to feed back to the class and discuss any interesting points further.

11 Improvisation

Divide the class into pairs. Tell students they are going to create a dialogue between Joel and his dad. Read through the instructions with students. Give students two minutes to plan their dialogue. Circulate and help with vocabulary as necessary. Encourage students to use expressions from Exercise 10. Students practise their dialogue in pairs. Listen to some of the best dialogues in open class.

12 Team Spirit DVD Episode 1

a Look at the photo with students and ask them to describe what is happening and to guess the answers to the questions. Listen to some of their ideas in open class.

Answers
Joel's special project is helping a drama group for people with disabilities. At the beginning, Joel hates the idea. After the first meeting, he realises that it is interesting and wants to go again.

b Ask students to match the words and definitions. Allow them to use a dictionary if necessary. Students check their answers with a partner before feedback in open class.

Answers
2 e 3 a 4 c 5 g 6 b 7 d 8 f

Now watch episode 1 of the DVD and find out what happened.

13 Write

The planning for this exercise can be done in class and the writing can be set for homework.

a Ask students to read through the instructions and then questions 1 to 6. Check any problems. If necessary, go through the first item as an example. Students read through the report and answer the questions. Check answers.

Answers
1 A football match.
2 Last Wednesday evening in London.
3 They both played really well. Ronaldo was excellent.
4 Ronaldo.
5 2–2.
6 Yes, he did. He saw some great players and he went for a pizza.

UNIT 2   27

b Students read through topics 1 to 3. Students read the report again, this time matching each paragraph with a topic. Check answers.

> **Answers**
> 1 B 2 C 3 A

c In pairs, students think of a sports event they have seen or watched on television. Students now write up their own reports. Encourage them to follow the report on page 24 as a model and to use as many adverbs and adjectives as they can to describe how they felt and what the atmosphere was like. This exercise can be set for homework. In the next session, collect in the reports to correct or students can swap reports with a partner.

14 Last but not least: more speaking

a Look at the example with students and check that they understand the concept of Yes/No questions. Students write questions based on the prompts. Check answers. Ask students to repeat the sentences after you and check they are using the correct intonation pattern.

> **Answers**
> 2 Do you play any sport?
> 3 Have you got a favourite sportsperson?
> 4 Do your parents like sport?
> 5 Does anyone in your family play a sport well?

b Follow the same procedure with the prompts in column C.

> **Answers**
> 2 What do you play?
> 3 Who is it?
> 4 What do they like?
> 5 Who plays a sport well? / What does he/she play?

c Tell students they are going to ask the questions to a number of different students. Ask students to stand up and circulate, and ask questions until they have found a different name for each of the five questions. If space is limited, organise students into small groups, then rearrange the groups when students have asked each other the questions.

d Divide the class into pairs. Students tell each other what they have learnt about their classmates. You may like to ask some students to read some of the examples in open class without mentioning a name, for the rest of the class to guess who they refer to.

Check your progress

1 Grammar

a 1 saw 2 was looking 3 started 4 was crossing
5 heard 6 was coming 7 stopped 8 didn't hit

b 2 easier; easiest 3 more exciting; most exciting
4 worse; worst

c 2 happily 3 fluently 4 badly 5 easily 6 well

2 Vocabulary

a 2 slow 3 expensive 4 ugly 5 messy
6 noisy 7 difficult

b 2 getting old 3 got a surprise 4 get home
5 gets good ideas 6 get the answer

How did you do?

Check that students are marking their scores. Collect these in and check them as necessary and discuss any further work needed with specific students.

Memo from Mario

He ran faster

1 A hero of yours

- In preparation think of a person that you really respect and feel is a model for you … a hero, if you like. This could be someone in public life, in sport or in your own circle of acquaintance.
- Write seven to eight short clear sentences about this person's characteristics, behaviour and beliefs.
- Photocopy the text for the students or have it ready to flash up on the IWB.
- In the lesson give out your text about your hero for the class to read.
- Allow them to ask you questions about what you have written.
- Now ask them to work on their own, and bring to mind a person they very much admire.
- Ask them to write seven to eight sentences about this person's characteristics, behaviour and beliefs. Tell them they have 10–15 minutes for this task.
- Go round helping with the language and correcting.
- When the writing phase is done, ask them to re-read what they have written and underline all the sentences that apply to them as well as to their hero.
- Group the students in fours to read what they have written and to explain what they have underlined.
- Round off the lesson with open class feedback about what they learnt from the activity.

> **RATIONALE**
> There is a fascinating range of heroes presented in Level 1 of English in Mind and in this book. In this exercise, by modeling the activity, you help the students think more intimately about their heroes.
>
> The fact that you, their teacher, looks up to people and learns from them can have quite an impact on the students.

Acknowledgement
I learned this activity in a Gestalt therapy workshop.

2 Four voice dictation

- Australia almost the champions (page 20)
- In preparation photocopy the reading text on page 20.
- Cut it into its four paragraphs. The first paragraph includes the title.
- Warn colleagues working near your room that you will be running a noisy activity for around ten minutes!
- In the classroom reorganise the class so that a quarter of the students are seated in each of the four corners of the room, facing the centre.
- Ask each group to send you a 'leader'.
- Give each leader a paragraph of the text and tell them to stand on the opposite side of the room from their groups.
- Ask the leaders to simultaneously dictate their paragraph to their group, on the other side of the room.
- When this is done, ask the students to return to their normal places, turn to page 20 and check that what they have written is correct.

> **RATIONALE**
> Four voice dictation is one of the most realistic listening exercises that I know.
>
> The student has to follow the voice of his leader and ignore the cacophony of the others.
>
> This is exactly what happens in a noisy railway station or in a party with a lot of people in a small space. Excellent practice for real life. Teenagers love this one.

Acknowledgement
This is one of many excellent techniques I have learned from Herbert Puchta.

UNIT 2

3 Our world

Unit overview

TOPIC: The environment

TEXTS

Reading and listening: a text about a free bicycle scheme
Listening: a radio interview about renewable forms of energy
Listening: a song: *Big Yellow Taxi* by Joni Mitchell
Writing: an article for a school website about water

SPEAKING AND FUNCTIONS

Discussing environmental problems
Predicting future events
Discussing the uses of water

LANGUAGE

Grammar: *will/won't* and *may/might* (*not*) for prediction; *if/unless* in first conditional
Vocabulary: The environment and forms of renewable energy

1 Read and listen

Warm up

As a class or in small groups, students discuss problems with the environment. You could elicit some of the vocabulary in the unit, e.g. *global warming, pollution, climate change,* etc. Ask them what sort of things they can do to help. Ask for some groups to feed back to the rest of the class and discuss any interesting ideas further. This can be discussed in L1 if appropriate.

a Students read the question and look at the photos. Elicit some ideas. Students then read the text quickly to check their ideas. Remind them they don't have to understand every word in the text at this stage. Check answers as a class.

> **Answer**
> They have introduced a free bicycle scheme.

b ▶ CD1 T14 Ask students to read through items 1 to 6 and a to f.

Stronger classes: Ask them to read the text and match the two parts of the sentence. Then play the recording for them to listen and check only.

Weaker classes: Play the recording, pausing it after the first item and ask them to match this as an example. Then play the rest of the recording while students read and listen and match the other sentences. Check answers. Play the recording again, pausing as necessary to clarify any problems.

TAPESCRIPT

See the reading text on page 26 of the Student's Book.

> **Answers**
> 2 a   3 d   4 b   5 c   6 e

c In small groups, students discuss the questions. Circulate and help with vocabulary as required. When students have discussed fully, you may like to divide them into pairs and present their answers to their new partner. Encourage students to speak at length without interruption. As feedback, listen to some of their ideas in open class and encourage further discussion.

2 Vocabulary

★ The environment

a Ask students to read through phrases 1 to 7. Go through the first item as an example, eliciting or explaining the meaning.

Students work out the meaning of the other expressions from context by looking at the other sentences in the text.

Check answers as a class or if students prefer they can check answers in a dictionary.

> **Answers**
> 1 lines of stationary traffic; dirty air; smoke from cars
> 2 make the air cleaner
> 3 smoke from industry
> 4 increase in temperatures around the world; big changes in weather and temperature
> 5 being lost
> 6 go up / increase
> 7 the natural world

b ▶ CD1 T15 Ask student to read through words 1 to 8 in the box and to look at the pictures.

Stronger classes: Elicit the words students know already and ask them to match them. Students then match the other words.

Weaker classes: Go through the first item as an example. Students then match the other words.

Students compare answers in pairs. Play the recording for students to listen and check or change their answers. Play the recording again, pausing for students to repeat each word.

> **Tapescript/Answers**
> 1 recycling D
> 2 litter E
> 3 pollution A
> 4 factory fumes C
> 5 rainforests F
> 6 rubbish B

c Students read through the verbs in the box. Check any problems. Go through the example, if necessary. Students complete the exercise. Check answers.

> **Answers**
> 1 pick … up 2 recycle 3 waste 4 clean up
> 5 pollute 6 cut down

Vocabulary notebook

Students should start a section called *The environment* and note down all the new words from Exercise 2.

3 Speak

a Divide the class into pairs. Read through the example sentences and explain to students that they must think of more problems in the environment and make a list. Give students a few minutes to complete the exercise. Ask for feedback and put a selection of ideas on the board or ask students to come out and write their ideas on the board.

b Students now rank the problems in order of seriousness. Give students a few minutes to continue to rank the other items in their lists. Then put each pair with a new pair to make groups of four and pairs compare lists. Ask for feedback and ask students to come out and rank the items on the board. Are there any interesting results? Does the whole class agree? Encourage students to discuss with the rest of the class why they feel certain problems are more or less important than others.

c In the same or different pairs, students now make a list of things ordinary people can do to help the environment. Put the examples on the board and elicit a few more. Give students a few minutes to discuss this. Ask for feedback and write their ideas on the board or ask some students to come out and write their ideas up.

d In small groups, students discuss which of the things from Exercise 3c they do to help the environment. Ask for feedback.

4 Grammar

★ *will/won't* and *might/may (not)* for prediction

a **Stronger classes:** Read through the examples with students, pointing out the use of *will* and *might*. Ask students if it is definite that people will still use their cars and elicit *Yes*. Ask them if it is definite that pollution levels will reduce and elicit *No, it is only possible*. To check understanding at this point, ask a few students to give you an example of their own for each verb. Students now go back through the text on page 26 and underline other examples of *will/won't* and *may/might (not)*.

Weaker classes: Books closed. Write a few examples of your own on the board, e.g. *I will/might be at school tomorrow. / It will/might rain tomorrow. / (Juventus) will/might win the league this year*. Ask students how likely each of these things is to happen. Elicit that it is very likely that you will come to school tomorrow and circle *will* in the example on the board. Ask a student to come out and choose the correct answer in the next example and another for a third example if you have used one. At this point, elicit or explain the difference between *will/won't* and *may/might (not)* and when we use them (*will/won't* for certainty and *may/might (not)* if there is an element of doubt).

To check understanding at this point, ask a few students to give you an example of their own for each verb. Students now open their book at page 28 and read through the examples from the text. Then they go back through the text on page 26 and underline further examples of *will/won't* and *may/might (not)*. Check answers.

> **Answers**
> Para 2: won't use
> Para 3: won't solve; might help; will be; will continue; will get

Students now read the rule box and complete it. Check answers.

> **Answers**
> will; might

> **Language note**
> Remind students that the negative form of *will* is *won't* and that it is the same for all persons.

b Students read through sentences 1 to 5. Go through the example as a class, if necessary. Students complete the exercise. Check answers.

UNIT 3

> **Answers**
> 2 will travel   3 will arrive   4 'll buy
> 5 won't take

c Students read through sentences 1 to 7. Go through the example, if necessary. Students complete the exercise. Check answers.

> **Answers**
> 2 might be   3 might not like   4 might break
> 5 might not pass   6 might live   7 might have

d This exercise can be set for homework. Students read through sentences 1 to 7. Check any problems. Go through the example, if necessary, making sure students understand why *might* is the correct answer. Students complete the exercise. Remind them to think about the degree of possibility before they choose their verb. Check answers.

> **Answers**
> 2 won't   3 might   4 will   5 might
> 6 A: will B: might   7 won't

Grammar notebook
Remind students to note down the rules for the use of *will/won't* and *may/might (not)* from this unit and some example sentences of their own.

6 Speak

a Divide the class into pairs. Students read through the topics in the box. Ask a stronger pair to read out the example exchange to the class. Draw students' attention to the use of *will* and *might* in the exchange. Give students a few minutes to discuss the topics in the box. Remind them to use *will/won't* and *might/may not* wherever possible. Monitor and check these are being used correctly and note down any errors or pronunciation problems to go through as a class later.

Weaker classes: They could choose three topics only from the box.

Ask for pairs to feed back to the class. If there are any interesting points, discuss these further as a class.

b Working individually, students make notes of what they think will/might (not) change. Circulate and help with vocabulary as necessary. In pairs, students compare ideas. As feedback, listen to some of their ideas in open class and encourage further discussion.

7 Grammar and speaking
★ First conditional

a **Stronger classes:** Read through the example sentence with students and ask them to offer suggestions to complete the gap. Students then turn to the text on page 26 again and check or change their answers. Remind students how to form the first conditional by asking them which verb goes in each half of the sentences. They read through the rule box and complete it using the examples to help them.

Weaker classes: Books closed. Write a few examples of your own on the board, e.g. *If I study hard for my exam, I ... / If it doesn't rain tomorrow, I ... / If I save up enough money, I ... .* Ask students to offer suggestions to complete each sentence. Ask students what they notice about the verbs in each half of the sentence. Elicit that the first one is present simple and the second one is *will/won't*. Students now open their books at page 29 and read through the example sentence. Students look back at the text on page 26 and complete the sentence. They read through the rule box and complete it using the examples to help them.

Check answers.

> **Answers**
> Sentence 1: ... they won't use a bicycle – they'll still use their cars.
> Rule: present; will

To check understanding of the first conditional at this point, ask students to produce an example sentence each about themselves.

b Students read through sentences 1 to 6. Go through the example, if necessary. Students complete the exercise. Check answers.

> **Answers**
> 2 are; will be
> 3 see; will give
> 4 increases; will die
> 5 won't tell; don't come
> 6 will be; see

> **Language notes**
> 1 Remind students that the *if* phrase can come first or second in the sentence but the present simple tense always goes with the *if* phrase.
> 2 Remind students to use the contracted form in conditional sentences. It is more natural in English to say *If the weather is good tomorrow, I'll go to the beach* than *... I will go to the beach.*
> 3 Students may produce sentences like *If I will go ... , I will ... .* Ask them to think about how these sentences work in their own language and to translate them if necessary.

32   UNIT 3

c This exercise can be set for homework. Students read through questions 1 to 6. Go through the example, if necessary, pointing out the word order in questions. Students complete the exercise. Remind them to use the correct question forms and to look for the *if* phrase carefully since it may not always be at the start of each question. Check answers.

> **Answers**
> 2 will, go; go
> 3 will, buy; go
> 4 don't go; will, do
> 5 doesn't give; will, do
> 6 phone; will, talk about

d Divide the class into pairs. Ask a stronger pair to read out the example exchange and draw students' attention to the use of the first conditional in the question and *might* in the answer. Remind students that *might* is used if we are unsure of something. Give students a few minutes to ask and answer the questions. Monitor and check that students are taking turns to ask and answer. Note down any problems they are having with the question and answer formation or pronunciation to go through later as a class. Ask for feedback from pairs on what each person answered.

e Divide the class into pairs (or keep the same pairs as Exercise 7d). Students look at the pictures. Go through the example sentence as a class, drawing students' attention to the use of the first conditional structure. Give students time to complete the exercise. Ask a few pairs to read out their sentences to the class.

Weaker classes: They may need more support with vocabulary here. Offer them the following prompts (or others of your own choice) for each picture:
2 borrow money / buy a computer
3 play football / break a window
4 turn the music down / father get angry
5 stop raining / play tennis
6 ride properly / have an accident

> **Example answers**
> 2 If he doesn't borrow some money, he won't be able to buy a computer.
> 3 If he plays football, he might break a window.
> 4 If she doesn't turn the music down, her father will be very angry.
> 5 If it doesn't stop raining, they won't be able to play tennis.
> 6 If she doesn't ride properly, she might have an accident.

Grammar notebook
Students should note down the rules for the first conditional from this unit and some example sentences of their own.

✱ *unless* in first conditional sentences

f **Stronger classes:** Students read through the example sentence from the text. Ask them what they notice about the verb following *unless* in the sentence and elicit that it is positive. Students complete the rule.

Weaker classes: Book closed. Write two examples on the board, e.g. *Unless you study hard, you won't pass your exams. / If you study hard, you'll pass your exams.* Ask students to identify the first conditional sentence (sentence 2) and then ask them what they notice about the *unless* sentence. Elicit or explain that the verb following *unless* is positive but the second verb is negative. Students now open their books at page 29 and look at the examples from the text. Students then complete the rule. Draw students' attention to the meaning of *unless*.

Check answers.

> **Answer**
> don't do

To check students have understood the meaning of *unless* at this point, ask them to produce a sentence with *unless* about themselves.

> **Language notes**
> 1 Remind students that *unless* means *if not*.
> 2 Students may produce statements like ~~Unless I don't work~~, I will ... Remind them that *unless* is always followed by a positive verb.
> 3 Students may find it useful to think about how this phrase works in their own language and translate some of the example sentences.

9 Students read through items 1 to 5 and a to e. Go through the example, if necessary. Students complete the exercise. Check answers.

> **Answers**
> 2 e 3 a 4 b 5 c

Grammar notebook
Encourage students to note down the rules for *unless* and an example sentence of their own.

Culture in mind

8 Listen

Warm up

Ask students what uses of water they can think of, elicit a few examples and put them on the board. Then ask them how they think water is used in other countries.

UNIT 3   33

a ▶ CD1 T17 Look at the pictures and ask students if they can describe any of them. Tell students they are going to hear seven facts about water. You may like to pre-teach the following words: *fresh water, salt water, iceberg, dripping tap, wells, diseases.*

Play the recording while students match the facts to the pictures. Check answers.

TAPESCRIPT

Narrator: Water, water – but it isn't everywhere.

Speaker 1: Water – it's easy for us, isn't it? It's everywhere. When we want water, it's there – we cook with it, we wash with it, and when we're thirsty we drink it. Water is very, very important for our survival on our planet. Here are some facts that perhaps you didn't know about water.

Speaker 2: One – there are two kinds of water on planet Earth: fresh water and salt water. We can only drink fresh water. Salt water isn't drinkable.

Speaker 1: Two – of all the fresh water on the planet, people can only get to and use about one per cent of it. Only about one per cent – the other 99 per cent of fresh water is in places we can't get to. For example …

Speaker 2: Three – about 70 per cent of all the fresh water on earth is in Antarctica, at the South Pole, in the ice and icebergs there. Lots of fresh water, but it's frozen, and very far away from where we live. So we can't use it.

Speaker 1: Four – most of us get our water at home out of a tap. Sometimes the tap drips because it's old or because someone hasn't turned it off properly. So what? Well, a dripping tap can sometimes waste about 75 litres of water every day.

Speaker 2: Five – in western homes – in the USA for example, or in Europe – one person can use as much as 500 litres of water a day. An African family might only use about 20 litres a day.

Speaker 1: Six – every day, millions of people – especially women and children – walk very long distances to get water, from rivers or lakes or wells, and sometimes the water is dirty and polluted. This means lots of bad things, for example …

Speaker 2: Seven – many people get sick because they drink dirty water. 88 per cent of all diseases in the world are caused by drinking dirty water.

Answers
1 D 2 F 3 B 4 E 5 G 6 A 7 C

b ▶ CD1 T17 Ask students to match the two parts of the sentences. Allow them to compare answers with a partner before listening to the recording to check answers. As a follow-up, ask students which part of the information they find most surprising and discuss in open class.

Answers
1 b 2 e 3 c 4 d 5 a

c ▶ CD1 T17 Before they listen, ask students what problems they think some people in the world have with getting water. Do this in L1 if necessary, translating/eliciting new vocabulary in English as students explain.

Weaker classes: You could write the new vocabulary on the board first. Students copy these and listen and tick the words as they hear them mentioned on the recording.

Answers
They have to walk very long distances to get water, from rivers or lakes or wells, and sometimes the water is dirty and polluted. This means many people get sick because they drink dirty water.

d ▶ CD1 T18 Students read through the questions. Check they understand difficult vocabulary: *polar ice caps, total rainfall.* Play the recording for students to listen and complete the exercise. Students can compare answers in pairs before a whole class check. Play the recording again pausing as necessary to clarify any problems.

TAPESCRIPT

Radio host: We're talking now to one of the organisers of SafeWater, Joanne Williams. Ms Williams, what exactly is SafeWater?

Expert: SafeWater is a non-profit organisation. We help people in developing countries to get safe drinking water and sanitation. It is our aim to make sure that one day, everyone in the world can get safe water to drink.

Radio host: Why is it that there are such problems with safe water? If it's true that people can only get to and use about one per cent of all the fresh water on the planet, then I'm sure a lot of listeners will ask 'Where's the rest?'

Expert: That's a very good question. First of all, when we talk about fresh water we have to remember that 97.5 per cent of the world's water is salt water, and only 2.5 per cent is fresh water. Now, of all the fresh water that there is in the world, 70 per cent is frozen in the polar ice caps.

Radio host: Well, but what about the rest? That still leaves us 30 per cent of all the fresh water, doesn't it?

Expert: Not really. Most of the 30 per cent is in the ground – we wouldn't have grass or plants or trees if the soil wasn't moist. Then there are also huge underground lakes, deep down in the ground, but we don't have access to them, because it would be too expensive to get to

UNIT 3

them, so we can only get to one per cent of the fresh water supply, and that's in lakes, rivers, reservoirs, and in underground sources that are not too deep in the ground, so we have access without huge costs.

Radio host: What about the rainfall? Can you tell us something about that?

Expert: Yes. Of all the water falling onto our planet, about two-thirds goes back up into the atmosphere through a process called evaporation, or else plants take it up. About one-third of the rainfall ends up in the world's rivers. The problem of course is that the world's population is growing very fast, and as a consequence there is about 40 per cent less fresh water available per person than there was, say, 50 years ago.

Radio host: I see. Can you give us a rough idea of …

> **Answers**
> 1 To make sure that everyone in the world can get safe water to drink.
> 2 In the ground or in underground lakes.
> 3 About one-third of total rainfall ends up in rivers, the rest is evaporated into the atmosphere or is taken up by plants.
> 4 The world's population is growing fast, so there is less water per person.

9 Speak

Divide the class into small groups. Ask students to read through the questions and discuss their answers to the questions. Ask groups to report back to the class and compare answers.

10 Listen

a ▶ CD1 T19 Tell students they are going to listen to a song called *Big Yellow Taxi*. In open class, ask students what they think might happen in the song. Read through the words in the box and check understanding. Students read the lyrics of the song. Tell them not to worry about unfamiliar vocabulary at this stage. Play the recording while students listen and fill the gaps with the words in the box. Students compare answers with a partner before you play the recording again, pausing if necessary.

> **Answers**
> 1 paradise 2 parking lot 3 gone 4 museum
> 5 dollar 6 apples 7 give

b Read through the lyrics of the song and deal with any new vocabulary. Tell students that *parking lot* is an American term for an outdoor car park and a *screen door* is a mesh door designed to keep flies out, but allow for ventilation.

Divide the class into pairs and ask students to discuss the environmental message of the song. Circulate and help with any questions. During feedback encourage open class discussion. Ask students if they know any other songs with an environmental message.

> **Possible answers**
> They paved paradise and put up a parking lot
> Don't it always seem to go that you don't know what you've got till it's gone?
> They took all the trees, put 'em in a tree museum
> Hey farmer, farmer, put away that DDT now.
> Give me spots on my apples, but give me the birds and the bees, please!

11 Write

a Ask students to read through the instructions and the questions. Students then read through the web article quickly to find the answers. Check answers.

> **Answers**
> Four (more cycle lanes; more clubs for teenagers; more places for teenagers to play sports; stop people dropping litter)

b Elicit any words/phrases students know to introduce ideas and to give opinions. Write them on the board under the headings *Introducing ideas / Giving opinions*. Ask students to read through the instructions. Go through the example in the web article as a class, making sure students understand which words are for opinions and which are for introducing the idea. Students complete the exercise. Check answers by asking students to come out and write their phrases under the relevant heading on the board.

> **Answers**
> Introducing ideas: Also; In addition; Finally
> Giving opinions: I think that …; I believe that …; In my opinion …; I'm sure that …

c This can be set for homework with the preparation done in class. Read through the bullet points as a class and the three-point plan in Exercise 1d. Give students time to plan their articles in class, answering any questions and helping them as necessary. Students then complete the exercise for homework.

Vocabulary notebook

Encourage students to note down the expressions from Exercise 11 and to use them whenever possible in their writing and speaking.

Memo from Mario

Our world

1 Running dictation

- In preparation make five or six photocopies of 'Bicycle revolution' on page 26 of the Student's Book.
- Stick them up at the front of your class.
- Ask the student to sit in groups of five to seven at the back of the class with a pen and paper.
- Tell them to close their books.
- Explain that one person from each group is to run to the front of the room, read a small bit of the text, run back and dictate it to the group, who all take it down. (Warn the students that trying to bring back too much text at a time can often be inefficient because you forget!) The runner must not take pen or paper with them.
- Then the next runner goes up to the wall to read the next bit of text.
- Start the running dictation.
- At the end of the competition the students return to their normal places and check what they have written against the text in the book.

> **RATIONALE**
> This technique can galvanise a sleepy class. It brings movement into reading and physical excitement into what is often a silent, quiet activity. The exercise has become a classical one around Europe because it keeps the 'naughty' (often highly kinaesthetic) kids more or less in order.

> **VARIATIONS**
> 1 Seat the students at one end of the room, with the texts at the other (as above). <u>Each</u> student goes up to the front wall, reads a bit of text goes back and writes it down. They then return to the wall for more text. You could call this 'self-dictation' and it suits the more intra-personally intelligent learners.
>
> 2 Put the texts up in the corridor outside your room, maybe five to six metres from the door.
>
> The students work in teams of three, A, B and C. The A students read a bit of text and come with it as far as the classroom door. The B students are crowding in the doorway and the A's tell them the first bit of text. The B's then run to the back of the room and dictate this bit to the C's. A student may not enter the classroom and B's may not go out into the corridor!
>
> You need to be sure your colleagues either side and opposite can cope with the sounds of teenage energy!
>
> My own feeling is that use of the corridor and other spaces in the school allows students to break out of the implicit mental prison that the classroom can become during the 16,000 hours of instruction between kindergarten and the school-leaving exam.
>
> 3 Use the same set-up as in 2 above but instead of putting a text up on the wall, stand there yourself reciting a short (eight line) poem or song lyric. Keep reciting in a continuous loop. The A students have to come and listen till they hear the next bit they need.
>
> Don't read yourself into trance!
>
> 4 Use the same set-up as in the main exercise above but have <u>two</u> students run to the front wall of the classroom. They read a short bit of the text and on the way back to their team, they translate it into their mother tongue. They dictate the mother tongue snippet. Then the next two run up to the wall, read, translate, come back and dictate.
>
> At then end of the running phase have the teams put their translations up on the board so you can give them a helping hand.
>
> The relationship between L1 and L2 fascinates linguistically gifted learners.

2 Guessing the picture

- Write these phrases on the board:

  Might it be a ... ?
  It might be a ...
  I think it's a ...
  It's got to be a ...
  It's a ...

- Tell the class you are going to draw an object, line by line, and they have to volunteer guesses as to what it is. (If you decide to draw, say, a bike, draw the cross bar, then a front wheel spoke, then the saddle stem, in other words build up your drawing mysteriously.)
- Make sure the students use *might* with a suitably tentative tone of voice.

> **RATIONALE**
> Fun!

4 Holiday or vacation?

Unit overview

TOPIC: Canada and the USA

TEXTS

Reading and listening: a quiz about Canada and the USA
Reading: a text about Wi-Fi in Vancouver
Listening: a dialogue about recently completed holiday activities
Writing: an email about a holiday

SPEAKING AND FUNCTIONS

Checking information
Talking about recently completed holiday activities

LANGUAGE

Grammar: Question tags; Present perfect with *just, already* and *yet*
Vocabulary: British vs. North American English
Everyday English: *You're not supposed to*; *in the middle of*; *What do you reckon?*; *the kind of thing*; *Have a look*; *No wonder*

1 Read and listen

If you set the background information as a homework research task, ask students to tell the class what they found out.

> **BACKGROUND INFORMATION**
>
> **Vancouver** is a city in the west of Canada situated in the south west of British Columbia.
>
> **British Columbia** is one of Canada's western provinces. It is almost entirely mountainous with the Rocky Mountains in the east and the Coast mountains in the west.

Warm up

Ask students to look at the pictures and ask them what the capital of Canada is (*Ottawa*) and the capital of the USA (*Washington DC*).

a Students then read the quiz and select their answers. Remind them to read all the answer options carefully before making their decision. Do not give answers at this point.

b ▶ CD1 T20 Ask students to read through the instruction. Play the recording once for students to check or change their answers. Play the recording again, pausing as necessary to clarify any problems.

TAPESCRIPT

Speaker 1: And, well – you're Canadian, aren't you?
Speaker 2: That's right. I'm from Edmonton.
Speaker 1: So I thought maybe you could tell me some things about Canada.
Speaker 2: Sure, OK. But it's a big country! I don't know everything about it.
Speaker 1: Yeah – but it's smaller than the USA, isn't it?
Speaker 2: No – no, it isn't. In terms of square kilometres, Canada's much bigger than the USA. But a lot more people live in the USA. About ten times as many.
Speaker 1: Really?
Speaker 2: Yes. Only about 30 million people live in Canada.
Speaker 1: Oh. And what's the biggest city? It isn't Vancouver, is it?
Speaker 2: No, no it isn't – the biggest city is Toronto. But it isn't very big – it has a population of only about two and a half million.
Speaker 1: Cities in the USA are much bigger than that, aren't they?
Speaker 2: Sure. I mean New York, that's got about eight or nine million people. It's the biggest city in the USA.
Speaker 1: Wow. But look, I'm more interested in Canada. Tell me about Vancouver. You've been there, haven't you?
Speaker 2: No, I haven't, actually. But I know a few things. Well, first, it's in a part of Canada called British Columbia …
Speaker 1: Where's that?
Speaker 2: It's in the west. Wow, you don't know much about Canada at all, do you?
Speaker 1: No – well, geography isn't my best subject. Anyway, if it's British Columbia, I guess they all speak English there.
Speaker 2: Uh huh.
Speaker 1: Oh but wait a minute – people speak French in Canada too, don't they?
Speaker 2: Well, over in the east, around Montreal, yes – but not in Vancouver. In fact, do you know what the two most common languages are in Vancouver?
Speaker 1: English and Spanish?
Speaker 2: No!! English and Chinese. Lots of Chinese people live there.

UNIT 4 | 37

Speaker 1: Really? I didn't know that. But listen – tell me about sport, I want to see some good sport when I'm there. Some baseball, for example.

Speaker 2: Well, you won't see a lot of baseball – but you could go to an ice hockey game, it's really popular. In fact, ice hockey's the most popular sport in Canada.

Speaker 1: Hmm, no thanks. I'm not really interested in ice hockey. Maybe I could see some baseball in the USA. We're thinking of going down to California too, to San Francisco. Dad says it isn't very far from Vancouver, he wants to drive there.

Speaker 2: Not far!!?? Wow, it's about 1,200 kilometres!! It's a 15-hour drive!

Speaker 1: Oh – then I should tell Dad that, shouldn't I?

Speaker 2: I think you should! But it's a beautiful drive to get there. You can drive down the coast, that's cool – or else, you can drive inland and go past the Rocky Mountains.

Speaker 1: But they're only in Canada, aren't they?

Speaker 2: No, Morgan! They're in the USA too. Wow, you haven't learned anything in geography, have you?

Speaker 1: No – that's what I said before, Janie ...

> **Answers**
> 1 a   2 b   3 c   4 a   5 b   6 c   7 b   8 b
> 9 c

2 Grammar
✶ Question tags

a ▶ CD1 T20 **Stronger classes:** Ask students to read through the gapped sentences. Go through the example and ask students why they think the tag is negative and elicit because the verb is positive. Students complete the exercise. Remind them to look carefully at the verb used before they decide which tag is required. Students can compare answers in pairs. Play the recording for students to listen and check or change their answers. At this point, elicit that where there is a positive verb there is a negative tag and where there is a negative verb there is a positive tag.

Weaker classes: Books closed. Ask a few questions with question tags of your own, e.g. *It isn't raining today, is it? / You saw the plane outside, didn't you?* etc. but do not explain the use of tags at the moment. Students open their books at page 33 and follow the procedure above for stronger classes. When students have finished the exercise focus again on your own examples and elicit the information from students.

TAPESCRIPT
See Exercise 1b.

> **Answers**
> 2 isn't   3 is   4 aren't   5 haven't   6 do

b Ask students to read through the instructions and then complete the rule. Remind them of the tags used in Exercise 2a and refer them back to their completed answers if necessary.

> **Answers**
> positive; do; did

To check understanding at this point, ask students to ask and answer a few questions of their own.

c Ask students to read through items 1 to 10 and the list of question tags. Go through the example with students. If students are still having problems, refer them back to the rules in Exercise 2b. Students complete the exercise. Check answers.

> **Answers**
> 2 f   3 g   4 i   5 c   6 a   7 e   8 d   9 j
> 10 b

d This exercise can be set for homework. Ask students to read through items 1 to 8. Go through the example, asking students to explain why the tag is *didn't he* (because the verb is in the past simple and we use the auxiliary *did/didn't* in past simple questions). Students complete the exercise. Students can compare answers in pairs before a whole class check.

> **Answers**
> 2 do they   3 doesn't she   4 can you
> 5 didn't they   6 doesn't she   7 haven't you
> 8 has she

Grammar notebook
Encourage students to note down the rules for question tags and a few examples of their own.

4 Speak

a Divide the class into groups of four. Ask students to read through the six questions. Explain that they must ask each person in their group the questions and try to remember their answers without writing them down. Monitor and check students are taking turns in asking and answering and note down any repeated errors to discuss later as a class.

b Go through the example pointing out the use of the question tag to check information. Remind them their intonation should go down at the end of a question if they are checking information and are sure of the answer, and up if they are not sure of the answer. Encourage some students to report their findings back to the whole class.

38 UNIT 4

Monitor and check students are using the correct question tags and the correct intonation. If students are still having problems with intonation at this stage, drill a few more examples as a class.

c Divide the class into pairs. Students read through the prompts on the page. Ask a student the example question, making your intonation go up to show you are not sure of the answer. Students ask and answer the question in their pairs, using question tags. Monitor and check students are using the correct tags and intonation and note down any problems for further discussion.

> **Answers**
> You're 14 years old, aren't you?
> You don't like basketball, do you?
> You live in a flat, don't you?
> You're not English, are you?
> You've been to the USA, haven't you?
> Your sister can't play the piano, can she?
> You can swim, can't you?

5 Read

Warm up

Write *Wi-Fi* on the board. Ask students if they have ever used a Wi-Fi network and discuss the advantages and disadvantages of it. Do they know how Wi-Fi works?

a Tell students they are going to read some posts on a website which is discussing Wi-Fi in Vancouver. Ask students to read through the questions. Encourage them to read the text quickly to check their answers. Remind them they don't need to understand every word. Students can compare answers in pairs before a whole class check.

> **Answers**
> Mike thinks it is a good idea, Anna and Tim think it is a bad idea.

b Read through the sentences with students and check understanding. Students read the text more carefully to answer the questions. Let them compare answers with a partner before feedback in open class. Encourage students to correct false sentences.

> **Answers**
> 1 T
> 2 F (other cities already have it)
> 3 T
> 4 F (she doesn't want to write emails in her garden)
> 5 F (she thinks the bus system could be better)
> 6 T

6 Vocabulary

✱ British vs. North American English

a Ask students if they know any words that mean the same but are different in North American and British English. Put any suggestions on the board. Read through the pairs of words in the box as a class and ask students to focus on the pictures. Go through the first item, eliciting the word to match the first picture in English. Students complete the exercise.

> **Answers**
> 2 sidewalk – pavement
> 3 lift – elevator
> 4 subway – underground
> 5 flat – apartment
> 6 garbage – rubbish
> 7 lorry – truck
> 8 football – soccer
> 9 cookies – biscuits
> 10 candy – sweets

b ▶ CD1 T22 Play the recording for students to check or change their answers. Play it again if necessary, pausing to clarify any problems.

TAPESCRIPT

Speaker 1: You have different words for lots of things, don't you?

Speaker 2: That's right. We Canadians use lots of the same words that Americans use, words that you guys in Britain don't use.

Speaker 1: For example?

Speaker 2: Well, for example … in Canada we say sidewalk, but you say pavement.

Speaker 1: Oh yes, that's right. And you say elevator when we say lift, don't you?

Speaker 2: Yeah – and in American English, pants are what you call trousers. And we say subway, but in Britain you say … oh what do you say?

Speaker 1: Underground. We say underground. Oh, I know another one – erm, the American word for flat is apartment, isn't it?

Speaker 2: Right. Oh, and we say garbage but you say rubbish …

Speaker 1: This is fun! How many more can we think of?

Speaker 2: Oh – I know! We say truck but you say lorry, and we say soccer instead of football.

Speaker 1: Oh, right – soccer.

Speaker 2: OK – one more! You British people say biscuits but we say cookies.

Speaker 1: True – and that reminds me, we say sweets but you say …

Speaker 2: Candy!

UNIT 4 39

Speaker 1: Wow – it's amazing. How do we understand each other? It's the same language but so many things are different!

Speaker 2: Yeah, but we Canadians aren't as different as the Americans. I mean, not so different from the British. For example, we spell lots of words the same way that you do – words like colour, which we spell with a 'u' – and we say the letter 'zed', not 'zee' like Americans.

Speaker 1: Oh yeah? I didn't know that. Tell me some more things that …

Answers

	Britain	North America
2	pavement	sidewalk
3	lift	elevator
4	underground	subway
5	flat	apartment
6	rubbish	garbage
7	lorry	truck
8	football	soccer
9	biscuits	cookies
10	sweets	candy

Vocabulary notebook

Encourage students to start a section called *British / North American English* and to note down the words from Exercise 6.

 Grammar

✱ Present perfect simple with *already* and *yet*

a **Stronger classes:** Elicit how to form the present perfect tense (*has/have* + past participle). Ask students to read through the examples and ask them what they notice about the position of *already* and *yet* (*already* goes between *has* and the past participle, *yet* goes at the end). Explain that *already* means that something has happened before the time of speaking and that *yet* means something has not happened up to the point of speaking but is likely/expected to happen. Ask students to practise a few questions and answers of their own in class to check they have understood.

Weaker classes: Books closed. Write a few examples of your own on the board, e.g. *I've already had my breakfast. / I haven't had my lunch yet.* Ask them: *Have I had my breakfast?* and elicit the answer *Yes.* Then ask: *Have I had my lunch?* Elicit the answer *No.* Ask students to practise a few questions and answers of their own to check they have understood. Students now open their books at page 35 and look at the examples. Follow the procedure for stronger classes.

Students now go through the text on page 34 and find other examples of the present perfect before completing the rule. Check answers.

Answers
have already tried; hasn't stayed; I've already said; I've never heard; it's stayed; I've just read; hasn't built
Rule: have / past participle
past participle / yet

b Ask students to read through dialogues 1 to 4. Check any problems. Go through the example, reminding them of the rules from Exercise 7a. Students complete the exercise. Students can compare answers in pairs before a whole class check. Ask a few stronger pairs to read out their completed dialogues to the rest of the class.

Answers
1 B: I have bought the DVD too.
2 A: Has your brother gone to university yet?
   B: I've already moved into his old bedroom.
3 A: I haven't bought their new CD yet.
   B: I've already listened to it.
4 A: Have you done your homework yet?
   B: I've already finished the Maths, but I haven't started the Geography yet.

Grammar notebook

Encourage students to note down the rules for this and a few examples of their own.

 Listen and speak

▶ **CD1 T23** Ask students to read through the instructions and prompts 1 to 8. Check any problems. Play the recording, pausing after the first prompt if necessary and elicit the correct answer. Play the recording while students complete the exercise. Do not check answers at this point.

TAPESCRIPT

Speaker 1: Hello?

Speaker 2: Maggie? Hi, it's me, Dan!

Speaker 1: Dan? But you're in New York, aren't you?

Speaker 2: That's right. I'm on holiday here!

Speaker 1: Lucky you! Are you having a good time?

Speaker 2: Brilliant, thanks! I've seen lots of things, it's great!

Speaker 1: So, tell me – have you been up the Empire State Building yet?

Speaker 2: Yes, I have. It was wonderful. And the lift's great, it goes up really fast!

Speaker 1: I know, it's fantastic. I think New York is brilliant. Have you had a ride in a yellow cab yet?

40 UNIT 4

Speaker 2: No, not yet. But I've already travelled on the underground several times.

Speaker 1: You mean the subway?

Speaker 2: Yeah, the subway! Sorry.

Speaker 1: And what about baseball? Have you seen a baseball game yet?

Speaker 2: No, not yet. I think we're going the day after tomorrow. And Maggie – something else, but you won't believe it!

Speaker 1: What?

Speaker 2: I haven't eaten an American hamburger yet!

Speaker 1: What??!! Dan, I don't believe it! But you love hamburgers, don't you?

Speaker 2: Yeah, well, I'm here for another four days so I've got time.

Speaker 1: Do you like the people there? Have you met many New Yorkers?

Speaker 2: Oh yes, I've met lots of wonderful people, they're great.

Speaker 1: And Dan, I want to see the photos when you come back. Have you taken lots of photos?

Speaker 2: Sorry Maggie, I haven't taken many photos yet – but I will, I promise! Oh – and one more thing.

Speaker 1: What?

Speaker 2: I've bought you a present!

Speaker 1: Dan! How nice, thanks! What is it?

Speaker 2: I'm not going to tell you – you'll have to wait and see …

Answers
1 ✓ 2 ✗ 3 ✓ 4 ✗ 5 ✗ 6 ✓ 7 ✗ 8 ✓

9 Grammar

✱ Present perfect simple with *just*

 Stronger classes: Students look at the example. Ask them what they notice about the position of *just* and elicit that it goes between *has/have* and the past participle. Ask them if they can explain what the example sentence means. Ask them a few questions to help them if necessary: *Did he/she read Ken's post a long time ago? (No) Has he/she read Ken's post recently? (Yes)* and explain that *just* means a short time ago.

Weaker classes: Books closed. Give students a few examples on the board, e.g. *We've just started Exercise 9. We've just finished Exercise 8.* Ask them what they notice about the position of *just* and elicit that it goes between *has/have* and the past participle. Ask students: *When did we start Exercise 9? When did we finish Exercise 8?* and elicit that

you finished it a few minutes ago. Explain that using *just* with the present perfect shows that something happened a short time ago. Students open their books at page 35 and look at the example sentence. Follow the procedure for stronger classes.

Students complete the rule. Check answers.

Answers
just
have; past participle

To check understanding at this point, ask students to think of a few questions of their own and to ask and answer them across the class.

Language notes
1 Students may have problems with this structure because of the way their own language works. Their own language may only have one verb to express this concept. Monitor them carefully when they are using this structure and check they are using it correctly.
2 It may be helpful to point out to students that *just* + present perfect is used mainly in positive statements.

 Ask students to look at pictures 1 to 6 and read the prompts. Go through the example. Remind students where *just* and *yet* go in their sentences. Students complete the exercise. Check answers.

Answers
2 She's just gone to bed, but she hasn't switched off the light yet.
2 He's just bought a new bike, but he hasn't ridden it yet.
4 She's just eaten dinner, but she done the washing-up yet.
5 He's just made some fruit juice, but he hasn't drunk it yet.
6 They've just scored a goal, but they haven't won the match yet.

Grammar notebook

Encourage students to note down the rules and examples from Exercise 9. They may find it useful to translate the examples into their own language.

✱ New girl

10 Read and listen

Warm up

Ask students to look at the photo story and tell you who the characters are (Joel, Pete, Jess and Debbie). What can they remember about Joel,

UNIT 4   41

the character from Unit 2? (Joel's father had run a marathon and Joel thought it was funny that his father was slow.) Students look at the title of the story and try to predict what is going to happen.

a ▶ CD1 T24 Read through the instructions and the questions with students. Play the recording for students to read and listen. Check answers.

> **Answers**
> She is from Tokyo. She falls asleep in class. Joel and Pete think she is dreaming about her boyfriend.

b Ask students to read through the questions and check understanding. Students answer the questions. Allow them to look back at the story if necessary. Allow them to discuss their answers with a partner before open class feedback.

> **Answers**
> 1 She goes on the internet to find out about life in Japan.
> 2 He realises why Natsumi might be tired.

TAPESCRIPT
See the text on page 36 of the Student's Book.

11 Everyday English

a Students must decide who said these expressions from the photo story. Do the first one as an example if necessary.

Stronger classes: Ask students to complete the exercise without looking back at the photo story.

Weaker classes: Allow students to refer back to the photo story.

> **Answers**
> 1 Joel 2 Pete 3 Joel 4 Joel 5 Debbie
> 6 Pete

b Read through the dialogues with students and check they understand. Ask students to use the expressions in Exercise 11a to complete the gaps. Students complete the exercise. In pairs, students compare answers before a whole class check.

> **Answers**
> 2 in the middle of   3 No wonder
> 4 the kind of thing   5 What do you reckon
> 6 You're not supposed to

Vocabulary notebook

Students should now note down the Everyday English expressions in that section of their vocabulary notebooks. Encourage them to use translations or other expressions from this unit to help them remember each one.

> **Discussion box**
> **Weaker classes:** Students can choose one question to discuss.
>
> **Stronger classes:** In pairs or small groups, students go through the questions in the box and discuss them.
>
> Monitor and help as necessary, encouraging students to express themselves in English and to use any vocabulary they have learned from the text. Ask pairs or groups to feed back to the class and discuss any interesting points further.

12 Improvisation

Divide the class into pairs. Tell students they are going to create a dialogue between Natsumi and Pete. Read through the instructions with students. Give students two minutes to plan their dialogue. Circulate and help with vocabulary as necessary. Encourage students to use expressions from Exercise 11. Students practise their dialogue in pairs. Listen to some of the best dialogues in open class.

13 Team Spirit ● DVD Episode 2

a Look at the photo with students and elicit some adjectives to describe the appearance of the people. In open class discuss students' reactions to the photo.

> **Language note**
> The word 'goth' is derived from gothic and is used to describe people, fashion and music inspired by gothic novels like Dracula and horror films.

b In open class, ask students how they think the characters in the photo story would react to goths.

c Divide the class into pairs. Read through the question with students and elicit some ideas. In pairs, students discuss the question. Listen to some of their ideas in open class as feedback.

d In the same pairs, or with a different partner, students discuss their ideas. Circulate and help with vocabulary as required.

e Watch episode 2 of the DVD and find out what happened.

14 Write

The preparation for this can be done in class and students can write the email for homework.

a Ask students to read through questions 1 to 5. Check any problems. Students read through the email and answer the questions. Check answers.

Answers
1 San Diego and Los Angeles.
2 Alcatraz prison. It was really interesting.
3 No, but she's seen it.
4 Yes.
5 A San Francisco Giants baseball cap.

b Ask students to read through questions 1 to 3. Check any problems. They may not need to read the email again to answer these questions. If they can do this from memory, they can read it only to check answers.

Answers
1 Hi Chris   2 Love, Laura   3 PS

Language note
PS in English means *post script*, literally 'after writing'. Ask students how they make these additions to letters or emails in their language and what the abbreviation stands for.

c Students may need time to do some research for this. They read through the cities in the box and choose one or they can choose a city of their own and research it, if necessary. Remind them to follow the model in Exercise 14a and write their own email. They can then send their email to a partner to read and check and correct any mistakes. Encourage students to read out their emails to the class.

15 Last but not least: more speaking

Books closed. Tell students that they are going to ask each other some questions about the USA and Canada. Divide the class into pairs and give each student a letter A or B. Ask students A to look at the questions on page 38 and students B to look at the questions on page 126.

a Students read through the instructions and mark what they think is the correct answer. Circulate and check students are on track.

b Students ask each other questions using question tags. Monitor to check students are using the correct intonation patterns. As feedback, listen to some of the dialogues to check students have used the correct question tag.

Check your progress

1 Grammar

a 2 'll phone; doesn't arrive   3 speak; won't understand   4 phones; will tell   5 won't know; don't tell

b 2 doesn't she   3 isn't he   4 aren't we   5 are they   6 has she

c 2 have already had   3 have … bought   4 have already finished   5 Has … seen

2 Vocabulary

a 2 lift   3 lorry   4 garbage   5 pavement   6 candy

b 2 moist   3 global   4 recycle   5 rubbish   6 waste   7 pick   8 forest   9 clean
Mystery word: pollution

How did you do?

Check that students are marking their scores. Collect these in and check them as necessary and discuss any further work needed with specific students.

UNIT 4

Memo from Mario

Holiday or vacation?

1 Sentence expansion and translation

▸ Write this utterance on the board or IWB:

No, she hasn't yet

▸ Then write these sentence expansion rules:
▸ Write ten new sentences by adding one or two words to the sentence on the board.
▸ None of your new sentences can be more than six words long.
▸ You can add the new words anywhere in the sentence that is OK grammatically.
▸ You cannot change anything in the original sentence.
▸ Write these example sentence expansions on the board:

No John, she hasn't yet left.
No, she hasn't yet kissed him.
Well no, she hasn't yet arrived.
No problem, she hasn't yet eaten.

▸ Pair the students and ask them to produce ten new sentences based on the one on the board.
▸ Go round the class helping and checking that students have understood the rules.
▸ When most people have finished, ask the pairs to write mother tongue translations of each sentence.
▸ Ask individual students to write one of their favourite sentences up on the board. If your class is monolingual ask them to also put up their translation. Work on the translations.

> **RATIONALE AND ACKNOWLEDGEMENT**
> This free but rule-governed expansion technique comes from the work of Caleb Gattegno who intended students to learn language by discovering all they could do with it.
> Within the rules, learners are invited to use their full linguistic creativity.
> Gattegno was a strict follower of the Direct Method and would turn in his grave at the suggestion of using translation. Here I feel it is important for students to fully realise just what the new sentences they have created actually mean.

2 British English words / North American English words

▸ The car is a lexical area where the British and North American varieties of English diverge considerably.
▸ Divide the board in two with a vertical line down the middle.
▸ Draw the bare outline of two cars; one on the left hand side and one on the right hand side.
▸ Your outlines should have no wheels and no other features:
▸ Over the left hand space write US CAR and over the right hand space write UK CAR.
▸ Divide your class into a right hand group and a left hand group facing the board.
▸ Each group sends two students to the front of the class with board markers at the ready.
▸ Explain that when you call out an item (from the list below) both students should draw the item and write the word next to it, only if the word is common to both British and North American English.
▸ Their teams will naturally shout out help.
▸ If the word is only North American English then only the US pair will draw the item and write the word.
▸ If the word is only British English then only the UK pair will draw the item and write the word.
▸ After each item ask the team to send out two new people to the front to do the drawing and writing.
▸ Here is the list:

US	BOTH	UK
	FRONT WHEEL	
HOOD		BONNET
	ROOF RACK	
FRONT FENDER		FRONT BUMPER
	STEERING WHEEL	
BOOT		TRUNK
	WING MIRROR	

▸ Now ask the students to draw two cars into their notebook, a US one and a British one. Tell them to label the two cars appropriately.

> **RATIONALE**
> It makes sense to teach things that are easy to visualize in a way that makes them memorable to the learner's inner eye. The trial and error aspect of the activity as students sometimes make the wrong decision makes this activity a change from "presentational teaching".
> Students with strong spatial intelligence may find this work fun.

44 UNIT 4

5 Growing up

Unit overview

TOPIC: Growing up in different parts of the world

TEXTS

Reading and listening: a text about a coming of age ceremony in Papua New Guinea
Listening: the origins of the coming of age ceremony
Reading and listening: a quiz about age limits
Writing: about a special day in your country

SPEAKING AND FUNCTIONS

Describing a ceremony
Retelling a story
Talking about permission
Discussing age limits

LANGUAGE

Grammar: Present simple passive; *let / be allowed to*
Vocabulary: Describing a person's age

1 Read and listen

If you set the background information as a homework research task, ask students to tell the class what they found out.

> **BACKGROUND INFORMATION**
>
> **Papua New Guinea** is a country in Oceania, occupying the eastern half of the island of New Guinea and numerous offshore islands. Its capital, and one of its few major cities, is Port Moresby.
>
> **The Sepik** is the longest river on the island of New Guinea. It is one of the great river systems of the world. It has a large catchment area and includes swamplands, tropical rainforests and mountains. Biologically, the river system is possibly the largest uncontaminated freshwater wetland system in the Asia-Pacific region.

Warm up

Ask students at what age someone is classified as an adult in their country. Ask them if they celebrate certain birthdays in special ways because of the age a person is. If so, how do they celebrate and what ages are special? Discuss this as a class or in L1 if appropriate.

a Ask students to look at the picture. Read through the two questions and ask them for their suggestions before they read the text. Students then read the text quickly to answer the questions. Remind them they don't need to understand every word in the text at this stage. Check answers.

> **Answers**
> 1 Papua New Guinea
> 2 Boys are becoming men.

b ▶ **CD1 T25** **Stronger classes:** Ask students to read through questions 1 to 5. Check any problems. Play the recording, pausing it after the second paragraph, and ask students to give you the answer to question 1. Play the recording while students read and listen to answer the questions. Check answers. Play the recording again, pausing as necessary to clarify any problems.

Weaker classes: You may want to pre-teach the following vocabulary: *skulls, ceremony, bamboo, beaten, painful*.

TAPESCRIPT
See the reading text on page 40 of the Student's Book.

> **Answers**
> 1 They live near a river full of crocodiles.
> 2 They believe that crocodiles made the Earth and its people.
> 3 It is a hut. The boys go there to become men.
> 4 They think about their crocodile 'mothers and fathers' and they play the drums.
> 5 He has adult responsibilities in the village.

c Divide the class into small groups. Ask students to read through the questions and discuss them in their groups. Listen to some of their ideas in open class as feedback.

2 Grammar

★ Present simple passive

a **Stronger classes:** Ask students to read through the instruction and the examples. Ask students to identify the verb *be* in each sentence and elicit why *are* is used in the first example (because *boys* is plural) and *is* in the second (because *bamboo* is singular/uncountable). Then ask them to point out the past participles.

Weaker classes: Books closed. Write the following items and countries on the board in jumbled order:

UNIT 5 45

olives/Spain/Portugal; Fiat cars/Italy; rice/China (and any other items of your own). Ask: *Where are olives grown?* and elicit: *They're grown in Spain.* Then ask: *Where is rice grown?* and elicit: *It's grown in China.* Put the singular and plural question and answer forms on the board and explain that this structure is called the present simple passive in English. Ask students what they notice about the verbs in each and elicit that the verb *be* is used in singular or plural and the past participle. Students now open their books at page 41 and look at the examples from the text.

b Students go back through the text on page 40 and find other examples of the present simple passive. Check answers.

> **Answers**
> the boys are told; they are beaten;
> the crocodile men are given

To check understanding at this point, ask students to think of one example sentence in the present simple passive about their own country.

> **Language notes**
> Students may have a different verb in their own language for this structure and they may have problems using this structure correctly. Monitor them carefully when they use it, making sure they are using the correct form.

c Students then read through the rule box. Go through the first example in the table as a class, asking them why *is* is used (*because boy is singular*). Check answers.

> **Answers**
> Rule: isn't important
> Positive: are
> Negative: aren't
> Question: Is/Are
> Short answer: is; aren't

d Students read through sentences 1 to 6. Check any problems. Go through the example, if necessary. Students complete the exercise. Remind them to check if the subject is singular or plural before they decide which part of the verb *be* to use and remind them that they can use the irregular verb list on page 127 if necessary. Check answers.

> **Answers**
> 2 are written
> 3 is sold
> 4 isn't grown / is grown
> 5 Are/sent
> 6 are made

e Students read through sentences 1 to 6. Check any problems. Go through the example, pointing out the changes from the active sentence to the passive sentence. Students complete the exercise. Check answers.

> **Answers**
> 2 ... is picked up every morning.
> 3 ... of trees are cut down every year.
> 4 ... water is wasted.
> 5 ... of letters are delivered by postal workers.
> 6 ... successful films made in Hollywood?

f This exercise can be set for homework. Students look at the pictures and read through prompts 1 to 4. Do the first prompt with them as an example, eliciting a passive sentence. Students complete the exercise, making passive sentences for the other pictures. Check answers.

> **Answers**
> 1 A torch is taken to the Olympic city.
> 2 A flag is carried into the stadium.
> 3 A flame is lit with the torch.
> 4 The Games are opened with a speech.

Grammar notebook

Encourage students to note down the rules and some examples of the passive. They may want to translate some examples if their own language uses a different construction to express this.

> ★ OPTIONAL ACTIVITY
>
> For further practice of this grammar, ask students to describe a process they know well using the present simple passive. To get them started, give them the example of making a cup of tea: *To make a cup of tea, you will need a cup, a teabag, a kettle, some milk, some water and some sugar. First, water is poured into the kettle and boiled. A cup is taken from the cupboard. A teabag is placed in the cup. When the water has boiled, it is poured on to the teabag. After two minutes, the teabag is removed and milk and sugar are added.*
>
> Students choose their own process and make notes of the order in which things happen before writing full sentences. Circulate and monitor, making sure students are using the present simple passive correctly. Ask students to explain their process to a partner and listen to some of the best examples in open class.

3 Listen and speak

a Divide the class into pairs. Read the instructions as a class. Students then look at the pictures and try to put them in order. Do the first one with them as an example, if necessary. Elicit some possibilities

46 UNIT 5

from the class and put them on the board but do not check answers at this point.

b ▶ **CD1 T26** Play the recording for students to listen and check or change their answers. Play the recording again, pausing as necessary to clarify any problems.

TAPESCRIPT

One day a man called Batangnorang was walking by the river. It was a beautiful day and he felt very happy with life. Suddenly he heard a noise, and when he looked round he saw a crocodile going towards the river. The man hid behind a bush and to his amazement he saw that the crocodile was carrying some gold back to his home, a hole in the river bank. Batangnorang wanted to get to the gold, so he thought of a plan. He went to find a tiger skin and some feathers, put them on and then went into the hole. 'If the crocodile sees me, it will think I'm an animal and not a man!' Batangnorang said. When he went into the hole, he was relieved to see that the crocodile wasn't there. But after a few minutes it suddenly came home. A crocodile has a good sense of smell, so it soon noticed Batangnorang's smell. 'Is this a man or an animal?' it thought. So the crocodile decided to give him a test – it gave Batangnorang some food that no human would normally ever eat.

Batangnorang realised that it was a test, and ate the food. The crocodile thought he was an animal and let him stay. A little while later Batangnorang pretended that he was leaving, but as he was going towards the door, he suddenly turned round and killed the crocodile with a spear. Then he took all the gold that he found in the crocodile's home. And that's why crocodiles and people have been enemies ever since.

Answers
2 B 3 F 4 A 5 C 6 E

Stronger classes: Students now retell the story with their partner.

Weaker classes: Students may find it useful to have a prompt for each picture before retelling the story. Elicit a prompt for each, and write the prompts on the board, replaying the recording as necessary. Students then retell the story with their partner. Monitor and check that they are both taking turns to retell it and note down any errors to go through later. Encourage some pairs to retell the story to the rest of the class.

4 Vocabulary
★ Describing a person's age

a ▶ **CD1 T27** Books closed. Draw a line on the board with 0 years at one end and 65 years at the other end. Elicit as many words as possible from students for different ages and write them on the line at various points. Students read through the words in the box and look at the pictures. Check the pronunciation of each item. Do the first item as an example, if necessary. Students complete the exercise. Play the recording for students to check or change their answers. Play the recording again, pausing after each word for students to repeat.

Tapescript/Answers
A a baby (4)
E a toddler (5)
F a child (2)
B a teenager (3)
D a young adult (1)
C a pensioner (6)

Language note
There are two possible ways to pronounce *adult*: /ˈædʌlt/ and /əˈdʌlt/.

b Students read through sentences 1 to 6. Check any problems. Go through the first item as an example, if necessary. Students complete the exercise. Students can compare answers with a partner before a whole class check.

Example answers
1 two   2 two to three and a half
3 12   4 13/19   5 18   6 65

c Divide the class into small groups. Students read through the questions and discuss them in their groups. Ask for groups to feed back to the class and see if everyone agrees. Are there any similarities in the students' own language?

Vocabulary notebook

Encourage students to start a section called *Describing a person's age* and to note down the words from this exercise. They may find it useful to note down translations of the words too.

5 Grammar
★ let / be allowed to

a ▶ **CD1 T28** Students read through the dialogue and questions 1 to 5. Check any problems. Go through the first question as an example, if necessary. Play the recording for students to listen and read. Give students a few minutes to answer the questions. Students can compare answers in

UNIT 5   **47**

pairs. Play the recording again for students to check or change their answers, pausing as necessary to clarify any problems.

TAPESCRIPT
See the dialogue on page 43 of the Student's Book.

> **Answers**
> 1 To a music festival in Leeds.
> 2 Because his parents say he is too young.
> 3 Because her mum didn't let her.
> 4 They let him stay out until midnight at weekends.
> 5 Stay up late and watch TV.

b **Stronger classes:** Students read through the examples. Elicit or explain that the first example means permission was not given and in the second example permission was given. Explain that *let* and *be allowed* are both used when permission is given and *don't/didn't let / not allowed* are used when permission is not given, and that they mean the same thing. Students then underline other examples of *let / be allowed* in the dialogue in Exercise 5a and complete the rules. Check answers.

Weaker classes: Books closed. Write the headings *Allowed / Not allowed* on the board. Ask students what sort of things their parents allow them to do during the week and at weekends. Give them a few prompts if necessary, e.g. *stay out late / watch TV / stay at friends' houses*, etc. Elicit a few examples and put them under the appropriate heading. Then elicit a sentence for *let* and *be allowed* for one of the examples on the board, e.g. *My parents let me stay up until midnight on a Saturday night. / I'm allowed to stay up until midnight on a Saturday night.* Explain to students that in both sentences permission is given to do something and that they mean the same. Students open their books at page 43 and read the examples. Students then underline other examples of *let / be allowed* in the dialogue in Exercise 5a and complete the rules. Check answers.

> **Answers**
> I'm not allowed ...
> ... didn't let me go
> ... usually let me ...
> I'm allowed to stay out ...
> ... never lets me do ...
> ... we're allowed to breathe ...
> ... let you stay up late ...

Students can now complete the rule.

> **Answers**
> be allowed to / let

To check understanding at this point, elicit a few more examples from the class of things they are allowed / not allowed to do.

> **Language note**
> Students may produce statements like ~~My dad let me to stay out late~~. Remind them that in English we don't use *to* after the expression *let someone do something*. Students may produce statements like ~~I'm allowed stay out late~~. The expression *allow someone to do something* is always followed by the infinitive with *to*.

c Students read through the instructions and sentences 1 to 6. Check any problems. Go through the example as a class, if necessary. Students complete the exercise. Remind them to use short forms where possible. Check answers.

> **Answers**
> 2 aren't allowed to
> 3 're allowed to
> 4 aren't allowed to
> 5 isn't allowed to
> 6 Are ... allowed to

d This exercise can be set for homework. Students read through the instructions and sentences 1 to 6. Check any problems. Go through the example as a class, if necessary. Students complete the exercise. Remind them to use short forms where possible. Check answers.

> **Answers**
> 2 My parents let me watch the late-night movie on Fridays.
> 3 I don't let my brother use my computer.
> 4 The teachers don't let us run in the corridors.
> 5 The head teacher doesn't let us wear trainers to school.
> 6 My dad lets me drive our car sometimes.

e Read through the instructions as a class. Individually, students note down things they are allowed / not allowed to do. Then divide the class into pairs. Students read through the instructions. Ask a stronger pair to demonstrate the example exchange. Students then ask and answer to exchange information. Monitor and check students are using the structures correctly and note down any repeated errors to go through as a class afterwards. Ask pairs to feed back to the class.

Grammar notebook
Remind students to note down the rules and explanations for this structure and to write a few examples of their own.

Culture in mind

7 Read and listen

If you set the background information as a homework research task, ask students to tell the class what they found out.

> **BACKGROUND INFORMATION**
>
> **Great Britain** (population 58.9 million) is three countries, England, Scotland and Wales. It lies to the north west of Continental Europe, with Ireland to the west. The countries' capital cities are London, Edinburgh and Cardiff respectively.
>
> **The United Kingdom (UK)** is made up of Great Britain, the north east part of Ireland, and many small islands. The UK is surrounded by the Atlantic Ocean, the North Sea, the English Channel and the Irish Sea.
>
> **Brazil** (population 191,908,000) is a country in South America. Bounded by the Atlantic Ocean on the east, Brazil has a coastline of over 7,491 kilometres.
>
> **Arizona** is a state in the south west of the United States. The capital and largest city is Phoenix. Arizona is noted for its desert climate, exceptionally hot summers and mild winters.
>
> **Germany** (population 82,369,000) is a country in Central Europe. It has the largest population of the states of the European Union. The capital and largest city is Berlin.
>
> **Mississippi** is a state located in the Deep South of the United States. Jackson is the state capital and largest city. The state's name comes from the Mississippi River, which flows along its western boundary.
>
> **Japan** (population 127,288,000) is an island country in East Asia, located in the Pacific Ocean. It comprises over 3,000 islands, most of which are mountainous. Japan's highest peak, Mount Fuji, is a volcano.

Warm up

Ask students to look at the pictures and discuss how old they think the people are in each one. What are the people doing in the pictures? Do they know anyone who has got married very young? What do they think of this? Do they know anyone who has just passed their driving test? Discuss this as a class or in L1 if appropriate.

a Ask students to read through the quiz and check any problems. You may want to pre-teach some vocabulary: *grounded, come of age, grown-up, vote, tattoo, bank account, glider* at this point. Students then answer the questions individually. Divide the class into pairs and students compare answers with a partner. Ask pairs to feedback to the class but do not give answers at this stage.

b ▶ **CD1 T31** Play the recording while students listen and check their answers. You may like to pause after each sentence to clarify any problems and to discuss in open class whether students are surprised by the information.

TAPESCRIPT

Speaker 1: And here are the answers to our quiz, 'How old do you have to be?' Question 1 is about the age you are allowed to vote in Britain. And the first statement is false. You can vote when you are 18, you have a right to, but you don't have to vote. Carol, over to you now and let's find out about the voting age in Brazil.

Speaker 2: Thank you Carl. Well, here's the answer. The statement is actually true. In most countries of the world, you are allowed to vote at 18, but it's different in a few countries, and Brazil is one of them. There, and in India, Switzerland, Austria, Nicaragua and the Isle of Man, for example, people can vote when they are 16.

Speaker 1: And now for a tricky one. Getting a tattoo. The statement is false, or shall we say it is half false? It's true that you can get a tattoo in Arizona, USA when you're only 14.

Speaker 2: Wow, that's really young.

Speaker 1: It is, isn't it? But the first part of the statement is false. The minimum age for getting a tattoo in Britain and in most states in the USA is 18.

Speaker 2: Really? And what did you think of the next one that in Mississippi you have to be 30 to get married without your parents' permission.

Speaker 1: It's a bit unlikely, isn't it?

Speaker 2: It is, yes, and of course, it's false. But it's interesting that in Mississippi you're not allowed to get married without your parents' OK before you're 21. That's still quite old!

Speaker 1: Yes, you're right, it is! OK, let's look now at how old you have to be to open a bank account in the UK. You might not believe this one, but the correct answer is … seven! So the statement is true. Although, of course, an adult has to open it for you.

Speaker 2: How about number 6? Are girls allowed to get married when they're 18, and boys when they're 16 in Japan?

Speaker 1: No, this one's wrong – it's the other way round. A girl has to be 16, and a boy has to be 18 to get married there.

Speaker 2: And last, but not least, would you believe it, in the USA you're allowed to fly a plane, a glider plane that is, a long time before you can drive a car?

UNIT 5 49

They let you fly a glider plane on your own at the age of 14, but you have to be 16 to drive a car!

Speaker 2: Who would have thought …

> **Answers**
> 1 F   2 T   3 F   4 F   5 T   6 F   7 F

c Read through the definitions with students and check understanding. Students look back at the text to find words or phrases that mean the same as the definitions. Check answers.

Stronger classes: Give them some time to attempt the exercise first, before looking at the text to check their answers.

> **Answers**
> 1 fed up
> 2 grounded
> 3 come of age
> 4 have a go
> 5 a couple
> 6 at least
> 7 without your parents' permission
> 8 turn

Speak

Read through the questions with students and clarify any difficulties.

Stronger classes: In pairs or small groups, students go through the questions and discuss them. If you have already discussed some of these in previous exercises, ask students to give more details here.

Weaker classes: They can choose one question only to discuss. If necessary, elicit a few prompts for the question they have chosen to help them with their discussion.

Monitor and help as necessary, encouraging students to express themselves in English.

Ask pairs or groups to feed back to the class and discuss any interesting points.

Write

If you set the background information as a homework research task, ask students to tell the class what they found out.

> **BACKGROUND INFORMATION**
>
> **Seijin no Hi ceremony:** This is a coming of age ceremony in Japan for 20-year-olds, celebrated on the second Monday in January every year. Young men and women visit a shrine and the day is a national holiday. Twenty is the legal age in Japan for voting, drinking and smoking.

Warm up

Ask students to look at the pictures and predict how old they think these girls are (*20*) and what the name is for the type of clothes they are wearing (*kimono*).

The preparation for this can be done in class and the writing set as a homework exercise.

a Students read through the question and then read the text quickly to find the answers to this and their Warm up predictions. Remind them they don't need to understand every word in the text. Check answers.

> **Answer**
> It is a coming of age ceremony.

b Students read through questions 1 to 3 and then match them with the paragraphs in the text. Do the first one with them as an example, if necessary. Check answers.

> **Answers**
> 1 A   2 C   3 B

c Elicit some special days which students celebrate and write them on the board.

Stronger classes: They can think about the things they do on the special day they have chosen and write their article using the model on page 45 to help them.

Weaker classes: Elicit prompts from them to help them with the special day they have chosen and encourage them to make notes from the prompts. Once they have made their notes, encourage them to expand them into a draft, using the model on page 45 to help them. At this point students can swap drafts with a partner and check their partner's work. Students can then produce the complete and final draft for homework.

Memo from Mario

Growing up

1 Present simple passive dictation

- Put the students into groups of three, and give each student a letter: A, B and C.
- Ask each group to tear some loose paper into 16 slips.
- Tell the students that Student A in each group will write the sentence you dictate.
- Student B will replace *banana* with the correct word/s at the beginning of each sentence and Student C will translate the full sentence into their mother tongue. If you have an international class, work with pairs and leave out the translation work.
- Give an example. Dictate:

  Banana is played out of doors with a very small hard ball.

  Student A in each group writes the sentence on a slip of paper.

  Student B takes the slip and replaces *Banana* with *Golf*.

  Student C translates the sentence into their mother tongue.

- Dictate the next headless sentence while Students B and C are at work on the first one.
- Start the dictation:

  Banana-ing is done down white-water rivers. *(kayaking/canoeing/rafting)*

  Banana is played with a large ball like an egg. *(rugby/American football)*

  Banana is played with a bat and a ball by men in white. *(cricket)*

  Banana matches with a little light ball are often won by the Chinese. *(table tennis)*

  Banana is played on a frozen rink – Canadians are good at it. *(ice-hockey)*

  Banana contests are held in Japan and are won by fat men. *(sumo)*

  Bows and arrows are used in banana. *(archery)*

  Banana is done very fast down mountains. *(skiing)*

- In open class ask students to read out their English sentences and their translations.
- Help with the translations. There may be room for some brief contrastive explanations.

> **RATIONALE**
> One reason for using the present simple passive is that it focuses on the subject of the sentence: for example, 'water is extracted from the ground …'
> In the exercise all the students' attention is firmly, if playfully, focused on the absent subject.

2 A spelling exercise

- Tell the class to open their books on page 40 and ask them to read through the 'Where boys become crocodile men' text.
- Demonstrate the activity with one student (with their book closed), working from paragraph three of the text. Ask the student to tell you the number of letters in each word you say. For example:

  You: *The*
  Student: *three*
  You: *boys*
  Student: *four*
  You: *are*
  Student: *three*
  You: *taken*

- Make sure everybody realises that the task is to say the number of letters in the word just heard.
- Pair the students so that one student can see the text while the other can't. The first student says the first word and his partner says the number of letters it has, and so on.
- They stop at the end of the paragraph.
- Ask the students to swap roles and do the exercise again.

> **RATIONALE**
> The activity encourages students to get the words up on their mental screen. We know that the best spellers in languages of spelling chaos like French and English are those who can visualize well.

> **VARIATION**
> If the students know a text by heart, for example a song, ask them to recite it word by word giving the number of letters after each word
> e.g.   *Jack 4 and 3 Jill 4 went 4 up 2 the 3 hill 4*
> A harder and more useful way is to say the numbers first.
> e.g.   *4 Mary 3 had 1 a 6 little 4 lamb*
> If the student only works auditorily they will probably say *5 little* and *3 lamb*

Acknowledgement

These techniques come from A. R. Orage whose book *On love and psychological exercises* first came out in 1934 (re-issued by Sam Weisner, New York, 1996).

UNIT 5   51

6 Have fun!

Unit overview

TOPIC: What makes people laugh

TEXTS
Reading and listening: a text about Comic Relief
Reading: a questionnaire
Listening: a song *Don't Worry, Be Happy* by Bobby McFerrin
Writing: an email reply to a friend

SPEAKING AND FUNCTIONS
Talking about unfinished situations
Asking and answering a questionnaire
Talking about having fun

LANGUAGE
Grammar: Present perfect simple; *for* vs. *since*
Vocabulary: Verb and noun pairs (*have/make*)
Everyday English: *Tell me about it*; *In other words*; *What's the point of?*, *Come on*; *Know what?*; *as long as*

1 Read and listen

If you set the background information as a homework research task, ask students to tell the class what they found out.

BACKGROUND INFORMATION
Comic Relief is a British charity organisation which started in the UK in 1985 in response to famine in Ethiopia. One of the fundamental principles behind working at Comic Relief is the 'Golden Pound Principle' where every single donated pound is spent on charitable projects. Currently, its two main supporters are the BBC and the supermarket chain Sainsbury's. The BBC is responsible for the live television extravaganza on Red Nose Day and Sainsbury's sells merchandise on behalf of the charity. Since it started in the 1980s, Comic Relief has raised over £600 million.

Warm up
Ask students if they ever get stressed and how it makes them feel. Ask them what they do to stop feeling stressed. Discuss this as a class or in L1 if appropriate.

a Refer students to the photos. Ask them what they think the text might be about (*feeling better through laughing*). Elicit students' predictions.

Students then read the text quickly to check their answers. Remind them that they do not need to know every word in a text to understand it. Check answers.

b ▶ CD1 T32 Students read through the statements, then read through the text and listen to the recording to decide if they are true or false. Check answers, asking students to correct false statements.

Answers
1 F (doctors say laughter is good for our health)
2 F (every two years)
3 F (more than 20 years)
4 T
5 F (New Zealand)

c Students read and answer the questions. They can compare answers in pairs before a whole class check.

Answers
1 They put on red noses and do silly things, e.g. watch funny films, hold talent shows, have red parties, make funny sculptures to raise money for poor people.
2 Laughter is good for the heart, blood circulation and immune system.

d Read through the questions with students. You may like to give students some individual thinking time before the discussion and ask them to make notes of any ideas. Divide the class into small groups and ask them to discuss the questions. Ask some students to tell the rest of the class what their group thinks.

★ OPTIONAL ACTIVITY

Ask students to plan a Red Nose Day for their school. Divide the class into groups and ask each group to think of a funny way to make money. Circulate and help with any difficult vocabulary. When students have their ideas, ask them to present them in open class. Ask students to decide which idea would raise most money or be the funniest.

2 Grammar
★ Present perfect simple

a **Stronger classes:** Students read the example. Elicit the answer to the questions and then students complete the rule. Check answers. Ask students how this tense is formed and elicit *has/have* + past participle.

Weaker classes: Books closed. Write the following example sentence (or one of your own) on the board: *I've been an English teacher for ten years.* Ask students the following questions: *Am I still an English teacher now?* (*Yes*) and elicit or explain that this action started in the past (*10 years ago*) and is still continuing now. Then ask students how this tense is formed and elicit *has/have* + past participle.

Students now open their books at page 47 and read the example from the text and the following question. If necessary, refer them back to the text where they can see the sentence in context. Students answer the question and try to complete the rule. Check answers.

> **Answers**
> Yes, it does.
> Rule: Present perfect simple

b Students go back through the article and underline more examples of the present perfect. Check answers.

> **Answers**
> have found; have they collected; has travelled, have made

At this point, ask some students to give you an example of their own to check they have understood the form and meaning correctly.

> **Language note**
> Ask students to translate the examples into their own language and compare the tense they use. If students use the present tense in their own language for this structure, point out that this can't be done in English.

c Students read through sentences 1 to 7. Check any problems. Go through the example sentence with them and ask if they can explain why the present perfect has been used (*because he/she still has his/her bicycle now*). Refer them to the rule they have just completed in Exercise 2a, if necessary. Students complete the exercise. Check answers.

> **Answers**
> 2 has worked 3 Has ... lived 4 have ... been
> 5 haven't seen 6 have been

✱ *for* vs. *since*

d **Stronger classes:** Students look at the examples from the text (refer them back to the text if necessary). Write the sentences on the board. Explain to students (using this year as a time marker) that Comic Relief has helped people for over 20 years and is still helping now. Students now try to answer the question.

Weaker classes: Write the following sentences on the board (or some of your own): *I've been an English teacher for three years. / I've been an English teacher since 1999.* Elicit or explain the difference between *for* and *since* in each sentence. Students now try to answer the question in their books.

> **Answers**
> We use *for* to show a period of time; we use *since* to show a point in time.

Students read through the words in the box. Go through the examples with the whole class (*for a week; since yesterday*). Remind them of the rule for *for* and *since*, if necessary. Students complete the exercise. Check answers as a class.

> **Answers**
> for: two years; an hour; a month; a long time; days
> since: Christmas; 1999; Saturday; I was 11; last weekend

Call out a few more time expressions at this point to check students have understood when to use *for* and when to use *since*, e.g. *December; ten years; half an hour; last week*.

e Look at the table as a class and do the first item, e.g. *I've studied English since I was 11 years old. / since 2001. / since yesterday. / for ages.* In pairs, students now make as many sentences as they can. Set a time limit of about three minutes. Remind them that there can be more than one possibility for each sentence. Check answers as a class.

> **Example answers**
> I've studied English since I was 11 years old. / since 2001. / since yesterday. / for ages.
> They've been married since I was 11 years old. / for 20 years. / since last Christmas. / for two weeks. / since 2001. / for ages. / since yesterday.
> John has had his bicycle since I was 11 years old. / for 20 years. / since last Christmas. / for two weeks. / since 2001. / for ages. / since yesterday.
> I haven't seen Mark since I was 11 years old. / for 20 years. / since last Christmas. / for two weeks. / since 2001. / for ages. / since yesterday.
> We've lived here since I was 11 years old. / for 20 years. / since last Christmas. / for two weeks. / since 2001. / for ages. / since yesterday.
> Maria hasn't spoken to John since I was 11 years old. / for 20 years. / since last Christmas. / for two weeks. / since 2001. / for ages. / since yesterday.

f This exercise can be set for homework. Students read through sentences 1 to 6. Check any problems. Go through the example and point out the time marker (*I was ten*). Students complete the exercise. Remind them to look for the time marker in each sentence to help them decide whether *for* or *since* is necessary. Remind them too that they will have to change the verb in each sentence. Check answers as a class.

> **Answers**
> 2 've had / for
> 3 's studied / for
> 4 haven't seen / since
> 5 haven't been / for

> **Language note**
> Students may produce statements like: ~~I am working here since two years ago~~. Remind them that in English we only use *ago* with the past simple in English.

Grammar notebook

Encourage students to note down the rules for the present perfect and expressions which follow *for/since* in their grammar notebooks.

✱ OPTIONAL ACTIVITY

Divide the class into pairs. Ask students to ask each other questions about their clothing and other belongings using the present perfect and *for/since*. Encourage students to continue their dialogues with other questions and comments:
A: How long have you had your watch?
B: I've had it since last October.
A: Did you buy it or was it a present?
B: My father bought it for me for my birthday.
A: You're very lucky. It's lovely!

This activity works well if students change partners regularly and speak to a lot of different students. You can organise this by clapping your hands and saying 'Change!' every two or three minutes. When students have changed partners several times, ask some of them to tell the class any interesting information they learnt about their partners.

Speak and read

Warm up

Books closed. Ask students if they enjoy doing questionnaires. Do they do them often? Students now open their books on page 48 and look at the questionnaire and the title. Elicit what they think some of the questions in the questionnaire will be about.

a Divide the class into pairs. Students read through the question prompts. Ask a stronger pair to read out the example exchange, drawing students' attention to the question and the use of *for/since* in the answers. Students ask and answer the questions in their pairs. Monitor and check students are taking turns to ask and answer and using the correct question forms and answering using *for* and *since*. Make a note of any repeated errors to go through later as a class.

Weaker classes: Elicit the past participles of the verbs in each prompt before they begin and put them on the board. This will help them form the questions correctly.

b Students read through the questionnaire. Check any problems and pre-teach any vocabulary and expressions, e.g. *lock, to make fun of, down* or ask students to look up the words in a dictionary. In the same pairs from Exercise 4a, students now ask and answer the questions in the questionnaire, then swap roles. Once both students have checked their scores and read the results on page 126, they compare results. Put pairs into groups to compare and discuss results. Ask for class feedback and put the results on the board to see if there is a personality type which dominates.

✱ OPTIONAL ACTIVITY

Stronger classes: Students can devise their own questionnaire, based on the one they have just completed. Then they can interview a partner and discuss the results.

Weaker classes: Students can put their results together and put them into a class bar chart to show personality types.

⑤ Vocabulary

✱ Verb and noun pairs

a Ask students if they can remember what people do on Red Nose Day. Accept all true answers but elicit *They have fun / make people laugh*. Ask students to read through the list of words in the box and then complete the exercise. Remind them to look back at the reading texts on pages 47 and 48 to help them find these expressions. Check answers, explaining that some expressions use *have* and some use *make*.

> **Answers**
> have: fun; a good time; a (good) laugh
> make: fun of someone; a fool of yourself; friends; plans; someone laugh/smile; funny faces

b This exercise can be set for homework. Students read through sentences 1 to 5. Check any problems. Go through the example, if necessary. Students

54 UNIT 6

complete the exercise. Students can compare answers in pairs before a whole class check.

> **Answers**
> 2 have   3 made   4 having; have   5 make

Vocabulary notebook

Encourage students to start a section called *Verb and noun pairs* and to note down any new vocabulary in their notebooks.

> **★ OPTIONAL ACTIVITY**
>
> Divide the class into small groups. One student mimes one of the expressions from Exercise 5 and the others guess what they are doing. The student who guesses correctly mimes the next expression, etc. Set a time limit for students to guess, e.g. 15 seconds. Alternatively, this could also be done as a whole class activity with one student standing at the front miming.

6 Listen

If you set the background information as a homework research task, ask students to tell the class what they found out.

> **BACKGROUND INFORMATION**
>
> *Don't Worry, Be Happy* is a song recorded by the American artist Bobby McFerrin in 1988. He was born to opera singer parents in New York in 1950 and moved to Hollywood in 1958. His father was the first African-American male soloist at the famous Metropolitan Opera.
>
> Bobby McFerrin formed various bands before going solo, starting at high school with the Bobby Mack Quartet. The album Simple Pleasures on which *Don't Worry, Be Happy* features was released in 1988 and soon became record of the year while the song itself was song of the year.

Warm up

Ask students to look at the title of the song and ask them the following questions: *Do they know this song? Have they heard it before? What do they think it is about?* Ask them what makes them worry and how they make themselves or other people happy when they are worried. Discuss this as a class and in L1 if appropriate.

a Students read the instructions and then translate 'Don't worry' into their own language.

b Pre-teach the vocabulary in the box by giving examples of the words in sentences or students can look up the words in a dictionary. In pairs, students check they know the words.

c Students read through the words in the two columns. Check any problems. Explain that the words in column one all rhyme with words in column two. Do the first one with them as an example (*smile – style*). Students then complete the matching part of the exercise. Check answers. Check students' pronunciation of each word and drill the words as necessary. Students now read through the whole song (remind them to ignore the gaps) and in pairs, complete the gaps.

> **Answers**
> 2 a   3 e   4 b   5 d

d ▶ CD1 T34   Play the first verse and pause the recording for students to check or change their answer to the first gap. Continue in this way until students have checked their answers.

> **Answers**
> 1 wrote   2 trouble   3 bed   4 smile   5 down

Vocabulary notebook

Remind students to note down any new vocabulary from the song.

> **★ OPTIONAL ACTIVITY**
>
> **Stronger classes:** In small groups, students write the next verse of the song. Ask for class feedback. The class votes for the verse they prefer.
>
> **Weaker classes:** Students find more rhyming words to continue Exercise 6c. This can be done as a chain round the class or students can discuss this in small groups and feed back as a class. Put all the rhyming words from the song on the board. For example:
> *smile; style; dial; file* etc.
> *trouble; double; bubble* etc.
> *frown; down; clown* etc.
> *wrote; note; goat; boat* etc.
> *bed; head; red; read; said* etc.
>
> If students enjoy this activity, you may like to give them other words to form rhyming chains starting with the numbers one to five, e.g. *one; sun; fun; gun; bun* etc.

★ Very funny!

7 Read and listen

Warm up

Ask students to look at the title of the photo story and the photos and to predict what they think this episode will be about (telling jokes). You could also ask them to remember the names of the characters and say where they are (in a cafe).

UNIT 6   55

a ▶ CD1 T35 Read through the instructions with students and see if students can guess the answers to the questions. Play the recording while students read. Check answers. Play the recording again, pausing as necessary for students to clarify any problems.

TAPESCRIPT
See the text on page 50 of the Student's Book.

> **Answers**
> Jess is telling a joke. Debbie finds it funny. Joel and Pete don't find it funny.

b Read through the questions with students and do the first one as an example if necessary. Students answer the questions, discussing their answers with a partner before feedback. Check answers.

> **Answers**
> 1 They feel depressed because they are studying very hard.
> 2 She thinks it's not very funny, but it makes her laugh.
> 3 He is being sarcastic.

8 Everyday English

a Read the expressions aloud with the class. Tell them to find them in the photo story and to try to match them with their meaning. Allow students to check answers with a partner before open class feedback.

> **Answers**
> 1 Pete 2 Debbie 3 Joel 4 Debbie 5 Jess
> 6 Pete

b Students read the dialogues and then complete them with the expressions from Exercise 8a. Go through the first item as an example, if necessary. Check answers.

> **Answers**
> 2 as long as 3 come on 4 In other words
> 5 What's the point of 6 Tell me about it

> Discussion box
>
> **Weaker classes:** Students can choose one question to discuss.
>
> **Stronger classes:** In pairs or small groups, students go through the questions in the box and discuss them.
>
> Monitor and help as necessary, encouraging students to express themselves in English and to use any vocabulary they have learned from the text. Ask pairs or groups to feed back to the class and discuss any interesting points further.

9 Improvisation

Divide the class into pairs. Tell students they are going to create a role play between Pete and Debbie. Read through the instructions with students. Give students two minutes to plan their dialogue. Circulate and help with vocabulary as necessary. Encourage students to use expressions from Exercise 8. Students practise their conversation in pairs. Listen to some of the best conversations in open class.

10 Team Spirit ⊙ DVD Episode 3

Read through the instructions with students. Ask students to work in pairs and write a short story to explain what happened in the photos. You may like to encourage students to plan their story first and spend some time thinking about the organisation of their story before writing. Circulate and help with vocabulary as necessary.

If there is time, listen to the students' stories in open class. If time is short, listen to some examples. You may like to pin stories around the classroom and ask students to circulate and read them, then vote on which was the best.

Watch episode 3 of the DVD and find out what happened.

11 Write

The preparation for this exercise can be done in class and the writing task done for homework with the replies collected in and marked.

Warm up
Ask students how often they send/receive emails. Who do they email? What do they talk about in their emails? Discuss this as a class or in L1 if appropriate.

a Students read the question, then read the emails silently or you could ask a stronger student to read it aloud. Remind students that they should only read the email to look for the answers to the questions, and it doesn't matter at this stage if they don't understand everything. Check answers.

> **Answers**
> Emily wants you to tell her what makes you laugh, what you do to have a good time, how often you do those things, how long you've done them for and why you think having fun is important. She wants this information because she is doing a project at school on how different teenagers round the world have fun.

56 UNIT 6

b Divide the class into pairs. Students look at the questions in the email. They take turns to ask and answer the questions. Remind them to use the expressions from Exercise 5 where possible. Monitor and check students are taking turns and that they are asking and answering correctly.

Now ask students to write a reply to Emily's email. Before they start, remind them that emails are informal ways of communicating and they don't have to include all the information they would on a letter, e.g. address, date, *Dear*, etc. Quickly brainstorm and write on the board some words and expressions which may be useful when writing an email, e.g. *Hi/Hello there; Thanks / Sorry / Must go / Be in touch soon / Let me know how the project goes,* etc. Go through the example email opening (*Sorry I haven't written sooner. I've been very busy at school / I've been ill / etc.; Anyway, you want to know how we have fun in England, well, let me tell you! ...*). Students write their replies and then send their emails to another student to read and check. Ask some students to read out their emails to the class.

✱ OPTIONAL ACTIVITY

Stronger classes: Email smileys. Ask students if they know any symbols which are used in emails to express things. Give them some examples:
:-)   :-(:-o

Can students think of any more to add? They could draw or print the symbols and use them to decorate their email noticeboard.

Weaker classes: Students set up an email noticeboard in class and display the replies to Emily's email on it.

12 Last but not least: more speaking

a Read through the questions with students and check understanding. Give students some silent time to think of their answers to the questions.

b Students make notes of their answers. Circulate and help with any questions about vocabulary. Tell students that they don't have to write complete sentences.

c Divide the class into small groups. Students tell each other their thoughts about laughter. Listen to some of the best ideas in open class as feedback.

Check your progress

1 Grammar

a 2 are produced   3 aren't held   4 is made
5 are sold   6 are bought   7 is; held

b 2 aren't allowed to   3 don't let
4 are allowed to   5 lets   6 are allowed to

c 2 has been; for   3 have lived; for
4 haven't seen; since   5 haven't listened; for
6 has phoned; since   7 haven't eaten; since

2 Vocabulary

a 2 young   3 child   4 middle   5 elderly
6 pensioner   7 teenager
Mystery word: toddler

b 2 makes   3 have   4 Have; made   5 have

How did you do?

Check that students are marking their scores. Collect these in and check them as necessary and discuss any further work needed with specific students.

Memo from Mario

Have fun

1 Laughter yoga

- One way of introducing Unit 6 would be to do a spot of laughter yoga with your class.
- Get the students to stand up and then start clapping, with a quick double beat to the right rhythm.
- Then, ask them to start clapping, with a quick double beat to the left rhythm.
- Continue until you have the whole group clapping with you.
- Stop, and ask the students to imitate you as you breathe in and draw yourself up.
- Drop forwards and breathe out.
- Come up slowly, inhaling.
- Hold for a moment upright with lungs full.
- Drop forwards and breathe out, etc.
- Repeat this four or five times.
- Now explain that you are going to show them the greeting laugh. Shake hands with a student near you, give them eye contact and laugh gently, do the same to the next student and then ask them to all try the greeting laugh, shaking hands with as many people as they can.
- Back to rhythmical two beat clapping.
- Back to the breathing exercise.
- Try the greeting laugh again.
- Back to clapping and breathing.
- Show the students the mosquito laugh which is a high pitched *hihihi* accompanied by a jabbing mosquito-like gesture with the forefinger.
- Back to clapping and breathing.
- Show the students the bear laugh. Stand back to back with a student, shoulders touching and knees bent. The bear laugh is a deep belly laugh *ho ho ho*.
- Finish with a final round of clapping.
- Ten minutes of laughter yoga will set the mood for 'The Power of Humour' text on page 46.

> **RATIONALE**
> A good lead-in to a reading text is for the students themselves to experience part of what the text is about. For excellent examples of this see the model lessons in *Teaching Teenagers*, Puchta et al, Pilgrim-Longman 1993.

Acknowledgement
I learnt this idea from Danny Singh, who credits it to Dr Madam Kataria, a medical practitioner from India.

2 Model grammar texts

- Photocopy these two texts before the lesson:

HIM
Oh I'm feeling low
Haven't had an email for a month
Haven't seen him since last Christmas
Haven't spoken on the phone
He hasn't texted me since Sunday
Oh I'm feeling low
Low, so low.
Who's that at the door?
Wow! It's you!

MY CAT
Oh I'm feeling bad
Haven't seen her for a week
Haven't seen her since she vanished
Haven't heard her purr or meow
She just hasn't been around
Oh I'm feeling bad
Oh how I miss her!
What's that at the door?
Wow! It's you!

- Hand out the texts and ask the students to read them.
- Deal with any new vocabulary, such as *low*, *Wow!*, *vanished*, *purr*, *meow*, *to miss*.
- Ask the students to stand up and then read *Him* with them chorally.
- Read the text again slowly and sadly. Then whisper it, shout it, read it in a high-pitched voice and read it fast and low.
- Do the same sequence of choral reading with *My cat*.
- Tell the students to sit down. Now ask them to think of other things or people they miss.
- Ask them to write a text imitating the pattern of the two model texts about the object or person that they miss.
- Put them into groups of six to read each other's texts.

> **RATIONALE**
> The choral readings allow the present perfect + *for/since* to sink into the students' unconscious minds. Note the omission of subject pronoun in the present perfect pattern, frequent in normal spoken English.
> (See Carter and McCarthy: *Cambridge Grammar of English*, Cambridge University Press, 2006).

Acknowledgement
I am grateful to Puchta, Gerngross and Thornbury for this guided writing technique from their book *Teaching Grammar Creatively*, Cambridge University Press/Helbling Languages, 2007. I have found the technique to be very popular with many teachers.

7 Disaster!

Unit overview

TOPIC: Natural disasters

TEXTS
Listening: a radio broadcast about a hurricane
Reading: a magazine article about a flying disaster
Reading: a text about the island of Tuvalu
Writing: a newspaper article about a disaster

SPEAKING AND FUNCTIONS
Talking about news events
Talking about and describing dreams
Agreeing and disagreeing

LANGUAGE
Grammar: Past simple passive; *a/an*, *the* or zero article
Vocabulary: Disasters

1 Vocabulary and listening

If you set the background information as a homework research task, ask students to tell the class what they found out.

BACKGROUND INFORMATION
Hurricane Katrina formed in August 2005 over the Bahamas, before passing over Florida and hitting New Orleans. The floodbanks failed and 80 per cent of the city was flooded. Over 1,500 people died and the estimated financial cost was $81.2 billion.

Warm up
Ask students if they can name any natural disasters. Ask them if they have ever experienced a natural disaster or seen any on television. If not, can they imagine what it would be like? Discuss this as a class or in L1 if appropriate.

a Students read through words 1 to 6 in the box and look at the photos. Students match the words to the pictures and compare answers in pairs.

Answers
1 F 2 D 3 C 4 B 5 E 6 A

b Students read the question. Elicit the reason why (*It is an unnatural/man-made disaster*).

Vocabulary notebook
Students should start a section called *Disasters* and note down words from this unit. Encourage them to use translations and illustrations if it will help them remember each word better.

c ▶ CD1 T36 Students look at the photo and read the question and in pairs or small groups discuss where and when they think it happened. Do not give answers at this point. Play the recording for students to listen and check their predictions. Play the recording again, pausing as necessary to clarify any problems.

TAPESCRIPT

Speaker 1: ... here today to talk to us about hurricanes and what happens when a hurricane hits a town or a city is Doctor Chloe Blaine. Good morning Dr Blaine.

Speaker 2: Good morning.

Speaker 1: I know that part of your research has been into, perhaps, one of the most well-known hurricanes in recent years ...

Speaker 2: That's right – Hurricane Katrina, as it was called, hit the city of New Orleans in 2005.

Speaker 1: That already seems so long ago.

Speaker 2: Yes, it does, and it's easy to forget just how terrible it was to ....

Answer
2005, in New Orleans

d Students read through the words and numbers in the box. Ask students to read through the summary, ignoring the gaps. Students now complete the exercise. They can compare answers in pairs but do not give answers at this point.

e ▶ CD1 T37 Play the second part of the recording for students to listen and check their answers. Play the recording again, pausing as necessary.

TAPESCRIPT

Speaker 1: So tell us about Hurricane Katrina.

Speaker 2: Hurricane Katrina was a Category 3 hurricane – that's very, very strong. It started in the Atlantic Ocean, crossed over Florida into the Gulf of Mexico, and hit the city of New Orleans, in the southern United States, on August 29th.

Speaker 1: Were many people killed?

Speaker 2: Yes, unfortunately. Many people left the city – in fact, on August 28th, the mayor of New Orleans told people to leave. But a lot of people stayed – many stayed because they had no way of leaving – and in the end, one thousand five hundred people were killed.

Speaker 1: That's terrible.

Speaker 2: Absolutely. But it could have been a lot worse. One good thing is that about seven thousand five hundred people were rescued by the police and firefighters – and probably even more people were rescued by friends and neighbours.

Speaker 1: And the city was very badly damaged, wasn't it?

Speaker 2: Oh yes indeed. Erm, this was one of the biggest disasters in US history. New Orleans was really badly damaged – erm, about 80 percent of the city was flooded.

Speaker 1: 80 per cent?

Speaker 2: Yes, 80 per cent. The problem was that the levees, the walls that were built to keep water out, well, they were destroyed by the hurricane and the water, and erm, the sea water just came into the city and flooded almost everything.

Speaker 1: People lost everything.

Speaker 2: Many people lost everything, yes. I mean, with this kind of disaster, it's very difficult to say how much the damage cost, but it was a huge amount of money – our estimate is about 90 billion dollars.

Speaker 1: That's a lot.

Speaker 2: It is, it is a lot ... but of course the worst thing was the effect that Katrina had on people's lives, you know, many people are still trying ...

> **Answers**
> killed; rescued; damaged; 80; lost; 90

2 Grammar

★ Past simple passive

a **Stronger classes:** Read the examples and the explanations with the class, and elicit the difference between the past and present simple passive which they saw in Unit 5 (the verb *be* is in the past tense in these examples). Students then go back through the summary in Exercise 1d and find more examples of the past passive.

Weaker classes: Books closed. Write some prompts and dates (in jumbled order) on the board, e.g. *last football World Cup/held/2006/Germany*; *Sistine Chapel/built/1473* (or another famous example from students' own country).

Elicit the past passive questions from students, e.g. *Where and when was the last football World Cup held? When was the Sistine Chapel built?* Then ask students to match each prompt with the correct date. Ask them if they can remember how to form the present simple passive from Unit 5. Elicit the form and then ask them what they notice about the verb in each question: it is the past tense of the verb *be* and the past participle. Students open their books at page 55 and read through the examples. Students go back through the summary in Exercise 1d and find more examples of the past passive.

Check answers. To check understanding at this point, ask students to give you an example of their own in the past passive.

Explain to students that this construction is usually used when we are more interested in the action and not the person who did it and we do not usually use '*by* + person' with it.

> **Answers**
> were rescued; was badly damaged; was flooded; was lost
> Rule: to be; past participle

b Students read through sentences 1 to 5. Go through the example as a class, if necessary. Ask students why it is *was* and not *were* and elicit that it is because *photo* is singular. Students complete the sentences. Check answers.

> **Answers**
> 2 was stolen 3 were built 4 was written
> 5 weren't used

c This exercise can be set for homework. Students read through sentences 1 to 8. Check any problems. Go through the example as a class, highlighting how the active sentence changes when it becomes a passive sentence. Elicit the differences (the active object becomes the passive subject 'the man'; we do not need to know who found the dead man so we do not use *by* + person). Students complete the sentences. Check answers.

> **Answers**
> 2 The house was robbed at midnight.
> 3 I am often confused with my older brother.
> 4 A lot of litter is dropped on the streets in our town.
> 5 A film was made about the earthquake.
> 6 She is called 'the Queen of Music'.
> 7 The Empire State Building was completed in 1932.
> 8 Our classroom window was broken last night.

Grammar notebook

Remind students to note down the rule and some examples of their own for the past passive.

4 Speak

a Divide the class into student A and B pairs. Tell Student As to read through the questions and answers on page 55 and Student Bs to turn to page 126 and look at their questions and answers. Make sure students understand that they have to make past passive questions and then they must choose the correct answer. Students should note down their partner's answers. Monitor and check students are using the correct forms and make a note of any repeated errors to go over as a class later.

b Ask a few pairs to read out their answers to the class and then give them the correct answers.

> **Answers**
> A 1 1989 2 Paris 3 volcano 4 830,000
> B 1 1925 2 1945 3 Colombia 4 1912

5 Read

Warm up

Write the following on the board: *Dogs; Birds; Spiders; Crocodiles*. In open class, ask students how they might cause problems for people. Encourage them to use their imagination and think of all possible dangerous situations.

a Students read through questions 1 to 4. Check any problems. Do the first question with students as an example, if necessary. Students complete the exercise. Remind them they don't need to understand every word in the text at this stage. Check answers.

Weaker classes: You may want to pre-teach the following vocabulary: *swarms, no wonder, harvest, hunger*.

> **Answers**
> 1 locusts
> 2 on their own
> 3 When they form swarms.
> 4 They destroy the harvests and bring hunger.

b Students read through topics 1 to 5, then match the topics with the paragraphs in the text. Check answers. Ask students to explain their choices.

> **Answers**
> 1 B 2 D 3 A 4 E 5 C

c Read through the questions with students and check understanding. Ask students to read the text more carefully and answer the questions. Allow them to compare answers with a partner before checking in open class.

> **Answers**
> 1 They cause damage to plants and people.
> 2 They are very small, they live on their own and they don't hurt anyone.
> 3 one-tenth
> 4 They swarm in massive numbers and they can eat their own weight in plants every day.
> 5 They destroy the harvest so people die of hunger.

d Students read through the definitions. Check any problems. In pairs, students find the words in the text to match the definitions. Set a time limit if you want to add a competitive element to this activity. Check answers. The pair that has the most correct answers is the winner.

> **Answers**
> 1 cause great damage 2 on its own 3 swarm
> 4 huge 5 It's no wonder 6 harvest

Vocabulary notebook

Students may find it useful to note down any new vocabulary from the reading text in their notebooks.

6 Grammar

★ *a/an, the* or *zero article*

a **Stronger classes:** Elicit the definition of 'an article' (*a, an* or *the*). Go through the text as a class. Students then underline the articles and the nouns they find while you read the rest of the text. Explain to students that *a/an* are used when we refer to something for the first time and *the* is used when we are referring to something we have already mentioned. Check answers.

Weaker classes: Books closed. Write the following sentences on the board (or some examples of your own): *I was in San Francisco in 1989 when there was an/the earthquake. The/An earthquake was not very strong.* Ask students to choose the correct alternatives. Explain to students that we use *an* in the first sentence because we are talking about the earthquake for the first time and *the* in the second sentence because we have already mentioned it. Students open their books at page 57. Follow the procedure for stronger classes from this point.

> **Answers**
> a volcanic eruption; The earthquake; the most powerful earthquake; the volcano; a Roman town

b Students read through the rule box and complete the rule.

> **Answers**
> a; an; the; zero article

UNIT 7

> **Language note**
> Students from many language backgrounds will make sentences like *The monkeys live in trees* or *The people are strange*. Point out and clarify that we do not use an article at all when talking about things in general.

c Students read through the sentences. Check any problems. Go through the example as a class. Students complete the sentences. Check answers.

> **Answers**
> 1 a, a, the, the
> 2 a, a, The, the
> 3 an, zero, zero, a, a, the, the
> 4 a, zero, a, zero, zero, zero

Grammar notebook
Remind students to note down the rules for this area and to make a note of a few examples of their own if necessary.

★ OPTIONAL ACTIVITY

Read out the following text and make a beep sound every time you come to *a/an* or *the*. Students must write down the word they think goes in each gap. They can compare answers in pairs before a whole class check.

It was a dark night in 1989. I was walking along the beach when I saw a boat. It was a very rough sea and the lighthouse was not working. I was sure the boat was going to hit the rocks. I had a white towel with me so I ran down to the shore and waved and waved the towel. Suddenly, the lighthouse light came on again and the boat turned and …

Stronger classes: They can then write their own ending for the story.

7 Speak

a Ask students to read through the gapped dialogue. Check any problems. Go through the example as a class. Students complete the dialogue using *a/an/the*. Students can compare answers in pairs before a whole class check.

> **Answers**
> 2 the 3 a 4 The 5 a 6 The 7 zero
> 8 a 9 a 10 the 11 zero 12 zero 13 an

b Divide the class into pairs. Read through the instructions as a class and make sure that students understand they must now make up their own dreams and use *a/an/the* in each sentence. Remind them of the model in Exercise 7a they have just completed.

Weaker classes: You could give them a first sentence to get them started, e.g. *Last night I dreamed I was very rich*. Monitor and check that students are taking turns to say a sentence and are using *a/an/the* in each sentence.

Ask pairs to read out their dreams to the class.

Culture in mind

8 Read and listen

If you set the background information as a homework research task ask students to tell the class what they found out.

> **BACKGROUND INFORMATION**
> **Tuvalu** is a Polynesian island nation in the Pacific Ocean which covers just 26km².
> **Fiji** is an island nation in the South Pacific Ocean.

Warm up
Write the words *South Pacific Island* on the board. Ask students what they think daily life is like on a Pacific island. Brainstorm advantages and disadvantages of living in a tropical paradise. Write any interesting new vocabulary on the board.

a Tell students they are going to read an article about a small group of South Pacific islands called Tuvalu. Look at the photo and map, and read through the questions to check understanding. You may like to ask them to explain the following, in L1 if necessary: *climate change, rising sea levels, global warming, emission of greenhouse gases*. Divide the class into pairs or small groups and ask students to discuss the questions. Ask some groups to briefly report back their ideas to the class. Do not give them the answers at this stage.

> **Example answers**
> 1 Rising sea levels and increased salt levels in water, climate change, hurricanes.
> 2 Hurricanes cause strong winds, storms and rough seas, which threaten life and cause damage. Rising sea levels increase salt in ground water, making it undrinkable.
> 3 Big ones produce more greenhouse gases.

b ▶ **CD2 T1** Ask students to read the text, listen and check their answers to Exercise 8a. Pre-teach difficult key words in the text: *uninhabitable, refused*. Tell them not to try to understand every word, but to look for the specific information required by the questions. Check answers in open class and encourage further discussion.

UNIT 7

c Read through the words and definitions with students. Ask them to look back at the text and match the words or phrases with the definitions.

> **Answers**
> 2 g 3 b 4 a 5 d 6 h 7 f 8 c

9 Speak

a As an introduction to this activity, ask students to tell you ways in which we can reduce the effects of global warming. Discuss in open class. Draw a horizontal line on the board and write *0 (I don't agree), 2, 3, 4, 5 (5 agree 100%)* along it. To give students an example, read the first sentence aloud and ask students where they would put a cross on the line. Ask them to give reasons for their decisions. Read through the other three sentences and check understanding. Ask students to work individually and decide how much they agree or disagree with the statement. Circulate and help less decisive students make a decision.

b Before asking students to write about their opinions, you may like to write the following phrases on the board to help them form sentences:
*0 I don't agree / I don't agree at all / I disagree
1/2/3/4 maybe / possibly / I partly agree / I'm not sure
5 I totally agree / That's absolutely right / I agree 100%*

Read through the example and ask students to write similar sentences to express their opinions on the statements. Circulate and help with any difficult vocabulary.

c Divide the class into small groups. Students discuss their opinions. Encourage them to each read aloud their sentences as part of the discussion. As feedback listen to some of their ideas in open class and expand any particularly interesting points into a class debate. Ask students to imagine that they have to work together to decide unanimously on a number between 0 and 5 in order to report their decision to the United Nations. The fate of Tuvalu and the world is in their hands!

10 Write

a Students read the newspaper story silently. Ask them the two questions.

> **Answers**
> A man was blown by a very strong wind off a cliff, into the sea.

✲ OPTIONAL ACTIVITY

Students underline the examples of the past simple passive in the text. Check answers.

> **Answers**
> Para 1: was rescued
> Para 2: was blown off; was taken
> Para 3: was saved

Elicit from them the reason the passive is used in the text. (The passive is often used in newspaper articles, in this case to place emphasis on the main person in the story.)

b Divide the class into pairs. Ask students to read through the phrases in the box. Check any problems. Ask a stronger student to describe picture 1 using phrases from the box. Students continue describing the pictures. Remind them to use the past simple passive where possible. Monitor and check students are using the construction properly and note down any repeated errors to go through as a class later. Ask a few pairs to feed back to the class.

> **Example answers**
> The weather was very hot. A cigarette end was dropped in the forest and the dry leaves caught fire. The fire was made worse by very strong winds. People had to leave their homes. The fire fighters could not control the fire and houses nearby were burnt.

c Students can do the preparation in class, and complete the writing at home.

They should organise their work so that each paragraph answers one of the three questions. They should use the passive where possible. When they have finished, ask them to read their article to the class or to a partner.

UNIT 7

Memo from Mario

Disaster!

1 Reduction exercise: past simple passive

▶ Dictate this sentence to a student who writes it on the board:

The secondary school, the one down by the bridge, was flooded late last night

by the rising water from the river, muddy brown water, and the school's roof was torn

off by hurricane-force winds in the greatest storm we've had in the last ten years.

▶ Check that students come to grips with any new words in the text. Write up mother tongue translations where needed.

▶ Ask several students to read the sentence aloud. After each reading underline sounds that have been mispronounced. Silently point to these and ask the student to read the word again. Usually the students themselves will correct the mistake or someone else in the class will shout out the correct form. Only give a model if no one else in the group can.

▶ Erase the mother tongue translations.

▶ Explain to the students that they are going to reduce this long sentence to perhaps one word. Tell them they can remove one word, two consecutive or three consecutive words at a time.

▶ A student who wants to delete a word (or words) comes to the board, erases the word/s and then reads the remaining sentence aloud to check if the grammar is correct and if the sentence is still meaningful. (During the exercise the meaning will change, sometimes radically.)

▶ Do not intervene if a student is intent on an incorrect deletion. Let him erase the words and read the remaining sentence. If the student does not realise the error, often someone in the group will. If no one detects the error, then quietly say to the deleter: '*Please put the words back in.*'

▶ Invite other students to get involved in the sentence reduction process.

▶ The activity ends when nothing more can, grammatically and syntactically, be taken out.

> **RATIONALE**
> While thinking about what can be deleted, the students are assimilating the past simple passive forms without noticing what is happening.
> Many other grammar points come up in the course of the deletion work and the structure to the activity has students think for themselves about these, without being spoon-fed by you.

Acknowledgement

The exercise comes from the work of Caleb Gattegno, the originator of the Silent Way.

2 Weed this passage

▶ Here is a good technique for getting students to revise any reading text you feel they need to.

▶ The passage used here is 'Man rescued from sea' (page 59).

▶ Give the students photocopies of the text below and ask them to take out any intrusive, unnecessary words.

Man rescued from sea

A 28-year-old man and woman was rescued by helicopter maybe yesterday after he fell into the sea near his good holiday home.

The accident always happened while the man, John Carter, was walking along the cliff. He was blown off by a very strong wind and fell upwards into the sea, 30 metres below. Luckily, a green woman saw Mr Carter in the water soon afterwards and she called the police rescue service rudely. He was taken to hospital with a useless broken arm.

Last night Mr Carter said from under his hospital bed, 'I am very lucky to be alive. My life was saved by the elephant woman who called the criminal police. I can't thank her grandmother enough.'

▶ (Key: words to be weeded out: *and woman maybe good always upwards green rudely useless under elephant criminal grandmother*)

▶ Ask the students to open their books on page 59 and compare their weeded text with the original.

> **RATIONALE**
> This technique, which has been used in the Cambridge ESOL CAE exam, encourages critical reading by the students.

> **VARIATION**
> Take two texts you want to revise. Divide your class in two. Give one text to one half of the group: their task is to re-write the text, adding eight to ten irrelevant words. Ask the other half of the class to do the same with the second text.
> Now pair people from the two halves of the class: the students exchange their texts with their partner and weed the texts.

8 Ways of living

Unit overview

TOPIC: Homes around the world

TEXTS
Reading and listening: a text and email about a cave holiday in Spain
Listening: people describing their homes
Writing: an email about holiday plans

SPEAKING AND FUNCTIONS
Describing quantity
Talking about your home
Discussing plans

LANGUAGE
Grammar: *too much/many, not enough; will* vs. *be going to*
Vocabulary: Homes
Everyday English: *There's no point in; There's nothing wrong with; It's up to you; Anything else?; all over the place; if you say so*

1 Read and listen

If you set the background information as a homework research task, ask students to tell the class what they found out.

BACKGROUND INFORMATION

Granada is a city in the region of Andalusia, Spain. The city of Granada is at the foot of the Sierra Nevada mountains and is 738 metres above sea level, yet only one hour from the Mediterranean coast.

Guadix is a city of southern Spain, in the province of Granada. Guadix is surrounded by ancient walls, and is home to a great cathedral, built between the 16th and 18th centuries on the site of a mosque which combines three architectural styles (Gothic, Renaissance and Baroque).

Andalusia is one of the autonomous communities of the Kingdom of Spain. Its capital and largest city is Seville.

Warm up

Ask students where they usually go on holiday and where they stay. What is the most exciting holiday they have been on? Discuss this as a class, in L1 if appropriate.

a Ask students to read the questions and look at the pictures. Students then read the text quickly to answer them. Encourage them to use the visual clues to help them. Remind them they don't have to understand every word at this stage. Check answers.

Answers
1 Guadix near Granada
2 You can stay in a cave.

b ▶ CD2 T2 Students read through items 1 to 3. They read the text again and listen to find the answers. Students can compare answers in pairs before a whole class check.

Weaker classes: You may want to pre-teach the following vocabulary: *lifetime, cave, primitive, luxurious, Jacuzzi, charm*.

Answers
1 Granada
2 electricity, phone, hot water, a broadband connection, Jacuzzi or swimming pool
3 The temperature is cool on hot days; they make you feel calm and safe

✱ OPTIONAL ACTIVITY

Write the following true/false questions about the reading text on the board and ask students to correct the false statements:
1 All of the caves are small.
2 You can use the Internet in some of the caves.
3 It is hot in the caves.
4 All the caves are different.

Answers
1 F (some are the size of a luxurious hotel)
2 T
3 F (temperatures are around 18–20° C)
4 T

c ▶ CD2 T3 Students read through the instructions and the questions. Check any problems. Play the recording while students read and listen for the answers.

Weaker classes: Pause the recording after the answer to the first question and go through this as an example. Continue playing the recording for students to answer the second question.

Check answers.

UNIT 8   65

TAPESCRIPT

See the reading text on page 60 of the Student's Book.

> **Answers**
> 1 He ate too much ice cream the day before.
> 2 Because there were too many tourists and they couldn't find a hotel.

2 Grammar

✱ too much/many, not enough

a Remind students of countable and uncountable nouns by eliciting a few examples of each. Remind students what the differences are by asking them, e.g. *Can we count water? (No) Can we count chairs? (Yes)*. Refer students to the examples and ask them to underline the countable and uncountable nouns.

> **Answers**
> countable: tourists; beds
> uncountable: ice cream; time

b Ask students to look at pictures 1 to 4 and the sentences. Ask them to give you the countable and uncountable nouns in each sentence and then ask them what they notice about the words used before the nouns. Elicit that *too many* is used with countable nouns and *too much* is used with uncountable nouns. Make sure students understand that *too + much/many + adjective* has a negative meaning (more than necessary) and compare it with *a lot of*. To make sure students understand, give them the following sentences and ask them to compare them and explain the difference in meaning: *My computer is very old now. My computer is too old now.*

c Students read through the rule box and complete it using the information from Exercise 2c. Check answers.

> **Answers**
> many; much

To check understanding at this point call out a few nouns, making sure you include a variety of countable and uncountable ones. Students have to say *too much/many* with the noun you call out. For example:
T: Nicolo, chairs.
S1: Too many chairs.
T: Francesco, milk.
S2: Too much milk. etc.

> **Language note**
> Students may produce statements like: ~~They are too much old~~. Remind them that we use *too + adjective* and *too much/many + noun*.

d Ask students to look at the four pictures and to read through the gapped sentences. Check any problems. Students complete the exercise. Remind them to look carefully at the noun before they choose *too much/many*.

Weaker classes: Ask students to underline the nouns and to identify them as countable or uncountable before they fill in the missing words. Check answers.

> **Answers**
> 1 too many   2 too many   3 too much
> 4 too much

e Students read through the examples from the email on page 60. Ask students to look carefully at the nouns and the verbs in each example and ask them if they are countable or uncountable (*beds* is countable and the verb is plural; *time* is uncountable and the verb is singular). Then ask them what they notice about the word *enough* and elicit that it doesn't change whether the noun is countable, uncountable, singular or plural. Students then read through the rule and complete it. Check answers.

> **Answers**
> countable; uncountable

> **Language notes**
> 1 Students may produce statements like: ~~There wasn't enoughs rooms~~. Remind them that *enough* always stays the same regardless of the noun being singular or plural in English.
> 2 Check students are pronouncing *enough* /ɪˈnʌf/ correctly.

f This exercise can be set for homework. Students read through the gapped text. Check any problems. Go through the example, asking them to explain why it is *too many*. Students complete the exercise. They can compare answers in pairs before a whole class check. Make sure students can explain their answer choices.

Weaker classes: Ask students to go through the text and underline all the nouns first. They can then identify if they are countable or uncountable and decide which phrase goes in each gap.

> **Answers**
> 1 too many   2 too much   3 enough
> 4 too many   5 enough

g Divide the class into pairs. Students read through the items in the box. Ask a stronger pair to demonstrate the example and point out the use of *not enough* and *too much*. Students make true

66   UNIT 8

statements about their town/country using the items in the box and exchange information with their partner. Monitor and check that students are taking turns to give information and make sure that they are using *too much/many / not enough* statements correctly.

Weaker classes: Allow them to write down their sentences before having their discussion. If there are repeated errors, note them down to go through later as a class. Ask for some pairs to feedback to the class and if there are any interesting statements, ask students to give more details.

Grammar notebook

Encourage students to note down the completed rules from this unit and some example sentences of their own. Students may find it useful to translate some of the examples.

✷ OPTIONAL ACTIVITY

Ask students to think about all the things they have in their bedrooms at home and create three lists: things they have too much or too many of, e.g. soft toys, pairs of shoes and things they haven't enough of, e.g. money, comics, CDs. When students have created a list, divide the class into small groups and ask students to take it in turns to describe their belongings. Students should try to find somebody to exchange things with, i.e. someone with too many CDs should find someone with not enough CDs.

4 Vocabulary

✷ Homes

a ▶ CD2 T6 Books closed. Elicit the names of different types of houses students know in English and write them on the board. Ask students to explain, in L1 if appropriate, what kind of house each one they mention is. Students now open their books at page 62 and read through the words in the box and look at the pictures. Students match as many of the words as they can, then compare answers in pairs. Play the recording for students to check or change their answers. Play the recording again, pausing for students to repeat each word.

> **Tapescript/Answers**
> A 2 a block of flats B 4 a cottage
> C 6 a caravan D 1 a detached house
> E 7 a semi-detached house F 5 a bungalow
> G 3 a housing estate H 8 a terraced house

b Students read through the words in the box. Check any problems. Go through the first item as an example, if necessary. Students complete the exercise and compare answers in pairs. Check answers as a class.

> **Example answers**
> Picture B: a chimney; a garden; a fence
> Picture C: a TV aerial
> Picture D: a garage; a garden
> Picture E: a gate; a chimney; a fence

c Students read through questions 1 to 3. Check any problems. In pairs, students discuss the questions. Ask for some pairs to feed back to the class.

> **Answers**
> 1 In a semi-detached house (picture E); a detached house (picture D); a block of flats (picture A); a cottage (picture B).
> 2 In a block of flats (picture A).
> 3 A bungalow (picture F); a caravan (picture C).

✷ OPTIONAL ACTIVITY

Students choose one of the types of homes from Exercise 4 or choose one of their own. They must decide why they want to live in it and why it is their ideal home.

5 Listen

▶ CD2 T7 Explain that students are going to hear six people talking about where they live. Students must listen and write the number of the speaker in the boxes in the photos in Exercise 4a. Elicit the kinds of words students think they might hear and write them on the board. Play the recording, pausing after the first type of home is mentioned and go through this as an example, if necessary. Play the recording again for students to listen and complete the exercise. Students can compare answers in pairs before a whole class check. Play the recording again, pausing as necessary to clarify any problems.

TAPESCRIPT

1 Our new house is smaller than our old one but it's really nice. Erm … it hasn't got a garage, but there's room for Mum's car in the drive. Er, it's semi-detached, you know, joined to another house, but our neighbours are nice, they don't make much noise … It's got a garden at the front with a fence round it.

2 I live in a place, erm, with my parents and my two brothers. We're on the seventh floor, so we've got a great view over the city. From my bedroom window I can see the river! But it's not so good when the lift is out of order. Then we have to climb up hundreds of stairs!

3 My house is small and I haven't got a garage, but the garden is big and I love gardening. My grandchildren like coming to see me and climbing the trees but they complain because I don't have a computer! The house is all on one floor – so there are no stairs to worry about.

UNIT 8 67

4 There are a lot of people who maybe wouldn't want to live where I do, but for me it's perfect. Just one floor, and it's quite small inside but I don't want a big kitchen or anything anyway. And the great thing, the really good thing about it, is that it's mobile. I've been in this place for more than two years now, but I can go somewhere else whenever I want to.

5 My husband and I always wanted to live in the country, and now that we don't have to go to work any more, we do! We've got a lovely little place with a thatched roof and a really pretty garden with a fence round it. It's very quiet at night and sometimes I miss the sound of the traffic! Can you believe that? But the country's a lovely place to be – I'm really happy here.

6 I'm pretty lucky because our house is quite big. We've got four bedrooms – they're all upstairs – and mine is the smallest because I'm the youngest. It's still quite big, though. And we've got a big garden where we can play football. And we haven't got any neighbours so I can play my music really loudly and there's no one next door to complain!

> **Answers**
> 1 E (semi-detached)   2 A (block of flats)
> 3 F (bungalow)   4 C (caravan)
> 5 B (cottage)   6 D (detached)

Vocabulary notebook
Students should start a section called *Homes* in their notebooks and note down all the new words and expressions from this exercise.

 Speak

a As an introduction to this exercise, students may be interested to hear about the place you live. Describe it to them in detail and ask them to guess which fact is not true. Read through the instructions with students. Ask them to make notes about the following things: *the type of house/flat they live in; the number of rooms it has; who sleeps in which room; how many other rooms it has; if it has a garden; what the neighbours are like; if they like it*. If time allows and you have an artistic class, ask them to draw a simple plan of their accommodation. Make sure they include one fact which is not true.

b Divide the class into pairs. Students take it in turns to describe their homes. Encourage them to go into as much detail as possible. Monitor and check students are taking turns and that they are able to express themselves clearly.

c When students have described their homes, their partners have to guess which thing is not true. As feedback, listen to a few examples in open class.

 Grammar
★ *will* vs. *be going to*

If you set the background information as a homework research task, ask students to tell the class what they found out.

> **BACKGROUND INFORMATION**
> **China** is officially known as The People's Republic of China and is situated in East Asia. It is the world's third largest country and the world's most highly populated country. The capital is Beijing and other major cities include Shanghai and Tianjin.
>
> **Qinghai** (or Tsinghai) is a province in western China. The capital of this province is Xining (Sining).
>
> **Tibet** is an autonomous region in south west China. The capital is Lhasa. Tibet is surrounded by incredible mountains including the Himalayas.

a ▶ **CD2 T8** Students read through the question and the dialogue. Check any problems. Play the recording for students to read and listen for the answers. Check answers.

TAPESCRIPT
See the dialogue on page 63 of the Student's Book.

> **Answers**
> 2 'm going to   3 Are … going to   4 will
> 5 will   6 won't   7 Will   8 'm going to   9 'll

b **Stronger classes:** Students read through the examples from the dialogue in Exercise 7a. Ask them if Jake decided to go to China before he spoke to Angie (*Yes*) and if he decided to send her a postcard before he spoke to her (*No*). Elicit that we use *going to* for future decisions made before the moment of speaking and *will* for decisions made at the moment of speaking. Students then read through the rule box and complete it.

Weaker classes: Books closed. Write the following examples on the board (or use some of your own): *I'm going to England for my holidays this summer. Here are my tickets. / My mobile phone's ringing. I'll answer it.*

Ask students which sentence shows something that has been planned already (example 1) and which sentence shows something that you decide to do at the moment of speaking (example 2). Students now open their books at page 63 and read the two examples from the dialogue. Follow the procedure for stronger classes from here.

68 UNIT 8

Check answers.

> **Answers**
> be going to; will/won't

To check students have understood the difference clearly, ask them to provide an example of their own for *will / going to*.

Students read through the examples. Make sure they understand that we don't usually use *going to + go*, and that we would normally say *I'm going swimming tomorrow* and *She's going to America next year*.

> **Language notes**
> 1 Students may produce statements like: ~~I will go to Brazil on holiday~~. Remind them that if something is already arranged, we use *going to*.
> 2 Students may find it useful to translate some of the examples in Exercise 7 into their own language to compare them.

c This exercise can be set for homework. Students read through dialogues 1 to 7. Go through the example as a class. Ask students to explain why *I'll carry them* is the correct answer. Students complete the exercise. Remind them to look carefully at each situation before deciding which verb is appropriate. Check answers, making sure students can explain why they made their choices by referring to the rule.

> **Answers**
> 2 he's going to have 3 I'll open
> 4 we're going to see 5 she's going to take
> 6 I'll lend 7 I'll have

d Read through the instructions. Students choose the correct form to complete each gap. Ask them to compare answers with a partner. During feedback, encourage students to explain why that option is correct.

> **Answers**
> 1 'm going to learn 2 's going to teach
> 3 'll probably be 4 'm going to take
> 5 'm going to buy 6 will show 7 'll want

Grammar notebook

Remind students to note down the rules for *will / going to* and some examples of their own.

✱ OPTIONAL ACTIVITY

Tell students they are going to plan a party. In open class, brainstorm all the things they will need to do in preparation, e.g. buy cakes, choose music, decorate the house, etc. When you have a good list, divide the class into small groups and ask students to offer to do things on the list and give a reason why they can do it, e.g. *I'll choose the music because I've got lots of CDs / I'll buy the cakes because I live next door to a cake shop*. When students have decided who is going to do what, regroup them into pairs and ask them to tell each other who is going to do what and why, e.g. *Sandra's going to buy the cakes because she lives next door to a cake shop*. Monitor and ensure students are using tenses correctly. As feedback, hold an open class discussion to decide who has had the best ideas for a party. If students enjoy this activity, you could expand it to plan a class party in the school.

All over the place

8 Read and listen

Warm up

Ask students which are their favourite subjects at school. Are there any subjects that they find difficult? What do they do if they are finding a subject hard? Do they ever study together? Listen to some of their ideas in open class.

a **CD2 T9** Read the questions through with students and ask students to guess the answers. Play the recording while students listen and read to find the answers. Play the recording again, pausing as necessary for students to check their predictions.

> **Answers**
> They are studying at school. Joel can't do his Maths because he hasn't studied.

TAPESCRIPT

See the text on page 64 of the Student's Book.

b Read through sentences 1–4 with students and check understanding of difficult vocabulary: *think very highly of; grateful*. Students complete the sentences in their own words. Circulate and help with vocabulary as required. Check answers in open class.

> **Answers**
> 1 … his ability in Maths.
> 2 … Pete offers to help him study.
> 3 … is very untidy.
> 4 … always finds his things quickly.

9 Everyday English

a Read the expressions aloud with the class. In pairs, students find them in the photo story and decide who said them. Check answers. Students can then translate them into their own language.

UNIT 8 69

> **Answers**
> 1 Joel 2 Pete 3 Pete 4 Pete 5 Pete
> 6 Pete

b Students complete the sentences with the vocabulary from Exercise 9a. Do the first item as an example, if necessary. Remind students to read through the whole dialogue before deciding which expressions to use. Check answers.

> **Answers**
> 2 if you say so 3 It's up to you
> 4 There's no point in 5 all over the place
> 6 There's nothing wrong with

✱ OPTIONAL ACTIVITY

Divide the class into pairs and ask them to practise the dialogue. You may like to read through the dialogue yourself first to give them an example. When students have practised the dialogue, students take it in turns to close their book and try to remember their part. Their partner can give them prompts to help them remember. Can any of the students remember the whole dialogue without looking at their books?

Vocabulary notebook

Encourage students to add these expressions to the *Everyday English* section in their vocabulary notebooks.

> **Discussion box**
>
> **Weaker classes:** Students can choose one question to discuss.
>
> **Stronger classes:** In pairs or small groups, students go through the questions in the box and discuss them.
>
> Monitor and help as necessary, encouraging students to express themselves in English and to use any vocabulary they have learned from the text. Ask pairs or groups to feed back to the class and discuss any interesting points further.

10 Improvisation

Divide the class into pairs. Tell students they are going to create a role play between Pete and Joel. Read through the instructions with students. Give students two minutes to plan their dialogue. Circulate and help with vocabulary as necessary. Encourage students to use expressions from Exercise 9. Students practise their conversation in pairs. Listen to some of the best conversations in open class.

11 Team Spirit (DVD Episode 4)

a Look at the photo with students and elicit adjectives to describe how Joel is feeling. Write some of the best ideas on the board and then ask students why they think he may feel like this.

b Divide the class into pairs. Read the instructions with students and ask them to work with their partner and make a list of strong feelings. Listen to some of their ideas in open class as feedback.

c With the same partner, students discuss the question. Circulate and help with vocabulary as required.

d In open class, discuss the question. Encourage students to use some of the language from Exercise 9 in their answers.

e Watch episode 4 and find out how the different people in the story act because of their feelings.

12 Write

The preparation for this can be done in class and the writing can be done for homework.

a Students read through questions 1 to 4. Check any problems. Students then read through the two adverts and answer the questions. Check answers.

Weaker classes: You may want to pre-teach the following vocabulary: *converted barn, guests, healthy, meal, chance*.

> **Answers**
> 1 A: four days; B: ten days
> 2 They are both in Britain; they are both staying in a home, with a family.
> 3 A: In a converted barn. B: In a family's house.
> 4 A: You learn how a farm works. B: You learn about life in Britain and improve your English.

b Students read through the questions and then quickly read the email to find the answers. Check answers.

> **Answers**
> 1 Her brother and her friend Anna from school.
> 2 To write to her when she gets back.

c Students read through the instructions and then re-read advert B. Students then plan their email using the model in their book. Remind them of the structure and format of emails and encourage them to plan their email before writing a final version.

Weaker classes: Go through the model with students, encouraging them to look at the content of each paragraph carefully:
- Opening greeting
- Para 1: Introduction

70 UNIT 8

- Para 2: Gives information about the type of holiday she's going on and what she is going to do.
- Para 3: What she will do now and what she intends to do when she gets back.
- Sign off

Once students have written their emails, they can send them to a partner.

13 Last but not least: more speaking

a Read through the prompts and example sentences. Give some further examples of your own if necessary. Students think about their plans for the next week and write sentences. Circulate and check students are using *going to / will* correctly.

b Ask two stronger students to read out the dialogue. With weaker classes, you may like to do some practice on the intonation of questions, reading B's questions aloud yourself and asking them to repeat. In pairs, students create dialogues. Listen to the most interesting ones in open class as feedback.

Check your progress

1 Grammar

a 2 were killed 3 wasn't injured 4 were beaten 5 was heard

b 2 an 3 a 4 a/zero 5 a/zero 6 a/zero 7 The 8 the/zero 9 the 10 zero

c 2 n't enough 3 too much 4 too many

d 2 'm going to wash 3 are ... going to meet 4 'll pay

2 Vocabulary

a 2 garage 3 bomb 4 semi-detached house 5 caravan

b 2 volcano 3 hurricanes 4 eventually 5 essential 6 TV aerial

How did you do?

Check that students are marking their scores. Collect these in and check them as necessary and discuss any further work needed with specific students.

UNIT 8

Memo from Mario

Ways of living

1 An alternative way of approaching Exercise 5 (Listen), page 62

- Make sure students' books are closed.
- Before playing the first text, ask the students to prepare to listen and tell them to create a mental picture of what they hear.
- Play the first text three times.
- Ask the students to draw what they have imagined.
- Follow the same procedure with the next five texts.
- Put the students into groups of six to compare their pictures.
- Tell the students to open their books on page 62 and compare their own pictures from the texts with the pictures in the book.

> **RATIONALE**
> This exercise uses the principle of personalisation, that the authors draw on throughout *English in Mind Second edition*, to make thoughts about houses more real to the students.

> **RATIONALE**
> Matching texts with photographs is a useful gist comprehension check but it is also good sometimes to allow the students to become aware of the mental pictures they naturally create as they listen to texts.
>
> Asking them to draw their mind pictures on the page is one way, an imperfect way, of getting them to share the huge realm of their imagination. It is an imperfect way because a brilliant visualiser may not manage to convey their inner pictures well through the medium of drawing.

2 Writing about my house

- In open class ask a confident student to tell you about the colours in their house, outside and inside. Write words the student cannot find but needs on the board.
- Ask another student to tell the group about noise, sound and silence in their house. Ask them to think of noise coming from outside as well as sounds from inside. Again, fill the board with the vocabulary the student needs.
- Ask a third student to tell you about the smells in his house.
- Ask a fourth student about the places they like best in their house.
- Now ask all the students to write two paragraphs describing their house. Go round the class helping students with their mini-compositions.
- Put the students in groups of six to read what they have written.
- Ask each group to choose one text they like. The writer of this text puts it up on the board for all to read.

9 Your mind

Unit overview

TOPIC: Memory

TEXTS
Reading and listening: a text about how to improve your memory
Listening: an interview about 'multiple intelligences'
Reading and listening: an article about a girl genius
Writing: a competition entry

SPEAKING AND FUNCTIONS
Discussing intelligence
Discussing memory
Discussing young intelligent people

LANGUAGE
Grammar: Determiners (*everyone, no one, someone* etc.); *must/mustn't* vs. *don't have to*
Vocabulary: Thinking

1 Read and listen

Warm up
Ask students if they are good at remembering things, e.g. birthdays, football scores, song lyrics, phone numbers, historical dates, etc. Ask them if they have any techniques for remembering things. Discuss this as a class or in L1 if appropriate.

a Explain to students that they are going to do a memory test. Students turn to page 102 and look at the picture for Unit 14. Explain that they have 30 seconds to look at the picture. After 30 seconds, tell students to close their books and give them a few minutes to write down all the things they saw in the picture. How many students remembered everything? In L1 you can discuss with students how they remembered the items they noted down.

b Students read the question and look at the title of the text. Elicit suggestions on ways to improve memory and then students read the text quickly to check their predictions.

> **Answers**
> take in lots of oxygen; tell a friend what you want to remember then think about your conversation later; go to sleep immediately after learning something; break big things down into smaller chunks to remember; relax; make pictures in your mind.

c ▶ **CD2 T10** Students read through sentences 1 to 6. Check any problems. Play the recording while students listen and read. Give them a few minutes to answer the true/false questions.

Weaker classes: You may want to pre-teach the following vocabulary: *take in, over-train, break it down, batteries, roller skates*.

Students can compare answers in pairs before a whole class check. Encourage students to correct the false answers. Play the recording again if necessary, pausing to clarify any problems.

TAPESCRIPT
See the reading text on page 68 of the Student's Book.

> **Answers**
> 1 F (it needs about 20 per cent of the oxygen that our body takes in)
> 2 T
> 3 T
> 4 F (it's easier to remember things you break down into smaller sections)
> 5 F (it works better when we are relaxed)
> 6 T

2 Grammar

✱ Determiners (*everyone, no one, someone* etc.)

a **Stronger classes:** Read through the examples as a class. Ask students what they notice about the words in bold and elicit or explain the meaning of the determiners in each sentence, asking students if they are used in this case to refer to people, places or things (*something*: things; *none of them; all of them*: people).

Explain that these words are called determiners in English. Then give students a few minutes to go back through the text on page 68 and find more. Elicit or explain that *none* is always followed by *of*.

Weaker classes: Books closed. Write the following examples (or a few of your own) on the board: *I can't remember everything in my diary for this week. Here are some dates. All of them are important but none of them are in my diary.*

Explain or elicit the meaning of the determiners in each sentence, asking students if they are used in this case to refer to people, places or things (*things*). Elicit or explain that *none* is always followed by *of*.

UNIT 9   73

Students now open their books at page 69 and read through the examples. Students then find more examples in the text on page 68.

Check answers.

> **Answers**
> no one   everything   everyone   something
> something   anyone   someone   everywhere

b Students read through the table while you copy it onto the board.

> **Answers**
> Column 1: all of them
> Column 2: someone
> Column 3: no one; none of them

c This exercise can be set for homework. Students read through the words in the box and sentences 1 to 7. Check any problems. Go through the example as a class. Students complete the exercise.

> **Answers**
> 2 no one   3 everyone   4 none of them
> 5 everything   6 everywhere   7 all of them

LOOK!

Students read through the examples in the Look! box. Make sure they understand that when we use a *no-* word we must use a positive verb in English and an *any-* word uses a negative verb. It may be helpful for students to translate these examples into their own language to see how they work.

Grammar notebook

Encourage students to note down the completed table and some examples of determiners from this exercise.

3 Vocabulary
✱ Thinking

a Discuss what these are in students' own language. Are there any similarities?

b This exercise can be set for homework. Students read the sentences. Check any problems and go through the first item as an example, if necessary. Students complete the exercise.

> **Answers**
> 2 recognise   3 believe in   4 suppose
> 5 guess   6 concentrate   7 imagine
> 8 wonder   9 think   10 realised

Vocabulary notebook

Students should start a section called *Thinking* in their notebooks and note down all the new words and expressions from this exercise.

4 Speak

In pairs or small groups, students go through the questions and discuss them. Monitor and help as necessary, encouraging students to express themselves in English using vocabulary they have learned from the text.

5 Listen

a ▶ **CD2 T11**   Divide the class into pairs. Ask students to read the question and look at the pictures on the page. Give them some time to discuss the question. Ask for feedback. Play the recording for students to listen and check their answers. Were any of them correct?

TAPESCRIPT

Speaker 1: Good morning, and welcome to the programme. Today we are discussing the human mind, and with us in the studio is the psychologist, Dr Rebecca Williams, who has been our guest many times before. Dr Williams, welcome back. Now, I'm going to ask you a very strange question: what is it that Leonardo da Vinci and Keira Knightley have in common?

Speaker 2: That's an interesting question, because when we first think of these two people, we probably think of what is different about them, and not what they have in common. Leonardo da Vinci, a man, lived about 500 years ago; Keira Knightley is a woman and is alive today. Leonardo was a great painter, designer, scientist and thinker. Keira Knightley is an actress who has acted in a lot of popular films. Leonardo was Italian; Knightley is British – and so on. But they have something in common. They both had certain problems with learning to read and write.

Speaker 1: That's really amazing, isn't it? When we think of Leonardo da Vinci, we would never imagine him with learning difficulties. What can you tell us about his learning problems?

Speaker 2: Well, I have to say that we don't know very much for certain. All we have is what some experts believe. It is difficult to prove, of course, because, as we said, Leonardo was born more than 500 years ago, and we can't ask him ... But what we do know is that Leonardo took a lot of notes, and he wrote his notes backwards, you know, from right to left. He wrote in mirror writing, so to speak – as if he was looking in a mirror while writing. And his notes also show quite a few problems with the spelling of words. All these are things that psychologists see in many left-handed dyslexic people.

Speaker 1: And is this what Leonardo da Vinci and Keira Knightley have in common?

74   UNIT 9

Speaker 2: Absolutely! An actor needs to learn long scripts, you know, all his or her lines for the play or the film. And that was really quite difficult for the young Keira. She was desperate to become an actress, even as an eight year old. But she could not read her lines.

Speaker 1: So how did she become such a successful actress?

Speaker 2: Well, she had very good teachers, and she really wanted to overcome her problems, and her mother helped her a lot too. When she was 11, her reading skills were already much better, and today she says she doesn't have any problems with learning her lines any more.

> **Answer**
> They are/were both left-handed dyslexics.

b ▶ **CD2 T11** Students read through questions 1 to 4. Check any problems. Play the recording again for students to answer the questions. Check answers. Play the recording again, pausing as necessary to clarify any problems.

> **Answers**
> 1 Leonardo da Vinci, a man, lived about 500 years ago; Keira Knightley is a woman and is alive today. Leonardo was a great painter, designer, scientist and thinker. Keira Knightley is an actress who has acted in a lot of popular films. Leonardo was Italian; Knightley is British.
> 2 He wrote in mirror writing.
> 3 Learning her lines.
> 4 She had very good teachers, and she really wanted to overcome her problems, and her mother helped her a lot too.

c ▶ **CD2 T12** Students look at the illustrations and captions and sentences 1 to 8. As a class, discuss what students think each type of intelligence is and what people with that type of intelligence will be good at. Go through the first sentence as an example. Students complete the exercise. Students can compare answers in pairs. Do not give the answers at this point. Play the recording, pausing as necessary to clarify any problems.

TAPESCRIPT

Speaker 1: Dr Williams, you are an expert in human intelligence, and you have written several articles about the fact that people can be intelligent in different ways. Now, if I'm right, this is called 'Multiple Intelligences', isn't it?

Speaker 2: That's right. Everyone has different strengths and weaknesses. No two people are the same. Usually, we call people intelligent when they are good at two intelligences: their logical-mathematical intelligence, and their verbal intelligence. Logical-mathematical intelligence means that someone is good at things like Maths, good at logic and good at problem-solving. And verbal intelligence means that someone is good with words – good at speaking, reading, story telling, writing – everything to do with words.

Speaker 1: So, if we come back to Leonardo da Vinci for a moment. He was a genius, right? Are you saying that his verbal intelligence was maybe not so good, but he was very good at other intelligences?

Speaker 2: Absolutely. He definitely had several intelligences where he was brilliant. First of all there was his visual intelligence, you know, we see it in his fantastic paintings, but also his detailed and precise illustrations, they all show what a visual genius he was. And he was also an incredible thinker, a great logical thinker. Just imagine that 500 years ago he came up with an idea of how to build a helicopter, and developed very precise drawings that showed his brilliant thinking.

Speaker 1: Are there other intelligences, Dr Williams?

Speaker 2: Oh yes, there is musical intelligence. Someone might be bad at school, but later in life become a famous composer or singer, because their musical intelligence is very developed for example. Or think of people who are very good at sports. And excellent dancers, for example – they would have a lot of body intelligence. And then there are the two personal intelligences, the interpersonal and the intrapersonal one. Your interpersonal intelligence helps you to understand other people, your intrapersonal intelligence helps you to understand yourself. Another intelligence is naturalistic intelligence. Someone who has a lot of it will be good at understanding nature, at noticing things like plants and animals, and so on. What is important is that …

> **Answers**
> 2 body intelligence
> 3 visual intelligence
> 4 interpersonal intelligence
> 5 musical intelligence
> 6 verbal intelligence
> 7 intrapersonal intelligence
> 8 naturalistic intelligence

6 Speak

✱ What's your strongest intelligence?

Warm up

In small groups, students discuss the question. Ask for feedback.

a Explain that you will give students three short memory tests to see what kind of intelligences they have, i.e. more strongly visual, verbal or body. Divide the class into students A and B pairs and keep those pairs for all three tasks.

Test 1: Tell students to write ten numbers from 1 to 50 on a piece of paper. Tell Student As to show Bs their numbers for ten seconds. Student B has to memorise the numbers and then write the numbers down after ten seconds. Student Bs then show Student As their numbers and Student As write them down after 10 seconds. Pairs then compare numbers to see how many numbers each person remembered.

Test 2: Students A and B write ten new numbers between 1 and 50 on a piece of paper. Student As then read out those numbers to Student Bs who must listen and write them down after hearing them. Student Bs then read out their numbers and Student As do the same. Students compare the numbers they wrote down and see how many they remembered correctly.

Test 3: Students write ten new numbers between 1 and 50 on a piece of paper. Student Bs then close their eyes while Student As trace the numbers out on their hand. Student Bs must open their eyes and write down all the numbers. Student Bs then follow the same procedure with Student As writing the numbers. Students compare lists and see how many numbers they remembered.

b Ask for a show of hands for each test result and write the results on the board. Go through the results as a class to see what different types of memory people have, more strongly visual, verbal or body.

7 Grammar
★ *must/mustn't* vs. *don't have to*

a Read through the questions as a class. Students then read the letter and decide which reply they prefer. Students compare answers in pairs before feeding back, giving reasons for their choice.

Weaker classes: You may want to pre-teach the following vocabulary: *grades, lazy, fair, waste time*.

b Students read through the examples from the letter and then underline more examples of *must / mustn't / don't have to* in the letters. Elicit or explain the difference in meanings between *must/ mustn't* and *don't/doesn't have to*. Students then complete the rules.

Weaker classes: Books closed. Write these three sentences on the board: *I must do my homework tonight. / I mustn't be late for the exam tomorrow. / I don't have to do any homework tonight.*

Sentence 1. Ask students: *Does the person have to do their homework tonight? (Yes) Can we use have to instead of must in this sentence to mean the same? (Yes).* Explain that *must* usually shows more urgency than *have to* for personal obligation.

Sentence 2. Ask students: *Can I be late for the exam? (No).* Explain that *mustn't* means it is important that you don't do something (i.e. arrive late) or something is not allowed.

Sentence 3. Ask students: *Is it necessary for the person to do homework that night? (No).* Explain that *don't/doesn't have to* means that there is no obligation to do something or it isn't necessary to do something. Contrast this sentence with *mustn't be late* in sentence 2 to show how these have completely different meanings.

Students open their books at page 71. Follow the procedure for stronger classes from here.

> **Answers**
> Letter: *I have to work; doesn't have to; mustn't waste your time; you must work harder*
> First reply: *You mustn't think; you must listen to*
> Second reply: *You don't have to do; you mustn't worry; you don't have to be*
> Rule: must; don't/doesn't have to

> **Language notes**
> 1 Students may produce statements like: ~~I mustn't to forget to do my homework~~. Remind them that in English *mustn't* is followed by an infinitive without *to*.
> 2 Check students' pronunciation of *mustn't* /ˈmʌsᵊnt/ and *have to* /ˈhæftə/.
> 3 Students may find it useful to translate some of the sentences from this exercise into their own language and compare them.

c Students look at pictures 1 to 4 and read through the sentences. Check any problems. Go through the first one as an example, if necessary. Students complete the exercise. Check answers, asking students to explain their choice of verb.

> **Answers**
> 2 don't have to   3 don't have to   4 mustn't

d This exercise can be set for homework. Students read through sentences 1 to 6. Go through the example, if necessary. Students complete the exercise. Check answers, asking students to explain their choice of verb.

> **Answers**
> 2 must   3 don't have to   4 doesn't have to
> 5 mustn't

Grammar notebook

Remind students to make a note of the rules for this grammar point and to note down some examples of their own and translations, if necessary.

9 Read and listen

a As an introduction to the topic, write the word *Genius* on the board and ask students to name famous people who they think are geniuses. Ask them to explain their choices. Tell students they are going to read a story about a girl genius. Students look at the title of the article and the pictures and write down six words they expect to see in the article. Circulate and help where necessary.

b Divide the class into pairs. Students compare their words and explain why they chose them. Listen to some of their ideas in open class.

c Students read the story quickly to choose the best title for each paragraph and to see if the words they chose in Exercise 9b are in the text. Pre-teach the following difficult vocabulary: *pyramid designs, jigsaw puzzles, scatterbrained, motivates, browses, hangs out*. Students compare answers with a partner before feedback.

Answers
A 4   B 2   C 1   D 5   E 3

d ▶ CD2 T14 Read through the questions with students and check understanding. Students read the article and listen to answer the questions. Check answers.

Answers
1 Because she was accepted into an American university at the age of 15.
2 She didn't speak until she was 22 months old, then she started using perfect speech.
3 That being under the pressure of a deadline pushes her to work well.
4 Because it helped her to be more like a normal teenager.

e Read through the words and phrases with students. With a partner, students look at the words in context and explain the meaning in their own words. With weaker classes, allow them to use L1 if necessary. Check answers.

Example answers
1 I think it's great.
2 I don't organise my thoughts very well.
3 It helped when she couldn't do something easily and had to try hard to get it right.
4 If you do something wrong, you learn more than if you get it right.

Discussion box

Divide the class into pairs. Students read through the questions and then discuss them.

10 Write

The preparation for this can be done in class and the writing task can be completed for homework.

a Students read through the advertisement to find out what they have to do. Check answers.

Answer
Write a composition of 120–150 words in English.

b Students read through the entry and find out Frances' answers to the questions. Check answers. Ask a few stronger students to give you an example answer for each question in the advertisement.

Answers
1 Swimming, dancing, Maths, Art.
2 Languages.
3 Swimming and dancing: good body intelligence; Maths and Art: good visual and logical intelligence; languages: difficult for her to memorise new words and understand grammar.
4 Architect because she's good at Maths and likes drawing things and she doesn't have to speak a foreign language.

c Students now write their own competition entry using the model on page 73 to help them. Remind them to think about the different types of intelligences they talked about earlier in the unit and encourage them to use *must / don't have to* structures where possible.

Encourage students to read out their entries to the rest of the class.

UNIT 9   77

Memo from Mario

Your mind

Determiners questionnaire

▶ Photocopy the questionnaire below before the lesson.

Questionnaire	Yes	No	Sometimes
Do you like being on your own?			
Do you enjoy hanging out with friends?			
Are you good at PE and sports?			
Can you sing well?			
When you read a story do you make pictures in your mind?			
Do you like Maths?			
Are you good with plants?			
Are you affected by the weather?			
Are you happy in mother tongue lessons?			
Are you good at reading a map?			
Do you enjoy talking to yourself?			
Do you think you're intelligent?			

▶ In the lesson, give out the questionnaire and check understanding of the questions.
▶ Ask each student to read the questionnaire and tick the appropriate column (*Yes*, *No* or *Sometimes*) about themselves.
▶ Then ask the students to get up and ask seven different classmates the questions, ticking the three columns appropriately.
▶ Tell the students to return to their seats and to count up the ticks in each column for each question.
▶ Write these sentence stems on the board:

Everyone/everybody I talked to …

Some people I …

A few of the people …

Nobody …

▶ Ask the students to write a 'determiner sentence' for each of the 12 questions, based on the number of ticks in each column. For example:

Some people I talked to like being on their own.

Everybody enjoys hanging out with friends.

▶ After the writing phase, put students in groups of three to see whether they agree with each other's sentences.

RATIONALE

This activity helps students revise simple present interrogatives and then practise the determiner phrases about their group.

The activity has everybody moving around the classroom and speaking. It is about the students themselves as people rather than about people on a page.

In some cultures you might want to conclude with a show of hands around the whole class about the answers to each question. My own sense is to leave this mysterious, as it provokes more thought.

Acknowledgement

The content of the questionnaire is based on Gardner's theory of eight intelligences.

10 Music makers

Unit overview

TOPIC: Music

TEXTS

Reading and listening: a text about a Brazilian musician and his school
Listening: people talking about music and musical instruments
Writing: a letter about your favourite type of music

SPEAKING AND FUNCTIONS

Describing recently completed and unfinished actions
Asking and answering questions about a famous person (David Bowie)
Discussing pop music and fashion

LANGUAGE

Grammar: Present perfect continuous; present perfect continuous and present perfect simple
Vocabulary: Music and musical instruments
Everyday English: *I have to say*; *What do you mean?*; *loads of*; *got nothing to do with*; *I'm just saying*; *Check it out*

1 Read and listen

If you set the background information as a homework research task, ask students to tell the class what they found out.

BACKGROUND INFORMATION

Berimbau is a single-string percussion instrument from Brazil. The berimbau is used in the practice of the Afro-Brazilian martial art capoeira.

Capoeira is an Afro-Brazilian art form that makes a ritual of movements from martial arts, games, and dance.

Samba is a Brazilian musical genre derived from African and European roots. It is recognised worldwide as a symbol of Brazil and Carnival.

Warm up

Ask students if they play a musical instrument. If so, which one do they play? If not, would they like to play one? Discuss this as a class, in L1 if appropriate.

a Students read the questions and look at the picture and the title of the text. Elicit suggestions for the first question. Students then read the text quickly to check their predictions. Remind them that they don't have to understand every word in the text at this point. Check answers.

Answers
1 He is from Brazil. He is a famous musician.
2 He opened a music school and trained hundreds of people to play instruments.

b ▶ CD2 T15 Students read through questions 1 to 5. Check any problems. Do the first question as an example, if necessary, reading through the text as a class or playing the first part of the recording. Play the recording while students complete the exercise. Students can compare answers in pairs before a whole class check.

Weaker classes: You may want to pre-teach the following vocabulary: *rhythm, percussionists, samba, containers, tin cans, drugs, violence, miracle, labour of love*.

TAPESCRIPT

See the reading text on page 74 of the Student's Book.

Answers
1 It's the capital of the state of Bahia in Brazil and you hear a lot of music there.
2 He saw music as a way of helping them escape drugs and violence.
3 They start by playing complex samba rhythms on plastic containers and tin cans.
4 It has started working together with government programmes.
5 Because it is a labour of love.

c In pairs or small groups students discuss this question. Monitor and check students are discussing this in English as far as possible. After a few minutes, ask for feedback and listen to some of the most interesting ideas in open class.

2 Grammar
★ Present perfect continuous

a **Stronger classes:** Students read through the examples. Ask them what they notice about how this tense is formed and elicit that is it *have/has + been + -ing* verb. To check students understand the meaning of the tense, ask them the following questions: *Is he still working there? (Yes) Are they still helping kids stay away from drugs? (Yes).* Elicit or explain that this tense is used to show that

UNIT 10   79

something started in the past and continues into the present. Ask students to give you an example of their own to check they have understood correctly.

Weaker classes: Books closed. Write the following examples (or some of your own) on the board: *I have been teaching English for X years. / She has been waiting for half an hour.* Ask them what they notice about how this tense is formed and elicit that it is *have/has + been + -ing* verb. To check students understand the meaning of the tense, ask them the following questions: *Do I still teach English (Yes) Is she still waiting? (Yes).* Elicit or explain that this tense is used to show that something started in the past and continues into the present. Students now open their books at page 75 and read the two examples on the page.

b Students go back through the text on page 74 and underline other examples of the tense. Check answers.

> **Answers**
> has been training; it's been doing; has been working

Students then read through the table and complete it. Check answers.

> **Answers**
> Positive: 's (has) been
> Negative: haven't (have not) been
> Question: Has/been
> Short answer: have/haven't/has/hasn't
> Rule: past

> **Language notes**
> 1 Students may find it useful to translate the sentences into their own language and compare them.
> 2 Remind students that we don't need to repeat the main verb in short answers with this tense.
> 3 Remind them that *it's* in *it's been working* = *it has been working* not *It is been working*.

c Students look at the pictures and read through prompts 1 to 6. Check any problems. Go through the example as a class, if necessary. Students complete the exercise. Check answers.

> **Answers**
> 2 He's been cooking all morning.
> 3 I haven't been feeling well.
> 4 You haven't been practising enough!
> 5 They have been playing football.
> 6 We have been watching too much TV!

d This exercise can be set for homework. Students read through sentences 1 to 8. Check any problems.

Go through the example as a class, if necessary. Students complete the exercise. Check answers.

> **Answers**
> 2 I've been waiting for you for ages!
> 3 He hasn't been sleeping enough.
> 4 I haven't been learning English very long.
> 5 How long have you been eating?
> 6 They've been doing their homework for three hours.

Grammar notebook
Remind students to note down the form and rules for this tense and any translations they may find helpful.

4 Grammar
✱ Present perfect continuous and present perfect simple

a Write the following examples on the board (or some of your own): *I've been teaching since X o'clock this morning. / I've drunk two cups of coffee this morning.*

Ask: *Am I still teaching now? (Yes)* and *Am I drinking coffee now? (No)*. Elicit or explain that the present perfect continuous often shows that an action started in the past and is still continuing in the present, and the present perfect simple is used when an action started in the past but has now finished. Tell them that this action may have a result in the present, or the time span may not have finished and the action may be continued later, e.g. *I've drunk two cups of coffee this morning.* (This morning hasn't finished yet and I may drink more coffee.) It may be helpful to compare the use of the past simple, e.g. *Charles Dickens wrote a lot of books. / J.K. Rowling has written a lot of books.* (Dickens is dead and won't write any more; Rowling is alive and may write more.) The present perfect continuous is often used when we want to stress the activity and the duration of the activity more than the result of the activity, whereas the present perfect simple is often used when we want to stress the completed result of the activity, e.g. *I'm tired because I've been working hard all day.* vs. *I've written ten emails today.* Students open their books at page 76 and read the example sentences. Students read through the examples. Ask: *Does the school still work with government programmes? (Yes)* and *Are the students becoming successful musicians now? (No).* Elicit or explain the difference in the two tenses used. The first example shows that something started in the past and continues to the present, while the second example shows several shorter, completed actions which started in the past and have now finished (but may continue

80 UNIT 10

in the future as the year described in the text is not finished yet).

Students then read through the rule box and complete the rules. Check answers.

> **Answers**
> present perfect simple; present perfect continuous
> present perfect simple; present perfect continuous

To check understanding at this point, ask students to give you an example of their own for each tense to make sure they are using the tenses correctly.

> **Language note**
> Students may produce statements like: ~~I am studying English for two years~~. Ask them to translate some of the examples from this exercise or examples of their own to compare how this structure works in English and their own language.

LOOK!

Students read through the Look! box. Give them some more examples of other verbs which are not normally used in continuous tenses in English: *see, hear, smell, taste, want, prefer, like, love, hate, think, feel, forget, remember.*

b Students read through sentences 1 to 8. Check any problems. Go through the example, if necessary, making sure students are clear why the present perfect simple is used. Students complete the exercise. Remind them to check the context of each sentence carefully before they choose the tense. Check answers, asking students to explain their choice of verb.

> **Answers**
> 2 read   3 had   4 cut   5 been cutting
> 6 won   7 has known   8 been reading

c This exercise can be set for homework. Students read through sentences 1 to 7. Check any problems. Go through the example if necessary, asking students to explain why the present perfect continuous is used. Students complete the exercise. Check answers.

> **Answers**
> 2 Haven't/finished   3 has/been doing
> 4 Has/made   5 haven't started
> 6 's cleaned   7 's been raining

Grammar notebook

Remind students to copy down the rules and some examples for this grammar point. They may also find it useful to translate some of the examples.

 Speak

Warm up

Books closed. Ask students if they have heard of David Bowie. If so, ask them what they know about him. Elicit information and write it on the board.

a Students open their books at page 76. Ask students to read the short text about David Bowie.

b Divide the class into Student A and B pairs. Tell Student As to read through the question prompts and their information on page 76. Student Bs look at their question prompts and information on page 126. Ask a stronger pair to demonstrate the example question and answer. Make sure students understand that they have to make questions, and answer their partner using the present perfect continuous and simple tenses. Give students a few minutes to complete the exercise. Monitor and check students are using the correct present perfect question and answer forms and make a note of any repeated errors to go over as a class later.

> **Answers**
> Student A
> He's been singing for more than 30 years. (How long has he been singing?)
> He's been playing / He's played the saxophone for more than 40 years.
> He's been making records since 1964. (How long has he been making records?)
> He has been in more than 15 films.
> He has been married for more than ten years.
> Student B
> He's been playing / He's played the saxophone for more than 40 years.
> He's made more than five films.

 Vocabulary

★ **Music and musical instruments**

If you set the background information as a homework research task, ask students to tell the class what they found out.

> **BACKGROUND INFORMATION**
> **Country** is based on traditional music from the west and south USA. The songs usually have a guitar as the main instrument.
>
> **Reggae** is a type of popular music from Jamaica with a strong second and fourth beat.
>
> **Hip-hop** began in New York in the 1970s. The main elements of hip-hop are rapping, DJ-ing, graffiti writing and breakdancing.

UNIT 10

Jazz is music that originates from African-Americans. Jazz has a strong rhythm and true jazz artists usually improvise.

Rock is music that is played with amplified electrical instruments and has a strong beat.

Classical tends to be associated with the music of famous composers such as Mozart, Beethoven and Brahms.

Warm up

Books closed. Ask students what type of music they like listening to and elicit a few answers. Now ask them what types of music they know and elicit the names and write them on the board.

a ▶ CD2 T17 Students open their books at page 77. Ask them to read through the types of music in the box and explain any they haven't heard of before. If there is time, ask students to give you an example of a group/singer for each type of music. Explain that they are going to hear examples of these types of music and that they must match the music they hear with the words in the box. Play the recording, pausing after the first piece of music and elicit the answer. Play the rest of the recording while students listen and complete the exercise. Students can compare answers in pairs before listening again to check or change their answers. Play the recording again, pausing for students to repeat each word.

Answers
1 classical 2 rock 3 jazz 4 reggae
5 country 6 hip-hop

b ▶ CD2 T18 Elicit as many words from students as they know for musical instruments and write them on the board. Students read through the words in the box and match the words with the pictures. Play the recording for students to listen and check or change their answers. Play the recording again, pausing after each word for students to repeat.

Tapescript/Answers
A 4 a violin
B 9 a synthesiser
C 6 an electric guitar
D 2 drums
E 8 a flute
F 3 a trumpet
G 1 a piano
H 5 a clarinet
I 7 a saxophone
J 10 a keyboard

c Divide the class into pairs. Students read through the questions and discuss them. Set a time limit for this and then ask for pairs to feed back.

Answers
1 live music: music that is seen or heard while it is happening; recorded music: music that is put onto magnetic tape or CDs using electronic equipment in a studio
2 an album: a CD or a record with several pieces of music/songs on it; a single: a CD or a record with one main piece of music/song on it
3 MP3: is a format that can play audio; MP4: is a format that can play audio and video

Vocabulary notebook

Remind students to start a section called *Music* and to note down all the new items from this unit. Students may find it helpful to illustrate or translate the new items.

7 Listen

 ▶ CD2 T19 Students read through the table. Play the first part of the recording pausing after Josh mentions the instrument he plays and go through the example as a class.

Stronger classes: Play the rest of the recording right through for students to listen and note down their answers. Remind them to think about the key words they should be listening for in each part of the table.

Weaker classes: Play the recording, pausing after each speaker to give students time to note down their answers. Remind them to think carefully about the kind of words they might hear in each part.

Check answers, playing and pausing the recording again as necessary.

TAPESCRIPT

Speaker 1: Hi, I'm Josh, Josh Thomas and I'm a guitarist, I play the guitar ... erm ... I've been playing since I was really young, I was about five years old when I started, so I guess I've been playing the guitar for about 11 years now. Sometimes I play the acoustic guitar and sometimes I play the electric guitar, and that's my favourite really. Erm ... I play in a band with some friends, we play rock music, that's definitely my favourite music, rock, I'm really into Pink Floyd for example, erm ... I like listening to music all the time if possible but I guess my favourite way is on my MP3 player because then I can listen to music just anywhere ... erm, except in class of course! And I'd love to get a new player where I can play MP4 formats, so I can watch video clips of my favourite songs.

Speaker 2: I'm Emma – hi – and I play the violin. The violin's a lovely instrument, and erm, but it's quite difficult to play, erm, it's not an easy instrument at all but I love it, erm … I've been playing it for about six years now so I'm not bad, but I still have lessons, I've got lots to learn and improve on … now, most people when you say 'violin' think of classical music and I do quite like that but my favourite kind of music is actually folk music, traditional English folk music, and erm, there's a folk club near my house and I go there quite a lot with my dad, he plays there sometimes. And actually you can play the violin in folk bands too, I do that sometimes – when I'm feeling brave! The folk club's great and I think the best way to listen to music is live, in a club or at a concert.

Speaker 3: Well, hi, I'm Jack and I'm a musician in a way, I mean, I play a bit, I play the piano but not very well because I only started about nine months ago, yeah, I've been learning for about nine months now, and it's really cool, I've always wanted to learn how to play, and, erm … when I get a bit better I want to play jazz piano 'cos jazz is definitely my favourite kind of music, I love jazz piano, Keith Jarrett and people like that, amazing … erm … and I usually listen to jazz at home, in my room, it's a shame but there's nowhere round here really where I can hear jazz live so, I listen at home. But my favourite way to listen to music, the best place to listen, is definitely in a car when you're driving, that's just great, I can't wait to get a car when I'm older and drive around with the music up loud! Not jazz of course – I'm into rock and things too!

Speaker 4: Hello, I'm Sophie, Sophie Greene, and I play the trumpet. I started when I was quite young, about eight, and I'm 14 now so I've been playing for about six years altogether. Yeah, I know, it's a bit unusual for a girl to play the trumpet but it's fun, I play in the school band, it's like a brass band and it's cool, I have a good time! Erm, but that's not really the music I listen to on our stereo at home or whatever, I mean, you know I like pop and rock and stuff, and rap, but my real favourite kind of music is actually classical, I'm just totally into Mozart and that, you know, all that classical stuff. So whenever I can I go to a concert, I'm lucky 'cos I live in London so there's loads of concerts on, and I get to hear really good orchestras and players. It's definitely the best way to listen to music – live, at a concert, it's brilliant. And then a pizza afterwards.

Answers

	Musical instrument	Time spent playing/ learning	Favourite type(s) of music	Favourite way of listening to music
1 Josh	guitar	11 years	rock	on an MP3 player
2 Emma	violin	6 years	folk	at a live concert
3 Jack	piano	9 months	jazz	in the car
4 Sophie	trumpet	6 years	classical	at a live concert

8 Speak

Divide the class into pairs. Students read through the questions. Give students a few minutes to discuss the questions. Put pairs with another pair to form small groups to compare answers before class feedback. If there are any interesting points, encourage students to give more information to the rest of the class.

Talent? Me?

9 Read and listen

Warm up

Ask students if they can play a musical instrument. If so, how did they learn? Was it difficult to learn? If not, ask students which instrument they would like to learn. Students then look at the photo story. Ask them who features in this story (Debbie, Joel and Pete) and ask them to predict what they might be discussing.

a ▶ CD2 T20 Students read the photo story and answer the questions. Play the recording for students to check their answers and their predictions from the Warm up. Were any of their predictions correct?

> **Answers**
> Debbie thinks Joel has a lot of talent. Pete doesn't care. Joel thinks anyone can learn an instrument.

b Read through items 1–6 with students and do the first one as an example if necessary. Students answer the questions. Check answers. Students can also correct the false statements.

UNIT 10 83

> **Answers**
> 1 True   2 False – music's not his thing
> 3 False – he thinks he's good
> 4 False – he tells her to watch some videos
> 5 True   6 False – she takes his advice

10 Everyday English

a Read the expressions aloud with the class. Ask students to try to remember who said them without looking back at the text. In pairs, students find them in the text of the photo story and discover who said them. Check answers. Students can then translate the expressions into their own language.

> **Answers**
> 1 Debbie   2 Debbie   3 Debbie   4 Joel
> 5 Joel   6 Joel

b Students read the dialogues and then complete them with the expressions from Exercise 10a. Go through the first item as an example, if necessary. Check answers.

> **Answers**
> 2 What do you mean?   3 loads of
> 4 I'm just saying that   5 I have to say
> 6 got nothing to do with

Vocabulary notebook

Encourage students to add the expressions to the *Everyday English* section in their vocabulary notebooks and, if necessary, to add translations to help them remember the meanings.

> **Discussion box**
>
> **Weaker classes:** Students can choose one question to discuss.
>
> **Stronger classes:** In pairs or small groups, students go through the questions in the box and discuss them.
>
> Monitor and help as necessary, encouraging students to express themselves in English and to use any vocabulary they have learned from the text. Ask pairs or groups to feed back to the class and discuss any interesting points further.

11 Improvisation

Divide the class into pairs. Tell students they are going to create a role play between Debbie and her mum. Read through the instructions with students. Give students two minutes to plan their dialogue. Circulate and help with vocabulary as necessary.

Encourage students to use expressions from Exercise 10. Students practise their conversation in pairs. Listen to some of the best conversations in open class.

12 Team Spirit (DVD Episode 5)

a–**d** Read through items a–d with the students. Divide them into pairs and ask them to predict the answers to the questions. Encourage them to give reasons for their answers. Circulate and help with vocabulary as necessary. As feedback, listen to some of their ideas in open class.

e Play episode 5 of the DVD while students check their predictions in 12a–d.

13 Write

> **BACKGROUND INFORMATION**
>
> **Faith Hill** (born Audrey Faith Perry in 1967) is an American country music singer.
>
> **Elbow** is an English alternative rock band formed in Manchester in 1990.
>
> **Arctic Monkeys** are an English rock band formed in Sheffield in 2002.
>
> **Willie Nelson** (born 1933) is an American country singer-songwriter author, poet and actor.
>
> **Garth Brooks** (born 1962) is an American country music artist.
>
> **Meredith Edwards** (born 1984) is an American county singer.
>
> **Jessica Andrews** (born 1983) is an American country singer.

The preparation for this can be done in class and the writing task set for homework.

a Students read the questions and the letter and answer the question. Check answers.

> **Answers**
> She wants to know what music Sandy likes and why, and how she prefers listening to music.

b Students read through the letter and find the answers to the questions in Exercise 13a.

> **Answers**
> She's been a country music fan for two years. She likes Faith Hill, Willie Nelson, Garth Brooks, Meredith Edwards and Jessica Andrews, because they have great voices and good lyrics. She listens to country music nearly all the time, usually on her headphones in her bedroom.

84   UNIT 10

c Students now write their own letters, replying to Jenny's questions using their own answers.

Weaker classes: They may find it useful to answer the questions first and then to expand their answers into a letter. They can draft their letter and then swap letters with a partner for them to check. They can then write a final version.

14 Last but not least: more speaking

If you set the background information as a homework research task, ask students to tell the class what they found out.

> **BACKGROUND INFORMATION**
> **Pop Idol** was a British talent show, broadcast in 2001 and 2003, to decide the best new young pop singer in the UK based on viewer voting.

a Read through the questions with students and check understanding. Ask students to work individually and make notes of their answers to the questions. Circulate and help with any questions about vocabulary. Tell students that they don't have to write complete sentences but just to make a note of their answers.

b Students tell each other their thoughts about music and talent shows. Listen to some of the best ideas in open class as feedback and encourage debate.

Check your progress

1 Grammar

a 2 nothing 3 someone 4 everything
5 somewhere 6 none of them 7 no one

b 2 don't have to 3 mustn't 4 mustn't
5 doesn't have to 6 mustn't

c 2 sent 3 been talking 4 been playing
5 visited 6 been reading; finished

2 Vocabulary

a 2 guess 3 concentrate 4 believe in
5 recognise 6 imagine

b Instruments: trombone; trumpet; guitar; clarinet
Types of music: reggae; jazz; rock; country

How did you do?

Check that students are marking their scores. Collect these in and check them as necessary and discuss any further work needed with specific students.

Memo from Mario

Music makers

1 Grammar sentence contraction and expansion: present perfect continuous

▶ Ask a 'Picasso' in your class to draw a picture of the Empire State Building, topped by Liberty, with a teenager standing next to the tower at the bottom.

▶ Tell them to draw this in the top left quarter of the board or IWB.

▶ Then draw a speech bubble coming from the teenager's mouth and taking up the whole of the right hand half of the board. Write this sentence in the speech bubble, leaving big gaps between the words:

> I've been learning this yukky language for nearly two years now.

▶ Explain to the class that they are going to transform the sentence by deleting <u>one</u> word and replacing it with <u>two</u> or <u>three</u> words.

▶ For example, delete *yukky* and replace it with *marvellous international* so the sentence reads:
I've been learning this marvellous international language for nearly two years now.

▶ Start the exercise with a volunteer student coming to the board, rubbing out one word, adding two or three words in its place and then reading out the resultant sentence.

▶ Do not correct the student if they are wrong – instead appeal silently to the other students. If they fail to correct the student, then simply delete the additional words and reinstate the original word.

▶ It is OK to delete a word that has been added at a previous stage.

▶ Then ask the next student to come out, and so on.

▶ Continue the activity until the sentence gets too unwieldy.

> **RATIONALE**
> Your students are reading, thinking of and saying the target structure over and over and focusing on its meaning.
>
> At this stage in their learning, your students may be ready to write and speak more complex sentences in English. This activity fosters a move forward from 'baby' English.

2 Text trimming: 'Music that changes lives' (page 74)

▶ Explain to the class that some writers use a lot of words to say something while others say the same with fewer words.

▶ Tell them that some people think that fewer words are better.

▶ Ask the students to help you 'trim' the first paragraph of the text on page 74.

In line 1 *take a* and *in* could be cut, leaving the sharper, more succinct:
If you walk the streets of Salvador ...

▶ Ask the students to work in pairs to tighten the rest of the passage by getting rid of between 15 and 20 words.

▶ When they have finished, ask the students to work in groups of four and compare what they have taken out and why.

▶ Offer them a trimmed version of your own. Read this out slowly.

> **RATIONALE**
> In pruning a text in this way the students have to do focused comprehension work on it.
>
> To be an editor is to wield power and this is something that mid-teenage people are sometimes short of in school.
>
> The activity is excellent training for editing texts students write themselves.

11 A visit to the doctor's

Unit overview

TOPIC: Medicine

TEXTS

Reading and listening: a text about medicine in the past
Listening: a dialogue about Dr Joseph Lister
Listening: a song: *Run That Body Down* by Paul Simon
Reading: a text about Médecins Sans Frontières
Writing: a magazine article about a famous scientist

SPEAKING AND FUNCTIONS

Expressing past habits
Discussing medical problems and their cures

LANGUAGE

Grammar: Defining relative clauses; *used to*
Vocabulary: Medicine

1 Read and listen

If you set the background information as a homework research task, ask students to tell the class what they found out.

BACKGROUND INFORMATION

Ancient Egypt an ancient civilization that began around 3150 BC and developed over the next three thousand years.

Ancient Greece refers to the period of Greek history lasting from c.1100 BC to 146 BC and the Roman conquest of Greece.

Scrofula is a form of tuberculosis, affecting the lymph nodes of the neck.

The Middle Ages European history from the 5th century to the 16th century.

Warm up
Write the following problems on the board: *headache, hiccoughs*. Ask students what they do if they have these problems and elicit a few suggestions.

Weaker classes: You may like to give them a few possible answer options to choose from, e.g. *lie down, take some medicine, have a drink of water, phone a doctor, call an ambulance*.

a Tell students they are going to read a text about medicine in the past. Ask students to describe what they can see in the pictures. Students read the text quickly to match each picture with a paragraph. Remind them they don't have to understand every word at this point. Check answers.

Answers
A 4 B 1 C 2 D 3

b ▶ CD2 T21 Students read through sentences 1 to 7. Check any problems. Play the recording while students read and listen and decide if the statements are true or false. If necessary, pause the recording after the first statement and go through this as an example.

Weaker classes: You may want to pre-teach the following vocabulary: *toothache, dead mouse, backache, pain, bone, tied, ladder, baldness, falling out, hippopotamus, rubbed, scrofula*.

Check answers and then ask students to correct the false statements.

TAPESCRIPT
See the reading text on page 82 of the Student's Book.

Answers
1 N 2 F (It was dead when they put it into their mouth) 3 T 4 N 5 N 6 T 7 N

c Divide the class into pairs or small groups. Students read through the question. Give them a few minutes to discuss it. Monitor and check students are discussing this in English and encourage them to express themselves as best they can. Ask pairs or groups to feed back and if there are any interesting points discuss these further as a class. If you are short of time, do this as a class discussion and elicit ideas from the class.

2 Grammar
✶ Defining relative clauses

a **Stronger classes:** Students read through the example sentences. Ask them: *Which people had toothache? (Ancient Egyptians)*. Explain or elicit that *who* refers to the people who had toothache. Then ask: *What is happening to the men who are not happy? (Their hair is falling out.)* Explain or elicit that *whose* in this sentence refers to the possession of hair. Students go through the text and find more examples of defining clauses. Check answers.

UNIT 11   87

Weaker classes: Books closed. Write the following examples (or some of your own) on the board: *Mr Brown is the teacher who teaches in class 2. / Those are the books which we use to learn English.* Ask students: *Which teacher teaches in class 2? (Mr Brown).* Explain or elicit that *who* refers to the teacher who teaches in class 2. Then ask: *Which books do we use to learn English? (Those books).* Explain or elicit that *which* in this sentence refers to the books. Students open their books at page 83 and read through the example sentences. Follow the procedure above from this point.

> **Answers**
> Para 3: people who suffer from it
> Para 5: people who had scrofula

b Students now read through and complete the rule box. Check answers.

> **Answers**
> who; which; that; when

To check understanding at this point, ask students to give you an example sentence of their own using a defining relative clause.

> **Language notes**
> 1 Students may produce statements like: *She is the woman which works in the library.* Remind them we can only use *who/that* for people.
> 2 Students may find it useful to translate the example sentences into their own language and compare the two.

c This exercise can be set for homework. Students read through sentences 1 to 6. Go through the example, if necessary. Ask students to explain why *that* is the correct answer. Students complete the exercise. Remind them to look carefully at the subject of each sentence before they decide which word to choose. Check answers, asking students to explain their choice.

> **Answers**
> 2 who 3 where 4 who 5 when 6 whose

Grammar notebook
Remind students to note down the rules for defining relative clauses with a few examples.

3 Vocabulary and listening
✱ Medicine

a Students read through parts 1 to 8. Check any problems. Go through the example, if necessary. Students complete the exercise. Remind students to think carefully about the subject of the first half and to look for some key words which relate to that subject in the second half. Check answers.

> **Answers**
> 2 a 3 g 4 e 5 h 6 d 7 b 8 f

b ▶ CD2 T22 Books closed. Elicit as many illnesses, aches and pains that students know in English. Write them on the board. Students open their books at page 83. Ask them to look at the pictures and read through sentences 1 to 8. Check any problems. Go through the first item as an example, if necessary. Students complete the exercise. Students can compare answers in pairs. Play the recording for students to listen and check or change their answers. Play the recording again, pausing for students to repeat.

> **Answers**
> 1 D 2 F 3 A 4 B 5 E 6 H 7 C 8 G

> **Language notes**
> 1 Students may produce statements like: *My head it is hurting me.* Remind them that in English we say *My ... hurts* or *I've got a sore ...*
> 2 Students may find it useful to translate some of the sentences in Exercise 3b into their own language and compare the two.

c ▶ CD2 T23 Students read through the instructions. Make sure they understand that they must choose from the illnesses in Exercise 3b. Play the recording, pausing after the first patient and ask students what the answer is. Continue playing the recording for students to complete the exercise. Students can compare answers in pairs. Play the recording again for students to check or change their answers. Play it again to clarify any problems.

TAPESCRIPT

Speaker 1: OK, I see. And how long has it been like this, Mr Parker?

Speaker 2: Since last Saturday. I was playing football in the park and I fell over.

Speaker 1: Does it still hurt a lot?

Speaker 2: Yes, it does.

Speaker 1: OK, take your shoe off, please, and your sock and let me have a look at it. Hmm, yes, that looks bad – does it hurt if ...

Speaker 1: And you've been like this since last week.

Speaker 3: That's right, doctor.

Speaker 1: Do you smoke, Mrs Jones?

Speaker 3: Me? No doctor, I don't smoke.

Speaker 1: OK, well let me have a look, please. Open your mouth – that's right. Now, say 'Aaaah'.

Speaker 3: Aaaah.

Speaker 1: And tell me, what did you have to eat last night?

Speaker 4: Nothing very much. Just some fish, erm ... with chips of course.

Speaker 1: Fried fish?

Speaker 4: Yes.

Speaker 1: Hmmm. And do you feel sick?

Speaker 4: Yes, I do – it really hurts, doctor!

Speaker 1: OK, Mr Johnson, don't worry. It might be food poisoning, but don't worry, we have good medicine for that ...

Speaker 1: And how long have you been like this, Mrs Smith?

Speaker 5: About a week, doctor. I stayed in bed yesterday and the day before.

Speaker 1: Have you taken any tablets?

Speaker 5: No, I haven't.

Speaker 1: Do your eyes hurt? Have you got a temperature?

Speaker 5: Yes, and I sneeze a lot too!

Speaker 1: Yes, well, nothing much to worry about, I think. It's just a cold, I think, though it's a bad one isn't it? Take this medicine which should help ...

> **Answers**
> 1 His ankle hurts.
> 2 She's got a sore throat.
> 3 He's got stomach ache.
> 4 She's got a cold.

4 Grammar

★ used to

a **Stronger classes:** Students read through the examples. Ask the following questions: *Is the action still going on? (No). Did it happen once in the past or lots of times? (Lots of times).* Elicit or explain that we use *used to* when we are talking about a repeated action in the past but which is finished now.

Weaker classes: Books closed. Write the following examples (or some of your own) on the board: *I used to work in Greece. / My brother used to like heavy metal music.*

Ask students the following questions: *Do I work there now? (No). Did I work there in the past? (Yes). Did I work there once or for a period of time in the past? (For a period of time).* Now ask: *Does he like heavy metal music now? (No). Did he like it once or over a period of time in the past? (Over a period of time).* Elicit or explain that we use *used to* when we are talking about a repeated action in the past but which is finished now. Students now open their books at page 84 and read the two examples.

Follow the procedure above if you need to check students have understood the concept correctly.

b Students look at the two sentences.

Stronger classes: Elicit the difference in meaning. Remind students of the explanations for the example sentences in Exercise 4a.

Weaker classes: Ask them the following questions about each picture: *Does he still listen to U2 now? (No). Did he listen to U2 in the past? (Yes). Did he listen once or over a period of time? (Over a period of time).* Now ask: *Did he listen to Alicia Keys this morning? (Yes). Is he listening to Alicia Keys now? (No). Did the action happen once or over a period of time in the past? (Once).* Elicit or explain that we use *used to* when we are talking about a repeated action in the past but which is finished now, but we use the past simple to show a completed action in the past.

To check understanding at this point, ask students to give you a sentence of their own using *used to*.

c **Stronger classes:** Students read through the rule and complete it.

Weaker classes: Encourage students to look back at the examples they have seen so far to help them work out the use of *used to*. Check answers.

> **Answers**
> past/now

> **Language notes**
> 1 Students may produce questions like: ~~Did he used to like punk music?~~ Remind them that the question form is *did + use to*.
> 2 They may also produce statements like: ~~Did she used to going to university?~~ Remind them that we use *used to* + infinitive without *to*.
> 3 Students may find it helpful to translate some examples into their own language and compare the two.

d This exercise can be set for homework. Students read through sentences 1 to 5 and a to e. Check any problems. Go through the first sentence as an example, if necessary. Ask students to explain their choice of answer. Students complete the exercise. Remind them to look for some key words in the second sentence which will link it with the first. Check answers, asking students to explain their choice of answer.

> **Answers**
> 1 d 2 a 3 e 4 b 5 c

UNIT 11

e This exercise can be set for homework. Students read through sentences 1 to 6. Check any problems. Go through the example, if necessary, focusing students' attention on the use of the present simple in the second part. Students complete the exercise. Remind them to read each one carefully and to think about which verb should be in the present simple. Check answers.

> **Answers**
> 2 used to be/say
> 3 doesn't smoke/used to smoke
> 4 isn't/used to be
> 5 Did you use to like/love
> 6 Did your father use to play/is

Grammar notebook

Remind students to copy down the rule from this exercise. They may also find it useful to write a few examples and some translations.

6 Speak

a Divide the class into Student A and B pairs. Tell Student As to read through the information on page 85 and Student Bs to turn to page 126 and look at their information. Ask students to think back to when they were five or six and give them a few minutes to tick the information that is true for them.

b Ask a stronger pair to demonstrate the example question and answer, with Student A starting first. Make sure students understand that they have to use *used to* in the statements they make. Give students a few minutes to ask and answer and tick their box about their friend. Monitor and check students are taking turns to ask and answer and that they are using the correct forms of *used to*. Make a note of any repeated errors to go over as a class later. Ask pairs to feedback to the rest of the class. If there are any interesting points, encourage students to discuss these further.

7 Listen

If you set the background information as a homework research task, ask students to tell the class what they found out.

> **BACKGROUND INFORMATION**
> **Joseph Lister** (1827–1912) was a British surgeon who introduced the principle of antiseptics to the medical world. He worked in Scotland and was the first doctor to carry out the first modern surgical operation in 1865. He used an acid called carbolic acid and encouraged the sterilisation of surgical instruments thus reducing the number of deaths following operations.

> **Antiseptics:** used before surgical procedures to clean the skin. They destroy or inhibit the growth of bacteria, thus preventing infection.

Warm up

Ask students if they have ever been in hospital? If so, what were they in for? What kind of experience did they have? If they haven't been in hospital, perhaps they can think about someone they know who has. Discuss this as a class or in L1 if appropriate.

a Students read through the question. Discuss this as a class and elicit suggestions.

b ▶ **CD2 T25** Students read the question. Play the recording for students to listen and find the answer. Check answers.

TAPESCRIPT

Speaker 1: Hi Vicky.

Speaker 2: Hi Andy. Hey, did you see that documentary on TV last night?

Speaker 1: No, I didn't watch TV last night. What was it about?

Speaker 2: A guy called Joseph Lister, a doctor from Scotland – the first doctor to use antiseptics in hospitals.

Speaker 1: Oh yeah?

Speaker 2: Yeah. He lived in the nineteenth century. You know, in those days, hospitals used to be really, really dirty.

Speaker 1: Is that right?

Speaker 2: Yeah, and patients used to die because everything was so dirty. You know, the doctors didn't use to wash their hands before they touched patients, or before they operated on them.

Speaker 1: Yuck!

Speaker 2: Yeah – just imagine! Anyway, Lister used to work in a hospital, in a city in Scotland, and he saw all these people dying, and he started to think 'Perhaps we just need to keep everything clean.' So he told the nurses to wash everything – but still, about 50% of patients died!

Speaker 1: 50%!! You're kidding!

Speaker 2: No, it's true! That's what they said in the programme! Isn't it incredible? Anyway, then he started to use antiseptics to wash the medical instruments and things – and after that, only 15% of the patients died.

Speaker 1: Only!? I mean 15% is still a lot, right?

Speaker 2: Yeah – but a lot less than 50%!

Speaker 1: True. So Lister was a big hero, yeah?

Speaker 2: Well, sort of. Do you know, when he tried to tell other doctors about antiseptics, a lot of the doctors laughed at him?

UNIT 11

Speaker 1: But in the end they saw that he was right, right?

Speaker 2: Yeah. I was impressed, you know – Lister was a really important man.

Speaker 1: Yeah, it sounds like it. It's amazing how there were these really important people but we never get to hear about them, do we? I mean, people who did so much …

Answers
Because the hospitals were very dirty, no one washed their hands before treating a patient or before operating on one.

c ▶ **CD2 T25** Students read through the summary. Check any problems.

Stronger classes: Go through the first item as an example, if necessary. Encourage students to guess the meaning from context and to think about what kind of word is missing, e.g. noun, verb, etc. Students complete the exercise. Play the recording for students to listen and check or change their answers. Play it again, pausing as necessary to clarify any problems. Check answers.

Answers
1 Scotland 2 19th 3 hospitals 4 dirty
5 died 6 wash 7 dying 8 nurses
9 50 10 antiseptic 11 15 12 right

✱ OPTIONAL ACTIVITY

Stronger classes: Ask students if they know anyone famous who has helped with medical research. Is there anyone from their own country? Students can choose a person and do some research on them for homework. They may want to use this later in Exercise 11.

Weaker classes: Write the word *antiseptics* on the board. Give students one minute to find as many words as they can from it. To make this more fun you can give points for every word students find, e.g. four points for a four-letter word, three points for a three-letter word, etc. The student with most points is the winner!

8 Listen

BACKGROUND INFORMATION
Paul Simon (born October 13, 1941) is an American singer-songwriter famous for his success beginning in 1965 as part of the duo Simon and Garfunkel. Their hits included *Sounds of Silence*, *Mrs Robinson* and *Bridge Over Troubled Water*. After the duo split in 1970, Simon began a successful solo career with hit albums such as *There Goes Rhymin' Simon*, *Still Crazy After All These Years* and *Graceland*. *Run That Body Down* appeared on the *Paul Simon* album in 1972.

a ▶ **CD2 T26** Tell students they are going to listen to a song called *Run That Body Down*. Students read the lyrics of the song. Play the recording while students listen and choose the correct options. Students compare answers with a partner before repeating the recording, pausing if necessary.

Answers
1 doctor 2 look around 3 fooling
4 head 5 boy 6 fooling 7 fooling

b Divide the class into pairs. Students discuss the meaning of the song. Discuss some of their answers in open class as feedback.

Culture in mind

9 Read and listen

If you set the background information as a homework research task, ask students to tell the class what they found out.

BACKGROUND INFORMATION
Nigeria is a country in Africa. The capital of Nigeria is Abuja.

Geneva is the second biggest city in Switzerland.

Afghanistan is a country in Central Asia. There has been civil war in Afghanistan since the late 1970s, as well as invasions by Russia in 1979 and the USA in 2001, the latter toppling the extremist Taliban government.

Nobel Peace Prize is one of five Nobel Prizes set up by the Swedish industrialist and inventor Alfred Nobel. The Peace Prize is presented annually in Oslo, Norway, on December 10.

Warm up
Books closed. Ask students to think about the life of doctors in their country. What do they do every day? Do they think their job is difficult? Would they like to be a doctor? Why / why not? Listen to some of their ideas in open class.

a Books open. Ask students to look at the photos and read the title of the text. What do they think the text will be about? Students read the text to find out what happened in each of the years.

Answers
1 There was a war in Biafra. Médecins Sans Frontières started.
2 Five MSF volunteers were killed in Afghanistan.
3 MSF won the Nobel Peace Prize.

> **Language note**
> Check students are aware of how we say years as two numbers: nineteen seventy-one etc. In many countries these are said as single numbers. Point out that this has changed in the first decade of the 21st century, as we say the years 2000–2009 as single numbers, e.g. two thousand and nine. We will revert to using two numbers in 2010 (twenty ten).

b ▶ CD2 T27 Read through the questions with students and check understanding. Ask students to read the text again and listen, using a dictionary for new words if they can't guess the meaning. Students answer the questions and compare answers with a partner before feedback.

Answers
1 It began during the war in Biafra in 1971 when French volunteer doctors were working there.
2 90 per cent comes from individual donations, the rest from governments and businesses.
3 It helps disaster victims all over the world.
4 They care for sick people, train local doctors and nurses, and help people do things like making wells.
5 Because volunteers are sometimes attacked, kidnapped or killed.

c Students find words or phrases in the text to match the definitions and compare answers with a partner. Check answers and pay attention to pronunciation of the words.

Answers
1 volunteer   2 was born   3 a famine
4 headquarters   5 care for   6 injured

d Read through the sentences with students and check understanding. Students complete the sentences with words from Exercise 10a. Check answers.

Answers
2 famine   3 volunteers   4 headquarters

Vocabulary notebook
Encourage students to make a note of new vocabulary. They may find it useful to note down translations of the expressions too.

10 Write

a Students read the question. Ask students if they know the answer and elicit their suggestions. Give them a few minutes to read the notes and the article to check their predictions. Check answers.

Answers
Because she discovered radium.

 The preparation for this can be done in class and the task set for homework. Students read through the notes about Alexander Fleming. Check any problems. Students choose either Alexander Fleming or someone of their own choice.

Stronger classes: Students expand their notes, using the article about Marie Skłodowska-Curie as a model and write up their article.

Weaker classes: Go through the model article as a class and look at how it is structured. Compare it with the notes where possible to show students how the information has been expanded. Students write out the notes for the person they have chosen into full sentences. They can swap these with a partner to check. Then they write their final version.

If students complete the task for homework, encourage them to add a picture of the person and any more information they can find.

11 Speak

In small groups students discuss which are the most important medical problems today. If they have difficulty thinking of examples, tell them to think about illnesses in other parts of the world as well as in their own country. Students then decide which disease they would like to find a cure for. As feedback, ask some groups for their ideas and write them on the board. Try to create a list of five problems that the whole class agrees on.

Memo from Mario

A visit to the doctor's

1 A *used to* / *would* dictation

- In preparation, think back to when you were between four and eight years old.
- Write a short text about what you would habitually do at that time.
- To start you thinking here is a text I have used in class about myself:

  I used to love riding my bike.
  I'd often go swimming.
  I used to carry a soft toy around with me, a lamb.
  My dad would get angry if I didn't finish my food.
  I used to read loads of books.

- Don't use my sentences. Your students know <u>you</u> and are interested in <u>you</u>.
- Photocopy your text.
- In the lesson explain that you are going to dictate some sentences to the students about when you were little and about things you used to do.
- If the students also did these things, tell them to write the sentences <u>in pen</u>.
- If they did <u>not</u> do the things you did, they are to write <u>in pencil</u>.
- Give the dictation, leaving time for pen/pencil swapping.
- Give out the photocopies of your text so they can check their spelling.
- Put the students into groups of four to talk about things they used to do between the ages of four and eight.

> **RATIONALE**
>
> The focus of human interest is on the teacher and on the students, which makes the structure (*used to / would*) more accessible and memorable.
>
> The students hear the structure, think about it, write it and then say it.

Acknowledgement

This activity comes from Christine Frank's *Grammar in Action* (Alemany, 1983).

2 Vocabulary picture revision – 'Médecins sans Frontières: Doctors without Borders' (page 86)

- Once the students have worked on the text in the ways suggested by the authors, do this word review exercise:
- Tell the students you are going to dictate ten words from the text to them.
- They will have 25 seconds to write the word down and to draw a picture of the word's meaning.
- Dictate these words and be strict about the timing:

  war   disease   volunteers   disaster
  tsunami   donations   politics   race
  sick   courage

- Then tell the students to get up, move around the room and try to find people with pictures similar to their own.

> **RATIONALE**
>
> The best use of this technique is for helping students to concretise and visualise abstract words. More thought is called for than when you ask them to draw objects or animals.
>
> Vocabulary books look more interesting with pictures in them. The pictures make revising more lively.

UNIT 11

12 If I had ...

Unit overview

TOPIC: Information technology and computers

TEXTS

Reading and listening: a text about teenagers and their internet usage
Reading: a text about young girls with websites
Reading: a text about the advantages and disadvantages of computers
Listening: people talking about problems caused by computers
Writing: a competition entry

SPEAKING AND FUNCTIONS
Giving advice
Talking about unreal situations
Discussing computers and the internet

LANGUAGE
Grammar: Second conditional
Vocabulary: Information technology and computers, the language of the internet
Everyday English: *at the same time*; *It's not worth it*; *It's a shame*; *Looks like*; *It's no good*; *It just goes to show*

1 Read and listen

Warm up

Ask students how many of them have computers at home. If they don't have a computer at home, do they have access to one? If so, where? Elicit answers and discuss them as a class or in L1 if appropriate.

a Students read through the questions. Elicit answers and discuss this as a class. Are there any interesting results? If so, encourage students to discuss these further as a class.

b Write the names of the people in the text on the board. Students read through the three bullet points and then read the text quickly to find the answers. Remind them they don't have to understand every word in the text at this point. Check answers.

> **Answers**
> Brett has his own web page.
> Kylie listens to podcasts.
> Brett would like to work in computing.

c ▶ CD2 T28   Students read through sentences 1 to 6. If necessary, play the recording, pausing after the answer to the first sentence and go through this as a class. Play the recording while students listen and read and complete the exercise. Students can compare answers in pairs. Play the recording again for students to check or change their answers and clarify any problems. Ask students to correct the false statements.

TAPESCRIPT
See the reading text on page 88 of the Student's Book.

> **Answers**
> 1 T
> 2 F (He posts videos quite often).
> 3 F (She thinks it is interesting).
> 4 F (He answered, but couldn't name a particular website).
> 5 F (He doesn't like podcasts).
> 6 T

✴ OPTIONAL ACTIVITY

Students must imagine they cannot use a computer for a whole day. They must work out a timetable for that day which includes all the things they would do instead of using a computer.

Weaker classes: Elicit or give them some ideas of things they could do instead, e.g. *go out with friends, phone friends, write letters, watch TV, read a book, do their homework,* etc.

2 Grammar

✴ Second conditional

a **Stronger classes:** Students read through the questions and the example sentences. Elicit the answer (*imagined*). Explain that this is the second conditional and that we use it when we talk about imaginary situations.

Weaker classes: Books closed. Write the following example (or some of your own) on the board: *If I had lots of money, I'd buy a new car.* Ask them: *Do I have lots of money? (No). Is the situation real or imagined? (Imagined).* Explain that this is the second conditional and that we use it when we talk about imaginary situations. Students open their books at page 89 and read through the example sentences. If necessary, follow the procedure for stronger classes from this point to check they have understood the concept.

b **Stronger classes:** Students go through the text on page 88 and find examples of the second conditional and then complete the rule. Check answers.

Weaker classes: After students have gone through the text, check the examples they have found and ask them what they notice about how this tense is formed. Elicit or give *If* + past simple + *would* + verb. Students can then complete the rule. Check answers.

> **Answers**
> If a friend asked you to recommend a really good website, which one would you recommend?
> But even if I had more time, I wouldn't listen to podcasts.
> If you were offered a job in computing, would you take it?
> If I had the chance, I'd like to work as a web designer.

> **Answers**
> past; would

At this point students may find it useful to compare the form of the first conditional with a second conditional sentence. You can put a first conditional sentence on the board and ask students to give you an example of a second conditional sentence, e.g. *If I win the lottery, I'll buy a new car. / If I had lots of money, I'd buy a new car.*

Language notes

1. Students may produce statements like: ~~If I would be rich, I would buy a new car.~~ Remind them that we can't use *would* in the *If* clause in the second conditional.
2. Explain to students that after *If I* in the second conditional we can use *was* or *were*, e.g. *If I were you, I'd …* or *If I was you, I'd …* Explain too that *were* can also be used with third person singulars in the second conditional.
3. Remind them that the *If* clause can go at the beginning or at the end of the conditional sentence.

c This exercise can be set for homework. Students read through sentences 1 to 6. Check any problems. Go through the example, if necessary. Students complete the exercise. Remind them to look carefully at the verbs and to see where the *If* clause is before they make their choice. Check answers.

> **Answers**
> 1 had / would buy
> 2 would pass / worked
> 3 lived / wouldn't have
> 4 would come / asked
> 5 was / would go
> 6 would give / knew

d This exercise can be set for homework. Students read through sentences 1 to 6. Check any problems. Go through the example, if necessary. Students complete the exercise. Remind them to look carefully at the sentences and to see where the *If* clause is before they choose which verb form to use. Check answers.

> **Answers**
> 2 would you do / ran
> 3 would talk / were
> 4 wouldn't tidy / didn't tell
> 5 had / would buy
> 6 would you invite / won

Grammar notebook

Remind students to copy down the rule for the second conditional from this exercise and to note down a few examples of their own and any translations if necessary.

> **✱ OPTIONAL ACTIVITY**
>
> Write the following prompts on the board and divide the class into small groups for students to decide on a suitable answer.
> *If you went to a park and a dog started chasing you, what would you do?*
> *If (insert name of famous person) invited you to dinner, what would you do?*
> *If you discovered a box full of gold in your back garden, what would you do?*
>
> Circulate and help students with any difficulties with pronunciation and intonation. Listen to some of their ideas in open class as feedback. As an extension to this activity, ask students to think up some situations of their own and ask the rest of the class what they would do.

4 Speak

a Divide the class into pairs. Remind students of the second conditional and elicit a few examples to check they remember how to form it correctly. Students then read through situations 1 to 6. Check any problems. Ask a stronger pair to read out the example exchange. Students then continue asking and answering each situation. Monitor and check students are taking turns to ask and give advice and that they are forming the second conditional

UNIT 12   95

correctly. Make a note of any repeated errors to go through as a class later.

Weaker classes: They may need more support with the advice they want to give. Elicit or give examples of advice they could give, e.g.
1   get a job; do more jobs round the house; ask for more pocket money; sell some of your CDs
2   talk to them more; ask your brother/sister what to do; think about how you could change your behaviour
3   take it to a shop; remove some files; buy a new computer
4   see a doctor; stop using the internet; watch television
5   go to the park; phone a friend; make a cake
6   study more; talk to the teachers; do all your homework

Ask some pairs to feed back to the class.

b Students in pairs read through questions 1 to 7. Check any problems. Ask a stronger pair to read out the example dialogue, drawing students' attention to the use of the second conditional in the question. Students complete the questions. Check answers. Students then ask and answer the questions. Monitor and check students are asking and answering the questions correctly and that they are forming the second conditional correctly. Note down any repeated errors to discuss later. Ask a few pairs to feed back to the rest of the class.

> **Answers**
> 2   Where would you live if you had to live in a different town?
> 3   If you could go to any event in the world you wanted, which one would you go to?
> 4   If you could meet an important person, who would you meet?
> 5   What would you do if you were invisible for a day?
> 6   If you could have one wish, what would you wish for?

✱ OPTIONAL ACTIVITY

Stronger classes: Students can choose one question from Exercise 4b and write up their story of what would happen if they made their wish, etc. If you are short of time, give students a few minutes to think about this and then ask them to tell the rest of the class.

Weaker classes: Give students the following short text and ask them to find seven mistakes in it in the second conditional sentences:
If I am winning the lottery I buy a new house. If I buy a new house I choose a big one. If I would choose a big house my friends could come and live with me. If my friends would come to live with me then we have parties all the time.

> **Answers**
> 1 won   2 would buy   3 bought   4 would choose   5 chose   6 came   7 would have

5 Read

Warm up
Ask students if they have ever designed a website. If so, what was it for? If not, would they like to and what would they design one for? Or do they know anyone who has? Discuss this as a class or in L1 if appropriate.

a Students read through the questions. Elicit suggestions. Students then read the text quickly and check their predictions. Remind them they don't need to understand every word of the text at this point. Check answers.

> **Answers**
> She is a girl who has designed her own website.

b Students read through questions 1 to 4. Check any problems. Go through the first item as an example, if necessary. Students complete the exercise. Check answers.

Weaker classes: You may want to pre-teach the following vocabulary: *icons, layouts, glitters, blogging, uploading, podcasts, fifth grade, enthusiastic.*

> **Answers**
> 1   She thinks that they are not patient enough.
> 2   Blogging, creating web pages and working on other people's websites.
> 3   They would need to be more interested in helping other people.
> 4   Women have only 27 per cent of computer-related jobs.

c Students read through the expressions from the text. Go through the first one as an example, encouraging students to guess the meaning from context. Students complete the exercise.

Weaker classes: Put the answers on the board in jumbled order. Students then match the expressions in their books with the definitions on the board.

Students can check answers in a dictionary before a whole class check.

> **Answers**
> 1   the people who create something new
> 2   more advanced than
> 3   an online magazine
> 4   looking for work

96   UNIT 12

Vocabulary notebook

Encourage students to note down the expressions from Exercise 5c and to provide some translations if necessary.

6 Vocabulary

★ Information technology and computers

a ▶ CD2 T31 Books closed. Elicit as many words to do with computers as students know and write them on the board or if there is time, ask students to come out and write them up. Students open their books at page 91 and look at the picture and read through the words in the box. Go through the first item as an example, if necessary. Students complete the exercise. Play the recording for students to listen and check or change their answers. Play the recording again, pausing after each word for students to repeat.

> **Tapescript/Answers**
> 1 adaptor   2 power lead   3 mouse
> 4 USB slot   5 screen   6 touch pad   7 printer
> 8 USB stick   9 CD drive   10 keyboard

b ▶ CD2 T32 Students read through the words in the box and the text. Tell them to ignore the gaps for the moment. Check any problems. Go through the example as a class, making sure students understand why *plug* is the correct answer. Students complete the exercise. Students can compare answers in pairs. Play the recording for students to check or change their answers. Play the recording again, pausing for students to repeat each word.

TAPESCRIPT/ANSWERS

My dad told me a story about when he was travelling some time ago and was in an airport VIP lounge. He decided to use his laptop to do some work. There was a place to plug his laptop in – but he hadn't got an adaptor with him, so he had to **run** the laptop on the battery.

Anyway, he switched the computer on and found there was a free Wi-Fi **network**. So he got a user name and a **password**, and **logged on** to the internet. He **surfed** the net for a while, and he found some interesting files connected to his work that he wanted to **save** on his hard disk. So he started to **download** them. While that was going on, he went off to get something to drink.

When he came back, he found that his computer had **crashed**! The battery had **run out**, of course. And not only that – his plane was delayed for three hours and he couldn't use his laptop any more!

★ The language of the internet

c Students read through words 1 to 5 and definitions a to f. Check any problems. Go through the first item as an example, if necessary. Students complete the exercise. Students can compare answers in pairs before a whole class check.

> **Answers**
> 1 c   2 d   3 e   4 a   5 f   6 b

Vocabulary notebook

Encourage students to start a section called *Information technology and computers* in their notebooks and to note down all the new words and expressions from this exercise. They can add illustrations and translations as necessary.

★ OPTIONAL ACTIVITY

Students discuss their favourite websites. Divide the class into pairs. Students think about a website they like and they explain to their partner what the website is and why they like it. Monitor and check students are taking turns to ask and answer and provide help and encouragement as necessary. Ask pairs to feed back.

7 Listen

Warm up

Ask students if they have ever had a problem with their computer. How did they fix it? Listen to some of their ideas and encourage them to use some of the vocabulary from Exercise 6.

a ▶ CD2 T33 **Stronger classes:** They can look at the pictures and predict what they think the problems are, then listen and check their predictions.

Weaker classes: Play the recording while students match each speaker to a problem. Remind students to listen for key words to do with computer problems.

Check answers.

TAPESCRIPT

Speaker 1: I use a computer a lot – you know, for my emails, to play games and to search for information on the internet. I do a lot of homework on my computer, too. I guess I spend about three hours a day on the computer – maybe more at the weekend. And it's making my eyes bad, I think – I already wear glasses, but very soon I'm going to need some new ones! My eyes get very tired, and sometimes I get headaches too. I try to make sure that I stop looking at the screen every ten minutes or so – but sometimes I forget!

Speaker 2: I haven't got any problems with using a computer – but my father has! He works at home – he's a writer, you know, he writes articles for magazines and things. And, er, … he doesn't really type very well, he isn't a typist, so now he's got problems with his wrist and fingers. It's because he's typing on the keyboard and using the mouse all the time. Now he has to wear a special kind of glove, and he's bought a better keyboard, one that supports his hands – but his hands and arms still hurt at the end of the day!

Speaker 3: Yeah, I've got a problem with computers – I'm addicted to the internet! I spend hours every day on the net, just surfing and going to chat rooms – I love it! You know, some people are addicted to chocolate and things like that, they have to eat it all the time – well, I have to surf the internet all the time. Some of my friends think I'm crazy, but for me it's the best way to relax. But my mother thinks I'm crazy, too – sometimes she has to pull me away from my computer!

Answers
1 B   2 C   3 A

b ▶ CD2 T33   Students read through questions 1 to 5. Check any problems.

Stronger classes: Students answer the questions first and then listen to check.

Weaker classes: Play the recording while students listen and answer the questions. Play the recording again for students to check or change their answers, pausing as necessary.

Answers
1 Three hours.
2 He stops looking at the screen every ten minutes.
3 He's a writer.
4 A special glove.
5 They think he's crazy.

8 Speak

Divide the class into pairs. Students read through the questions and then discuss them.

Weaker classes: They can choose one question only and discuss it.

Monitor and check students are taking turns to ask and answer. Help and encourage students to express themselves in English as far as possible. Ask pairs to feed back to the class.

Don't judge a book …

9 Read and listen

Warm up
Ask students which type of things they like reading. Do they prefer novels, history books, magazines, comics? Write *self-help book* on the board and explain the meaning. Ask them if they have ever read a book that teaches them things about themselves. Perhaps somebody in their family reads this type of book. Listen to some of their ideas in open class.

a ▶ CD2 T34   Students look at the pictures and answer the questions. Play the recording while students read and listen to check their answers. If students ask questions about vocabulary, write the words on the board, but do not explain the meaning at this stage.

Answers
It means you shouldn't judge things only by how they look. Debbie is reading a self-help book.

b Read through sentences 1–6 with students and check understanding of difficult vocabulary: *confirm, try it out*. In pairs, students complete the exercise. Encourage them to order the sentences without looking back at the text. Check answers in open class.

Answers
Order: 5 3 2 1 6 4

10 Everyday English

a Ask students to locate the expressions 1 to 6 in the text on page 92 and decide who says or thinks them. Ask students to translate the expressions into their own language. Check answers.

Answers
1 Debbie   2 Pete   3 Debbie   4 Debbie
5 Pete   6 Pete

b Ask students to read through the sentences and complete the answers. Go through the first sentence with them as an example if necessary. Check answers.

Answers
2 Looks like   3 It just goes to show
4 It's not worth it   5 it's no good
6 at the same time

Vocabulary notebook

Encourage students to add the expressions to the *Everyday English* section in their vocabulary notebooks and, if necessary, to add translations to help them remember the meanings.

> **OPTIONAL ACTIVITY**
>
> **Weaker classes:** Students can act out the dialogues. Make sure they are saying them with the correct intonation and expression and in the right context.
>
> **Stronger classes:** Students can write their own short dialogues using the expressions. They can then act them out in front of the class. Make sure they are saying them with the correct intonation and expression and in the right context.

> **Discussion box**
>
> **Weaker classes:** Students can choose one question to discuss.
>
> **Stronger classes:** In pairs or small groups, students go through the questions in the box and discuss them.
>
> Monitor and help as necessary, encouraging students to express themselves in English and to use any vocabulary they have learned from the text. Ask pairs or groups to feed back to the class and discuss any interesting points further.

11 Improvisation

Divide the class into pairs. Tell students they are going to create a role play between Pete and his teacher. Read through the instructions with students. Give students two minutes to plan their dialogue. Circulate and help with vocabulary as necessary. Encourage students to use expressions from Exercise 10. Students practise their conversation in pairs. Listen to some of the best conversations in open class.

12 Team Spirit (DVD Episode 6)

a In small groups, students discuss the meaning of the vocabulary items. Do not allow them to use a dictionary at this stage. If students cannot guess the meanings, allow them to use dictionaries. Check answers.

> **OPTIONAL ACTIVITY**
>
> You may like to do Exercise 12a as a competition and give students two minutes to guess the meanings. Check answers and award a point for each correct definition. If nobody in the class has the correct definition, hold a dictionary race and give a point for the first team to look up the correct definition.

b Read through the instructions and listen to some of the students' ideas. Encourage them to use words from Exercise 12a. Play episode 6 of the DVD for students to check their predictions.

13 Write

a The preparation for this can be done in class and the writing task set for homework. Students read the questions. Students then read the advertisement and the article to find the answers. Check answers.

> **Answer**
> Topic 1

b Students find the five underlined expressions. Elicit or explain that *probably* shows less certainty than the other four expressions.

c Students decide if they are going to write about topic 2 or 3.

Stronger classes: Give them a few minutes to make notes for their topic. Go through Ahmed's article with them and ask them to think about the structure of the article and the topic of each paragraph. Students then expand their notes into full sentences and put them into paragraphs. Remind students to refer back to Ahmed's article if they have problems.

Weaker classes: Elicit some ideas from them and help them with their note taking. Encourage students to expand their notes into full sentences. Students can swap their sentences with a partner for their partner to check. Once their partner has checked them, students write out a final version putting their sentences into paragraphs.

14 Last but not least: more speaking

a Give students time to read through the sentences and check understanding. You may need to pre-teach *concentration*, *reliable* and *stressed*. Do sentence 1 as an example in open class. Ask students to decide who they think said each of the sentences. Tell them there is no right answer. Students then decide how they feel about each statement and tick one of the boxes.

b Students work together and discuss their answers. Circulate and encourage them to give reasons for their choices. Monitor to check progress and ensure students are using language correctly.

c In small groups, students discuss the two statements they feel most strongly about. Get feedback from some of the groups. Write the most interesting ideas on the board and invite comments.

Check your progress

1 Grammar

a 2 where 3 that/who 4 that 5 which/that 6 who/that

b 2 live; used to live 3 enjoy; used to hate 4 used to eat; doesn't like 5 didn't use to use; use 6 Did ... use to have; don't have

c 2 knew; 'd tell 3 Would ... surf; had 4 got; would ... be 5 would go; asked 6 was; wouldn't buy

2 Vocabulary

a 2 pain 3 patient 4 temperature 5 hurt 6 injection

b Parts of a computer: CD drive; mouse; USB slot; power lead
The internet: download; crash; network
Using a computer: save; log on

How did you do?

Check that students are marking their scores. Collect these in and check them as necessary and discuss any further work needed with specific students.

Memo from Mario

If I had …
Second conditional letter writing exercise

- This exercise is best done as a follow-up to the work the authors propose on the new grammar.
- Ask each student to write their name on two small pieces of paper. The pieces of paper are then folded over and one student collects them in a box or bag.
- The same student then goes round the room and each student takes two names (not their own) from the bag.
- Tell the students to write a two paragraph letter to one of the two classmates whose names they have, expressing their thoughts and dreams using the second conditional, for example:

  I really like football and if I could run faster I'd play on the wing.

  I'd train to be ballerina if I had stronger ankles.

- Make it clear that when a student finishes their letter to their first correspondent they should get up and deliver it. They then write a different letter to their second correspondent, and deliver this, too.
- When a student receives a letter from someone they answer it.
- Begin to draw the activity to a close when the fastest students have had time to answer the two letters they have received.

> **RATIONALE**
> In this activity students are using their own creativity to say what they decide to say to their classmates and to do this in English. The exercise is a powerful way of getting students used to using the patterns of the unlikely/unreal conditional.

Acknowledgement
The letters-across-the-class technique was first noted in *Letters*, Burbidge et.al. Oxford University Press, 1996.

UNIT 12   101

13 Lost worlds

Unit overview

TOPIC: Lost worlds

TEXTS

Reading and listening: a text about the discovery of Tikal
Listening: a radio programme about the paintings of Lascaux
Reading: a text about three mythical cities
Writing: a short story

SPEAKING AND FUNCTIONS

Describing events in the past and earlier past
Telling a picture story
Discussing mythical cities

LANGUAGE

Grammar: Past perfect
Vocabulary: Noun suffixes: -r, -er, -or, -ist

1 Read and listen

If you set the background information as a homework research task, ask students to tell the rest of the class what they found out.

BACKGROUND INFORMATION

Guatemala is a country in Central America. Its capital is Guatemala City. Guatemala is home to an incredible variety of biologically significant and unique ecosystems.

Belize (formerly British Honduras) is a country in Central America. Belize was a British territory until 1981 and is the only country in Central America with English as the official language.

El Salvador is the smallest and most densely populated country in Central America.

Christopher Columbus (1451–1506) was a Genoese navigator, coloniser and explorer.

Warm up

Ask students what they would do if they found an important historical object. Would they keep it / phone a newspaper / take it to a museum? What about if they were walking in a forest and came across an ancient village – how would they feel? Listen to some of their ideas in open class.

a Students read the questions and then read the text quickly to find the answers. Remind them that they don't need to understand every word at this point. Check answers.

> **Answers**
> Tikal is in Guatemala; Mayans lived there.

b ▶ CD2 T35 Students read through questions 1 to 5. Check any problems. Play the recording while students listen and read and answer the questions. Check answers, playing and pausing the recording again as necessary.

TAPESCRIPT

See the reading text on page 96 of the Student's Book.

> **Answers**
> 1 He was looking for gum.
> 2 An ancient Mayan city.
> 3 Between 200 and 900 AD.
> 4 Around 900 AD, no one knows why.
> 5 Local Indians.

c Give students time to think about places or things which were 'found again' before pooling information in open class. You may like to give them an example of your own to get them started.

2 Grammar
★ Past perfect

a **Stronger classes:** Students read through the information in the box and sentences 1 to 6. Check any problems. If you think it will help students, draw a line on the board and mark two points on it. Then go through the first sentence as an example marking on the line in this way:

● *before Tut climbed*   ● *after Tut climbed*
_____X_____

He ran to tell the governor

Students work out when the other sentences happened using the line on the board to help them. Check answers, asking students to come out and write the sentence on the line on the board where it happened (before or after Tut climbed the tree).

Weaker classes: Books closed. Write the following sentence (or an example of your own) on the board: *I had finished my homework when the phone rang.*

Ask students what happened first (*I finished my homework*). Students now open their books at

102   UNIT 13

page 97 and read through the information in Exercise 2a. Follow the procedure for stronger classes from this point.

> **Answers**
> 1 B   2 A   3 A   4 B   5 A   6 A

b Ask students what they notice about the verb in all the sentences which happened before Tut climbed the tree and elicit or explain that they use *had* + past participle. Explain that this tense is called the past perfect and is used to make clear that one action happened before another in the past.

Stronger classes: Students go through the text on page 96 and complete the rule box and the table.

Weaker classes: Students go through the text. Check answers. Then read through the rule as a class and elicit the missing words. Students read through the table and complete it. Check answers.

> **Answers**
> Para 2: Tut didn't really know what he had seen; the city that the Mayans had built; palaces where kings had lived
> Para 3: local people had known
> Para 4: explorers had gone to; no one had listened to them; the lost city had been found

> **Answers**
> Rule: before
> Negative: hadn't
> Question: Had/hadn't
> Short answer: had/hadn't

To check understanding, ask students to give you a few examples of their own using the past perfect.

> **Language notes**
> 1 Students may confuse the past perfect with the present perfect and produce statements like: *I have finished my homework when the phone rang*. Remind them of the use of the past perfect in English.
> 2 Students may find it useful to translate a few examples into their own language and compare the two.
> 3 Remind them that we don't repeat the main verb in short answers. We don't say: *Yes, I had played*.

c This exercise can be set for homework. Students read through sentences 1 to 6. Check any problems. Go through the example as a class, making sure students understand the form. Students complete the exercise. Remind them to think carefully about the past participle and if they need a regular or an irregular past participle. Check answers.

> **Answers**
> 2 had lost ('d lost)   3 hadn't got   4 hadn't invited   5 had changed ('d changed)
> 6 had/left

d This exercise can be set for homework. Students read through the texts. Check any problems. Go through the example as a class, asking students to explain why the past simple is correct. Students complete the exercise. Check answers, asking students to explain their choice of verb.

> **Answers**
> 1 had built; had lived
> 2 was; had built; had sailed; went

e This exercise can be set for homework. Students read through sentences 1 to 3. Check any problems. Go through the example as a class. Students complete the exercise. Check answers, asking students to explain their choice of verb.

> **Answers**
> 2 hadn't seen   3 found; went

Grammar notebook

Remind students to note down the rules for the past perfect and the completed table from Exercise 2b. They may also find it useful to note down some examples and translations of their own.

4 Speak

a Divide the class into pairs. Students read through the table. Check any problems. Ask a stronger pair to read the example to the rest of the class. Give students a few minutes to make as many sentences as they can. Monitor and check they are using the correct verb forms and note down any repeated errors to go through as a class later. Ask some pairs to read out some of their sentences to the class.

b In pairs, students read through the words in the box and look at pictures. Students complete the exercise. Check answers.

> **Answers**
> A and E Two teenagers; B a bandage;
> B an ambulance; A and F an American football;
> D a small girl crying

c Ask pairs to talk about why they think picture A is the first one in the story and elicit the answer. Students then work out the order of the pictures to tell the story. Remind them to think carefully about the order of events and which things happened before others. Check answers.

> **Answers**
> 1 A   2 F   3 E   4 C   5 D   6 B

UNIT 13

d and **e** Students read the instructions. Ask a stronger pair to read out the example sentences to the rest of the class. Draw students' attention to the use of the past continuous and past perfect tenses. Students continue to retell the story in their pairs. Monitor and check students are taking turns to do this and make sure they are using the correct verb forms. Note down any repeated errors to go through later as a class.

f Students work in the same or different pairs, and read through the instructions. Then ask a stronger pair to read out the example sentences. Draw students' attention to the use of the past perfect in the example and remind them to use this in their own situations. Give students a few minutes to discuss their situation. Monitor and check that students are taking turns to ask and answer and that they are using the past perfect correctly. Ask pairs to feed back and if there are any interesting stories encourage students to give more information to the rest of the class.

5 Listen

Warm up

Ask students to look at the pictures. Do they know where the paintings come from? Has anyone heard of them? If so, what can they tell the class about them? Discuss this as a class or in L1 if appropriate.

a ▶ **CD2 T37** Students read the instructions and look at the pictures. Play the recording while students listen and check their order and check their Warm up predictions. Check answers.

TAPESCRIPT

Speaker 1: … and with us today is Doctor Joanne Williams who is going to tell us about the remarkable paintings in the caves at Lascaux, in southern France. They were found in 1940 – is that right?

Speaker 2: Yes, indeed. And it's quite a story, because the paintings were actually found by four teenage boys. Now, one day the boys went out walking with a dog – the dog belonged to a boy called Marcel, and its name was Robot – and Robot fell into a hole and couldn't get out again. So the boys went home and the next day they came back with a lantern …

Speaker 1: A light?

Speaker 2: That's right. And Marcel – the owner of the dog – went into the hole, and started to crawl down a very, very dark passageway, holding the lantern so that he could see. And he went crawling slowly along to try to find Robot, and when he got to the end of the passageway, he held up the lantern and saw that he was in a cave, and on the walls of the cave were these amazing paintings – hundreds of prehistoric paintings in beautiful colours.

Speaker 1: So he went back and told people about them?

Speaker 2: Well, not immediately, no! The four boys decided that they didn't want to tell anyone, they wanted to keep it a secret – but after two or three days they couldn't keep the secret any longer and they told their teacher. And the teacher told a friend who was an archaeologist, and soon everyone knew about the paintings.

Speaker 1: And what happened to the dog?

Speaker 2: You know, I really don't know!

Answers
1 D   2 F   3 E   4 C   5 B   6 A

b ▶ **CD2 T38** Students read through questions 1 to 5. Check any problems. If necessary, play the recording and stop it after the answer to the first question and go through this as an example. Play the recording for students to listen and answer the questions. Remind them to listen for key words to help them find the answers. Check answers, pausing the recording to clarify any problems.

TAPESCRIPT

Speaker 1: And this was an amazing discovery, wasn't it?

Speaker 2: Oh yes, it really was. I mean, of course, there were other caves in the world with prehistoric paintings, but the caves in Lascaux are very big and the paintings are very, very old … erm …

Speaker 1: How old?

Speaker 2: Well, we think that they are 16,000 years old.

Speaker 1: Incredible.

Speaker 2: And there are so many of them, too – almost 2,000 paintings on the walls. Most of them are paintings of animals – horses, cows, bulls, things like that.

Speaker 1: Can people go and see the caves?

Speaker 2: Well, this is what happened. After the boys found the caves, and after the archaeologists had studied them, the caves were opened to visitors … and after a few years, there were about a thousand visitors every day to the caves …

Speaker 1: A thousand people every day? Wouldn't that cause some problems?

Speaker 2: Well, yes, exactly. You see, what happened is that the carbon dioxide from people's breath started to destroy the paintings, they began to lose their colour, so in 1963 the caves were closed …

Speaker 1: And now people can't go in?

Speaker 2: No, not any more. However, there is a museum with replicas of the caves and the paintings that people can go and see …

> **Answers**
> 1 16,000 years old
> 2 about 2,000
> 3 animals – horses, cows, bulls etc.
> 4 about a thousand
> 5 in 1963

6 Vocabulary

★ Noun suffixes: -r, -er, -or and -ist

a Write the suffixes on the board and elicit as many jobs as students know for each suffix. Leave these on the board as you will need them in Exercise 6b.

Stronger classes: Students then read through the definitions. Go through the first item as an example, eliciting the job from students. Students then complete the exercise.

Weaker classes: Write the following jobs in jumbled order on the board: *collector, explorer, governor, traveller, archaeologist, astronomer*. Ask students to read through the definitions. Go through the first item with them as an example. Students then match the other jobs on the board with the definitions.

> **Answers**
> 1 collector 2 explorer 3 governor
> 4 traveller 5 archaeologist 6 astronomer

> **Language note**
> Explain to students that the stress on words often changes when we make a new noun, e.g. 'photograph – pho'tographer.

b Students read through the list of words. Check any problems. Go through the example, if necessary. Students complete the exercise.

Weaker classes: Ask students to come out and write the correct noun under the suffixes you put on the board in Exercise 6a.

Students can check their answers in a dictionary before a whole class check.

> **Answers**
> 2 journalist 3 presenter 4 cyclist
> 5 artist 6 farmer 7 inventor 8 juggler
> 9 decorator 10 receptionist

c Students read through sentences 1 to 6. Check any problems. Go through the example, if necessary. Students complete the sentences. Remind them to think carefully about the context of each sentence

before choosing which noun they need. Students can check answers in pairs before a whole class check.

> **Answers**
> 2 plumber 3 juggler 4 presenter
> 5 cyclists 6 farmer

Ask students to give you any more jobs they know with these suffixes, at this point.

Vocabulary notebook
Remind students to start a section for each suffix from this unit and to note down any new words from this exercise under the relevant suffix.

Culture in mind

7 Read and listen

If you set the background information as a homework research task, ask students to tell the rest of the class what they found out.

> **BACKGROUND INFORMATION**
> **Borobudur** is a 9th century Mahayana Buddhist monument in Magelang, Central Java, Indonesia.
>
> **Machu Picchu** is an Inca site located 2,430 metres above sea level on a mountain ridge above the Urubamba Valley in Peru, 80 kilometres north west of Cuzco.
>
> **Angkor Wat** is a temple complex at Angkor, Cambodia, built for King Suryavarman II in the 12th century as his state temple and capital city.
>
> **Plato** (428/427 BC/348/347 BC) was a Classical Greek philosopher and mathematician. Along with his mentor, Socrates, and his student, Aristotle, Plato helped to lay the foundations of Western philosophy.
>
> **Tibetan Buddhism** is a religion practised in Tibet and certain regions of the Himalayas, including northern Nepal, Bhutan and India.
>
> **Himalayas** is a mountain range in Asia, separating the Indian subcontinent from the Tibetan plateau.

Warm-up
Books closed. Write *Mythical cities* on the board. Explain the meaning of mythical and ask students if they can think of any examples of mythical cities or people. Listen to some of their ideas and write any interesting vocabulary on the board.

a Books open. Tell students they are going to read about three mythical cities. Students look at the names of

UNIT 13 105

the cities and guess the answers to the questions, before reading the text quickly to check their ideas. Tell them not to worry if they don't understand every word at this stage. Check answers.

> **Answers**
> in Asia: Shambhala; in South America: El Dorado; on an island in the ocean: Atlantis

b ▶ **CD3 T1** Read through the text and listen, pausing where necessary to check comprehension and help with difficult vocabulary: *explorers, gold, swallowed, mystical, Golden Age*. Students read and answer the questions and compare answers with a partner before feedback.

> **Answers**
> 1 1537
> 2 A place where you can get rich quickly.
> 3 Due to the natural resources on their island.
> 4 They became greedy and wanted power.
> 5 It was swallowed by the sea.
> 6 The city is inhabited by beautiful people who live in fabulous houses and there is no war.
> 7 A huge army will come out of Shambhala, destroy the world's bad rulers and start a new Golden Age.

c Students find words or phrases in the text to match the definitions and compare answers with a partner. Check answers and pay attention to pronunciation of the words.

> **Answers**
> 1 legend   2 resources   3 greedy   4 peaks
> 5 fabulous   6 rulers

d Read the sentences with students and check understanding. Students complete the sentences with words from Exercise 7c. Check answers.

> **Answers**
> 2 fabulous   3 rulers   4 resources   5 greedy

8 Write
✱ A short story

The preparation for this can be done in class and the writing task set for homework.

a Students look at pictures 1 to 3 and read the text. Check answers, asking students to explain their choice.

Weaker classes: You may want to pre-teach the following vocabulary: *alone, relax, reddish-brown, bomb, fortunately, blow up, dangerous*.

> **Answer**
> Picture 2

b Students read topics 1 to 4. Check any problems. Go through the first item as an example, if necessary. Students complete the exercise. Check answers.

> **Answers**
> 1 B   2 D   3 A   4 C

c Students read the three questions. Draw their attention to the underlined expressions in the text and elicit the answers.

> **Answers**
> 1 about a month ago; 15 minutes later
> 2 first; then; the next day
> 3 suddenly; immediately; fortunately

d Students read the instructions. Give them a few minutes to decide if they are going to choose one of the other pictures or something of their own choice.

Stronger classes: Encourage them to make notes about the sequence of events, using the model in Exercise 8a to help them. Students then expand their notes into full sentences and put them into paragraphs. Remind students to refer back to the short story if they have problems.

Weaker classes: Encourage them to choose one of the other pictures in Exercise 8a. Elicit or give some prompts for each picture and help them make some notes about the sequence of events and the content of their story. Refer them back to Exercise 8b to think about the order of events. Encourage students to expand their notes into full sentences. Students can swap their sentences with a partner for their partner to check. Students then write out a final version putting their sentences into paragraphs. Remind them to use the model story if they have any problems.

9 Speak

In pairs or small groups, students go through the questions in the box and discuss them.

Monitor and help as necessary, encouraging students to express themselves in English and to use any vocabulary they have learned from the text. Ask pairs or groups to feed back to the class and discuss any interesting points further.

Memo from Mario

Lost worlds

Comprehension questions – or are they?
'A City in the Jungle' (page 96)

▶ In preparation, photocopy the question sheet below (one per student). Write in the names of two students in the group to replace X and Y.

1. Have you ever been in a jungle? Where? When?
2. What temperature was it when Tut went out into the jungle?
3. What was Ambosio Tut wearing that day?
4. What was Tut's job?
5. Do you like climbing trees? Do you have a good head for heights?
6. What kind of man was Tut, in your opinion?
7. Why on earth was he at the top of a tree?
8. Do snakes also climb trees in this part of the world?
9. What did Tut see through the trees?
10. Do you think Tut was an educated man?
11. Was Tut in a hurry to tell the Governor? How do you know?
12. Who was the other man who walked through the jungle with Tut?
13. What could they hear as the walked?
14. Could they smell anything?
15. Does X like this text?
16. What was the name of the city the Mayans had built hundreds of years before?
17. Why have only ordinary Mayans lived there before? How do you know?
18. What time of day was it when the two men entered Tikai?
19. What had locals known before Tut's find?
20. For how many years had Tikai been the main city on the region?
21. What had the two British people done seven years before?
22. Once Tut and the Governor found Tikai who were the people who came next?
23. Do you think the Governor made money from the two men's discovery? If so, how?
24. Was their coming a good thing?
25. Does Y like this text?
26. Did the archaeologists steal the things they found and take them home with them?
27. Have you ever seen temples and palaces in the middle of a jungle?
28. Do you find this story interesting?
29. What would have made it more interesting?
30. Is the past important to you? If so, why?

▶ In the lesson ask the students to read the text on page 96 silently. Go through any difficult vocabulary with them.
▶ Give out the question sheet and ask students to cross out all the questions they don't like for whatever reason.
▶ Tell them they must keep at least ten questions.
▶ Go round the class, helping students with comprehension of the questions.
▶ Put the students into pairs (Student A and Student B). Tell them to exchange question sheets. Student A puts the questions Student B has not crossed out to Student B and Student B answers them.
▶ They then work the other way round.
▶ Leave time at the end of the activity for general feedback.

RATIONALE

This technique has the students doing a lot more detailed reading then they would normally do, and doubles their exposure to the past perfect patterns.

The request to cross out questions they do not like puts power in the students' hands.

Some of the questions make some students laugh.

The technique is designed to offer the students the chance to think divergently, without forcing natural convergent thinkers from doing what they do best, that is answering the traditional comprehension questions.

UNIT 13

14 A stroke of luck

Unit overview

TOPIC: Good and bad luck; superstitions

TEXTS

Reading and listening: a text about a man who has a lot of accidents
Listening: a dialogue about an unlucky day
Listening: a song: *Lucky Day* by Chris Rea
Writing: an email to apologise for something

SPEAKING AND FUNCTIONS

Reporting statements
Discussing superstitions

LANGUAGE

Grammar: Reported statements; Third conditional
Vocabulary: Noun suffixes *-ation* and *-ment*
Everyday English: *It's a bit like*; *Surely*; *What's going on?*; *was like*; *have a word with*; *It's just that*

1 Read and listen

Warm up

Ask students to translate the unit title into their own language. Ask them if they have had any good or bad luck recently. If so, encourage them to explain to the rest of the class what happened. Discuss this as a class or in L1 if appropriate.

a Students read the question and look at the pictures. Elicit suggestions. Students then read the text quickly to check their predictions. Remind students they don't have to understand every word at this point. Did any of the students choose the correct order?

Answers
2, 4, 1, 3

b ▶ CD3 T2 Students read through questions 1 to 6. Check any problems. Play the recording, pausing after the answer to the first question and go through this as an example. Play the recording while students listen and read and answer the other questions. Students can compare answers in pairs before a whole class check. Play the recording again as necessary, pausing to clarify any problems.

Weaker classes: You may want to pre-teach the following vocabulary: *near-death, shore, treatment, haystack, injuries, lottery ticket, advert, survived*.

TAPESCRIPT
See the reading text on page 102 of the Student's Book.

Answers
1 Many years ago.
2 He landed in a haystack.
3 He had no major injuries.
4 Because a lorry was coming straight at him.
5 Lucky.
6 He was afraid he would have an accident.

★ OPTIONAL ACTIVITY

Give students the following true/false exercise based on the text.

Stronger classes: They can answer the questions and read or listen to check answers only.

Weaker classes: Play the recording again then students answer the questions.

Check answers and ask students to correct the false statements.
1 Chevalier is Italian.
2 His train fell into the sea.
3 More people were killed on the plane than on the train.
4 A few years later his car exploded.
5 Chevalier bought a lottery ticket every week.

Answers
1 F (French)
2 F (river)
3 T
4 T
5 F (He bought his first one for 50 years when he was 71.)

2 Grammar

★ Reported statements

a Students read through statements 1 to 4. Go through the example, if necessary. Students then go back through the text on page 102 and find who said each one.

Stronger classes: They can do this from memory and can refer back to the text to check answers only.

Check answers.

Answers
3 A TV company   4 Chevalier

108 UNIT 14

b Students read through the instruction and look back at the text to find how the statements are reported. Ask students what they notice about the verb in the first statement and the verb in the reported statement. Elicit or explain that the verb changes from past simple to past perfect. Ask them if they notice any other changes in the sentences and elicit or explain that the pronouns and the tenses change.

Check answers.

> **Answers**
> 1 The doctors told him he had been lucky.
> 2 Chevalier said he was going to enjoy his life from then on.
> 3 A TV company in America said they wanted him to make an advert.
> 4 Chevalier said he wouldn't fly to Los Angeles.

c Students read through the table. Elicit the first item as an example. Explain to students that each tense in direct speech moves back a tense in reported speech. Students complete the exercise. Remind them to think carefully about how each tense will move back a tense before they write their answer. Check answers.

> **Answers**
> Present simple – Past simple
> Past simple – Past perfect simple
> Present perfect – Past perfect simple
> am/is/are going to – was/was/were going to
> can/can't – could/couldn't
> will/won't – would/wouldn't

To check understanding at this point, give students a few example sentences of your own and ask them to put them into reported speech.

Language notes

1 Students may fail to change the tenses in reported speech and produce statements like: *He said they want to leave at 8 o'clock*. Tell them that this is only correct if the fact is still true or hasn't happened yet. For example, in the above sentence the student may be talking about the future, in which case it is correct and the past simple would also be correct. However, if the student is referring to what has already happened he/she will need to use the past simple.

2 Remind students that pronouns may also need changing in reported speech and some time words, e.g. *this – that*; *here – there*, etc.

3 Students may find it useful to translate some direct speech into reported speech in their own language and notice if the same changes take place.

LOOK!

Students often make the mistake of using object pronouns after the verb *say*, e.g. *He said me that he was tired*. Read through the Look! box with students and ask them to translate the sentences into their own language to help them see the difference.

d Students read through sentences 1 to 6. Go through the example, drawing students' attention to the verb and pronoun changes. Students complete the exercise. Remind them to look carefully at the verbs and pronouns in the reported speech before they decide how it will be said in direct speech. They can also refer back to the completed table in Exercise 2c to help them. Check answers.

> **Answers**
> 2 'I've had a lot of luck in my life.'
> 3 'I'm going to marry my girlfriend.'
> 4 'I want to enjoy the rest of my life.'
> 5 'You'll be really good in an advert.'
> 6 'You can earn a lot of money.'

e This exercise can be set for homework. Students read through sentences 1 to 6. Go through the example, drawing students' attention to the changes in tense and pronouns. Students complete the exercise. Remind them to look carefully at the verbs and pronouns in each sentence before they make their decisions about the tense changes. Check answers.

> **Answers**
> 2 was going
> 3 had worked
> 4 would do his homework
> 5 could phone
> 6 had never had

Grammar notebook

Remind students to note down the completed table from Exercise 2c and some examples of their own.

★ OPTIONAL ACTIVITY

Stronger classes: Divide the class into small groups of four or five. One student thinks of a sentence about themselves in direct speech. They whisper it to the next person in the group who must then report the first student's sentence to the next person and add a new sentence in direct speech about themselves. This continues until the last person in the group can report back all the sentences. Continue like this until everyone has had a turn at reporting back all the sentences. For example:
S1 to S2: *I'm going to the cinema tonight.*
S2 to S3: *Marco said he was going to the cinema tonight. I'm studying for a test tonight.*

UNIT 14

S3 to S4: *Marco said he was going to the cinema tonight. Magda said she was studying for a test tonight. I'm ...* etc.

Weaker classes: Give them the following sentences to put into reported speech. Check answers.
1 'I'm going to the cinema,' said Maria.
2 'We're studying for our exam,' they said.
3 'My dad goes to the gym every day,' Laura said.
4 'You have to work harder,' the teacher said.
5 'I feel sick and I want to go home,' said the boy.

> **Answers**
> 1 Maria said she was going to the cinema.
> 2 They said they were studying for their exam.
> 3 Laura said her dad went to the gym every day.
> 4 The teacher said I had to work harder.
> 5 The boy said that he felt sick and wanted to go home.

3 Speak

Divide the class into pairs and give each partner a letter A or B. Student A looks at the three questions in exercise 3 on page 103, student B turns to page 126 and looks at the questions there. Ask students to take it in turns to ask their questions. Tell students that they mustn't make notes. Divide the class into different pairs for students to tell each other what they found out about their previous partner. Encourage students to use reported speech in their answers. Circulate and check students are using the language correctly. Listen to a few sample answers in open class as feedback.

4 Vocabulary

★ Noun suffixes -ation and -ment

a Write the endings -ation and -ment on the board. Elicit as many nouns with these endings as students know and write them up under the relevant suffix. If there is time, you can ask students to come out and write up the nouns themselves. Students now read through sentences 1 to 8. Check any problems. Go through the example, drawing students' attention to the connection between the noun and the verb it comes from. Students complete the exercise. Remind them to think carefully about each verb before they decide whether to add -ation or -ment. Check answers.

> **Answers**
> 2 invitation 3 improvement 4 equipment
> 5 calculation 6 management 7 information
> 8 entertainment

> **Language notes**
> 1 Remind students when they are spelling nouns with -ation endings that we usually need to delete the –e on the end of the root verb before adding -ion, e.g. *educate – education*.
> 2 Check students' pronunciation of the -ation ending /eɪʃən/.

b Read through the words in the box with students and check understanding. Ask students to complete the text with the correct noun form.

Weaker classes: Pre-teach *tents, hire, in advance*. Allow students to compare answers with a partner before feedback.

> **Answers**
> 2 entertainment 3 equipment 4 treatment
> 5 information 6 reservation 7 payment
> 8 cancellation

Vocabulary notebook

Encourage students to note down the noun suffixes and the new nouns from this exercise. They may find it useful to add some translations.

★ **OPTIONAL ACTIVITY**

Give students the following verbs and ask them to work out the -ment and -ation nouns from them. Check answers.
1 enjoy
2 advertise
3 present
4 motivate
5 explore
6 agree

> **Answers**
> 1 enjoyment 2 advertisement
> 3 presentation 4 motivation
> 5 exploration 6 agreement

5 Listen

a ▶ **CD3 T3** Students read the questions. Play the recording for students to listen for the answers. Remind them that they will be listening for a place in question 1 and a time in question 2. Students can compare answers in pairs before a whole class check.

TAPESCRIPT

Speaker 2: Hello?

Speaker 1: Hi, it's Sebastian. Is that you, Emily?

Speaker 2: Oh, hi, Sebastian. It's me, yes.

Speaker 1: Look, we're going for a bike trip on Saturday. Would you like to come along?

Speaker 2: Bike trip? Who's 'we'?

Speaker 1: Well, the group. Lizzy, Simon, Nick, James, Caroline, myself, and you hopefully!

Speaker 2: When are you going?

Speaker 1: We're meeting at 9.30 at the car park near the supermarket.

Speaker 2: OK. 9.30 it is!

Speaker 1: Great, Emily. See you tomorrow then.

Speaker 2: See you!

> **Answers**
> 1 On a bike trip.
> 2 At half past nine.

b ▶ CD3 T4 Divide the class into pairs. Students look at the pictures. Go through the first picture as an example. Students complete the exercise. Ask students for their answers and put them on the board. Do not give the answers at this point. Play the recording for students to check or change their answers. Play the recording again, pausing as necessary to clarify any problems.

TAPESCRIPT

Speaker 3: Sebastian! Your foot's in plaster! What happened?

Speaker 1: Oh, hi Melinda. Oh, it was just bad luck. It wouldn't have happened if I hadn't gone on that bike trip.

Speaker 3: Bike trip?

Speaker 1: We went for a bike trip on Saturday. You know, me, Simon, Nick and all the others ... and we were just riding across this field when the sun came out, so I put my sunglasses on.

Speaker 3: And?

Speaker 1: Well, a minute later we were in the woods, and the sun was gone, and it was really dark, and I didn't see this big stone and I fell off and broke my ankle.

Speaker 3: Oh, dear. So if you hadn't put your glasses on, you wouldn't have fallen off. That's bad luck.

Speaker 1: Well, I'm not sure. Maybe it was good luck. If I hadn't put them on in the first place, the sun would have blinded me. If the sun had blinded me, I would have fallen off earlier maybe. And who knows: maybe I would have broken both my ankles.

Speaker 3: Oh, Sebastian, you can be so funny.

Speaker 1: And there's another reason why I think it was good luck!

Speaker 3: What's that?

Speaker 1: If I hadn't broken my ankle, you wouldn't have stopped to talk to me!

> **Answers**
> D C A B

c ▶ CD3 T4 Tell students they are going to listen to part of the conversation again.

Play the recording while students listen, read and complete the gaps with the correct information. Students compare answers with a partner. Play the recording again, pausing if necessary for clarification. Check answers in open class.

> **Answers**
> 1 hadn't   2 have fallen   3 hadn't put
> 4 have broken   5 wouldn't have

6 Grammar
✶ Third conditional

a **Stronger classes:** Students read through the examples. Ask them some questions and elicit the answers, e.g. *Did he go on the bike trip? (Yes) Is the situation real or imagined? (Imagined) Is the situation in the past or the present? (Past)* Ask students to look at the verbs used and elicit the form of the third conditional. Then ask, e.g. *Did the sun blind him? (No) Would he have fallen off if the sun had blinded him? (Probably)* Elicit or explain that the sentence is showing the person imagining how things might have been different in the past. Students then read and complete the rule. Check answers.

Weaker classes: Books closed. Write the following example (or some of your own) on the board: *If I had studied more, I would have done better in the exam.*

Now ask the following questions: *Did he study hard? (No) Did he do well in the exam? (No) Is the situation in the present or the past? (Past) Is it real or imagined? (Imagined)* Students open their books at page 105 and read the examples. Follow the procedure for stronger classes from this point.

> **Answers**
> past perfect/have

b Refer students back to the dialogue in Exercise 5b. Go through the first example of a third conditional as a class. Students then underline other examples. Check answers.

> **Answers**
> If the sun had blinded me, I would have fallen off earlier maybe.
> If I hadn't broken my ankle, you wouldn't have stopped to talk to me.

UNIT 14   111

> **Language notes**
> 1 Students may produce statements like: *If I looked at my watch, I'd have been OK*. Remind them of the form of the third conditional if necessary.
> 2 Remind them that the *if* clause can go at the beginning or the end, as in all conditional sentences.

c Students match the beginnings and endings of the sentences. Let them compare answers with a partner before checking answers. During feedback, point out that the *if* clause and *would* clause can be reversed.

> **Answers**
> 1 b 2 d 3 e 4 a 5 c

d This exercise can be set for homework. Students read through sentences 1 to 5. Check any problems. Go through the example, if necessary. Students complete the exercise. Remind them of the form of the third conditional before they begin. Check answers.

> **Answers**
> 2 had studied; would have passed
> 3 wouldn't have won; hadn't played
> 4 would have bought; had had
> 5 would have gone; had asked

8 Listen

If you set the background information as a homework research task, ask students to tell the rest of the class what they found out.

> **BACKGROUND INFORMATION**
> **Chris Rea** (born 1951 in Middlesborough, England) is a rock and pop singer who became popular with the release of the albums *The Road to Hell* (1989) and *Auberge* (1991). He has sold over 30 million albums worldwide.

a ▶ CD3 T6 Look at the lyrics of the song and ask students to guess which words in italics they will hear. Play the recording. Students listen and check their predictions. Play the recording again, pausing to clarify any difficult vocabulary.

> **Answers**
> 1 pillow 2 morning 3 crystals 4 dawn
> 5 forever 6 complications

b Divide the class into pairs and ask students to read the phrases from the song and discuss their meaning. Circulate and help with any difficult vocabulary as required. As feedback, listen to some of the students' ideas in open class. Ask students if they agree with the phrases and encourage debate.

> **Answers**
> 1 a 2 b 3 d 4 c

c ▶ CD3 T6 Play the recording again and encourage students to sing the song. You may like to split the class in two and ask each half to take it in turns to sing a line. At the end of the song you can decide which group was best at singing.

Nervous about the exams

9 Read and Listen

Warm up

Ask students what they remember about the previous episode of the photo story in unit 12 and what happened (Debbie showed Pete a self-help book. He tried a questionnaire, but he wasn't impressed with the results).

a ▶ CD3 T7 Ask students to read the questions and predict the answers but do not comment at this stage. Play the recording while students read and check their predictions. Tell students to underline the answers in the dialogue. Check answers in open class. If students ask questions about vocabulary, write the words on the board, but do not comment at this stage.

TAPESCRIPT

See the text on page 106 of the Student's Book.

> **Answers**
> She feels stressed. Pete is not interested and is rude at first, then he feels sorry and admits he was nervous. Debbie is surprised and feels better.

b Read through the sentences. Students read the text again and complete the sentences. Students can then work with a partner to check each other's sentences. Circulate and help with vocabulary as required. Listen to some of their answers in open class as feedback.

112 UNIT 14

> **Answers**
> 1 … she is stressed and can't sleep.
> 2 … you don't know exactly what is going to happen.
> 3 … exams are stressful.
> 4 … nervous.
> 5 … being rude to Debbie.
> 6 … surprised.

10 Everyday English

a Read through the expressions from the dialogue with students. Do the first item as an example. Ask students if they can remember (without looking back) who said this (Debbie). Students complete the exercise, only looking back at the dialogue if they need to. Ask students to translate the expressions into their own languages. Is the translation always literal or do they use other words to express the same idea? Check answers.

> **Answers**
> 1 Jess 2 Pete 3 Joel 4 Debbie 5 Pete
> 6 Pete

b Students read the dialogues and then complete them with the expressions from Exercise 10a. Go through the first item as an example, if necessary. Check answers.

> **Answers**
> 2 It's just that 3 was like 4 It's a bit like
> 5 Surely 6 What's going on

★ OPTIONAL ACTIVITY

Weaker classes: Students can act out the dialogues. Make sure they are saying them with the correct intonation and expression and in the right context.

Stronger classes: Students can write their own short dialogues using the expressions. They can then act them out in front of the class. Make sure they are saying them with the correct intonation and expression and in the right context.

Discussion box

Weaker classes: Students can choose one question to discuss.

Stronger classes: In pairs or small groups, students go through the questions in the box and discuss them.

Monitor and help as necessary, encouraging students to express themselves in English and to use any vocabulary they have learned from the text. Ask pairs or groups to feed back to the class and discuss any interesting points further.

11 Improvisation

Divide the class into pairs. Tell students they are going to create a role play. Read through the instructions with students. Give students two minutes to plan their dialogue. Circulate and help with vocabulary as necessary. Encourage students to use expressions from Exercise 10. Students practise their conversation in pairs. Listen to some of the best conversations in open class.

12 Team Spirit DVD Episode 7

a – b Look at the photo with students and ask them to guess answers to the questions. Listen to some of their ideas in open class.

c Divide the class into pairs. Ask students to discuss the questions. Do they have any other good luck charms or mascots?

d Play the DVD while students watch episode 7 and check their answers.

13 Write

The preparation for this can be done in class and the writing task set for homework.

a Divide the class into pairs. Students read the instructions and then the email and find the three reasons for his lateness. Check answers.

> **Example answers**
> His watch broke and he didn't know what time it was.
> He had to walk because he'd missed the bus.
> He fell over a cat and got his trousers dirty.
> The second bus was late.

b **Stronger classes:** Students read the questions and then read the email again to find the answers. Check answers.

Weaker classes: You can elicit words they know for apologising and inviting before they do this exercise. They can then use those words to help them find Jack's words.

> **Answers**
> 1 apologise; really sorry; sorry again
> 2 Can we go out …?; Would you like to come with me …?

c Students read the instructions. Give them a few minutes to discuss some reasons in pairs. Ask for their suggestions and write them on the board.

Weaker classes: This can be done as a whole class activity. Elicit the reasons from students and write them on the board. Encourage student to think of reasons why they have been late for things.

UNIT 14   113

d **Stronger classes:** Students now plan their email using Jack's one as a model. Encourage students to think about how the email is structured and to think carefully about what they must put in each paragraph. Students complete the exercise. They can then send their emails to a partner to read.

Weaker classes: Go through Jack's email in more detail before students begin. Ask them to say what information is given in each paragraph:
Para 1: Reason for writing
Para 2: What happened
Para 3: A new invitation
Para 4: Signing off

Students then make notes for each paragraph of their own email using the information above. They can then expand their notes into full sentences and swap with a partner to check. After their draft is checked, they can write their final version and send them to a new partner to read.

14 Last but not least: more speaking

Warm up

Write *The early bird catches the worm* on the board. Tell students that this type of phrase is called a saying because it has a meaning other than its literal meaning (If you get there first, you will be successful). Ask students if they can think of any sayings in their own language and listen to some of their ideas.

a Divide the class into pairs. Ask students to read the sayings and discuss their meanings. Circulate and help with vocabulary as necessary. Check answers.

> **Example answers**
> 1 Some people are always lucky.
> 2 Stupid people are always unlucky or not clever enough to realise when they are lucky.
> 3 People waste so much time looking for luck that they miss out on a lot of good things.
> 4 Luck is temporary.
> 5 You make your own luck.

b Students work individually to decide whether they agree with the sayings. Encourage them to think of reasons why / why not.

c In small groups, students choose three of the sayings and discuss their meaning and whether they agree with them. Feedback in open class.

d Ask individual students to tell you about a time when they were lucky. You may like to give them an example of your own to get them started.

Check your progress

1 Grammar

a 2 felt; hadn't slept   3 had; hadn't been
4 was; had forgotten   5 Had … lived; moved
6 Had … known; got married

b 2 My little brother said he wanted to go home.
3 He told the teacher he hadn't done his homework.
4 Luis said he would pay for the meal.
5 My aunt told me my brother couldn't come.
6 He said he had never been to the USA.

c 2 wouldn't have bought; had known
3 had known; would have told
4 would've phoned; hadn't forgotten
5 would you have done; had found

2 Vocabulary

a 2 collector   3 artist   4 journalist   5 plumber
6 receptionist   7 archaeologist

b 2 reservation   3 invitation   4 improvement
5 equipment   6 information   7 calculation

How did you do?

Check that students are marking their scores. Collect these in and check them as necessary and discuss any further work needed with specific students.

Memo from Mario

A stroke of luck

1 Near-miss third conditional stories

- Here is an alternative way of presenting the so-called third conditional.
- In preparation, think of a time when you or someone you know had a close shave.
- Prepare to end your story with a third conditional, a bit like this:

I left the toddler in the car to go to the chemists'.
He clambered out of the driver's door.
A lorry just stopped in time.
If the lorry wheel had been a centimetre closer, it would have killed the child.

- It is your near-miss story that will move your students, not mine nor that of anybody on a page.
- In the lesson tell the students your near-miss story. Write your punch line on the board.
- Ask if anyone in the class has had a close shave with disaster or knows of someone who has.
- When a student volunteers, help them to tell their story to the class. Supply vocabulary and elicit their third conditional punch line.
- Repeat with a couple more students in open class.
- Ask the students to work in groups of four to come up with their near-miss stories and their final lines.
- After this oral phase ask around ten students to come up and write their punch lines on the board. Help to get these correct.
- If there is curiosity about the stories behind the third conditional sentences, let some students tell theirs to the whole class.

> **RATIONALE**
> Many people find they can assimilate L2 grammar most quickly when they meet it in a firmly affective context, as this near-miss one certainly is.
>
> In this activity, weaker students will need a great deal of help.

2 Success stories

- When you prepare your students for exams it is useful to help them to walk into the exam hall feeling good about themselves. Knowing the English you have tried to teach them is vital to exam success, but so is measured self-confidence.
- One way to boost this is to do a couple of lessons on success stories with them in the week before the exam.
- In preparation, think of a success story of your own – this could be a success in sport, cooking, teaching, painting or a success in your own inner thinking process.
- In class tell your success story to the group.
- Put the students in groups of four to tell their own success stories. Go round the class helping with language.
- In the case of the weakest students, let them tell their stories in their mother tongue.
- Round off the class by asking a couple of mother tongue tellers to re-tell their stories to the group.
- Get the students to shout out the English for what they are saying, and write this on the board, modifying it where necessary.
- Suggest that the students should bring their success stories back to mind as they enter the exam hall. You want them to walk tall.

> **RATIONALE**
> Just as you can shake your self-confidence by dwelling on bad moments from the past, so too can you change your body's feeling by recalling past highs. It is vital for students who are less sure of themselves to be given the chance to publicly shine on the eve of exams.
>
> For more thinking of this sort and more practical exam-lead-up exercises see Judy Baker's book, *Unlocking Self-expression through NLP* (Delta, 2005).

Pronunciation

Unit 1 Exercise 3
✱ *was* and *were*

a ▶ CD1 T6   Students turn to page 110 and read through items 1 to 3. Write the first item on the board. Play the recording, pausing it after the first item to do as an example. Ask a student to come out and underline or circle as appropriate. Remind students that they are circling when the form is weak and underlining when the form is stressed. Play the recording for students to complete the exercise. Check answers.

Weaker classes: They may find it helpful to listen to the recording twice, once for weak forms and the second time for stressed forms.

TAPESCRIPT/ANSWERS
1   He wasn't watching TV.
4   (Was) it raining?
5   Yes, it was.

b ▶ CD1 T7   Write the first sentence on the board and say it yourself as an example and ask if *were* is stressed or unstressed (unstressed). Circle *were*.

Play the recording for students to listen and circle or underline *were/weren't*. Students can compare answers in pairs. Play the recording again for students to check or change their answers.

Weaker classes: They may find it helpful to listen to the recording twice, once for weak forms and the second time for stressed forms.

TAPESCRIPT/ANSWERS
1   What were they doing?
2   (Were) they listening to music?
3   No, they weren't.

c ▶ CD1 T7   Play the recording again, pausing for students to repeat.

Unit 2 Exercise 4
✱ *than* and *as*

a ▶ CD1 T12   Students turn to page 110 and read through sentences 1 to 4. Play the recording, pausing it after the first item and go through the example. Play the recording again for students to listen and underline the stressed syllables. Play the recording again, pausing as necessary for students to check or change their answers.

TAPESCRIPT/ANSWERS
1   Sarah's brother isn't as old as her.
2   Peter isn't as messy as his sister.
4   Travelling by train is faster than travelling by bus.
5   Jo thinks Spanish is easier than French.

b ▶ CD1 T12   Play the recording, pausing for students to listen to the pronunciation of *as* and *than*. Play the recording again, pausing for students to repeat each sentence.

Unit 3 Exercise 5
✱ /əʊ/ *won't*

▶ CD1 T16   Students turn to page 110 and read through sentences 1 to 4. Play the recording, pausing after each sentence for students to repeat. If students are still having problems, play the recording again and drill the sound a few times.

TAPESCRIPT
1   I won't open it.
2   He won't answer the question.
3   She won't tell me.
4   They won't come.

Unit 4 Exercise 3
✱ Intonation in question tags

a ▶ CD1 T21   Students turn to page 110. Read through the explanation as a class and give students an example of your own for each type of intonation. Ask students to say if your voice goes up or down at the end of each question. Students now read through questions 1 to 6. Play the recording, pausing it after question 1 and go through this as a class. Make sure students understand that they only have to write U or D. Play the recording again for students to listen and complete the exercise. Check answers as a class, playing and pausing the recording as necessary.

TAPESCRIPT/ANSWERS
1   You're from Canada, aren't you? U
2   You're from Canada, aren't you? D
3   You don't know a lot about Canada, do you? D
4   There are 50 states in the USA, aren't there? U
5   People talk differently in the USA, don't they? U
6   You haven't been to New York, have you? D

b ▶ CD1 T21   Play the recording again, pausing after each question for students to repeat.

Unit 5 Exercise 6
✱ /aʊ/ allowed

a ▶ CD1 T29 Students turn to page 110 and read through words 1 to 6. Play the recording, pausing after the first word for students to repeat. Make sure students are pronouncing them correctly. Continue playing the recording, pausing after each word for students to repeat.

TAPESCRIPT

1	now	4	shout
2	how	5	loud
3	out	6	allowed

b ▶ CD1 T30 Students read through items 1 to 4 and underline the /aʊ/ sound. Go through the first one with them as an example, if necessary. Play the recording for students to listen and check or change their answers. Play the recording again, pausing after each item for students to repeat.

TAPESCRIPT/ANSWERS

1 H<u>ow</u> are you n<u>ow</u>?
2 I'm all<u>ow</u>ed to go <u>ou</u>t.
3 We're all<u>ow</u>ed to play l<u>ou</u>d music.
4 You aren't all<u>ow</u>ed to sh<u>ou</u>t.

Unit 6 Exercise 3
have, has and *for*

a ▶ CD1 T33 Students turn to page 110 and read through the sentences. Play the recording, pausing it after the first item and go through this as an example, making sure students understand which words are stressed. Play the recording again for students to listen and underline the stressed words in the other items. Check answers.

TAPESCRIPT/ANSWERS

1 <u>How long</u> have you <u>lived</u> here?
  For <u>three years</u>.
2 <u>How long</u> has she <u>worked</u> in <u>London</u>?
  For a <u>year</u>.

b ▶ CD1 T33 Discuss the pronunciation of *has/have* and *for* as a class, making sure students are clear about how to pronounce them. Play the recording again, pausing for students to repeat.

Unit 7 Exercise 3
✱ 'Silent' letters

▶ CD1 T38 Students turn to page 110. Read through the instructions as a class and elicit some examples of words with silent letters. Students read through words 1 to 6. Go through the first word as an example, then students underline the silent letters in the other words. Students can compare answers in pairs. Play the recording for students to check or change their answers. Play the recording again, pausing after each word for students to repeat.

TAPESCRIPT/ANSWERS

1	bom<u>b</u>	4	ans<u>w</u>er
2	bu<u>i</u>ld	5	mount<u>ai</u>n
3	<u>k</u>nocked	6	woul<u>d</u>

✱ **OPTIONAL ACTIVITY**

Stronger classes: In pairs, students think of as many words as they can with silent letters and write sentences using as many of them as they can. Can they write one sentence (or short paragraph) which makes sense and uses them all? Students can swap sentences and ask other pairs to read out theirs.

Weaker classes: In pairs, students think of as many words as they can with silent letters. Students can then practise saying them.

Unit 8 Exercise 3
✱ Sound and spelling: *-ou*

a ▶ CD2 T4 Ask students to turn to page 111 and read the words. Play the recording, pausing after each word for students to repeat. If they are still having problems, play the recording again or drill the problem words as a class.

TAPESCRIPT

1	enough	3	famous
2	out	4	could

b Divide the class into pairs. Ask students to read through the words in the box and decide which sound of *-ou* they have. Listen to some of their ideas in open class, but do not give the answers at this stage.

ANSWERS

en<u>ou</u>gh: tough, young   fam<u>ou</u>s: dangerous
<u>ou</u>t: house, around, found   c<u>ou</u>ld: would, should

c ▶ CD2 T5 Play the recording for students to listen and check. Play the recording again, pausing after each word for students to repeat.

✱ **OPTIONAL ACTIVITY**

In pairs, students make one sentence using as many of the *-ou* words as they can in it. Ask pairs to read out their sentences to the rest of the class. The class can vote on the best sentence.

Unit 9 Exercise 8
must

a ▶ CD2 T13 Students turn to page 111. Read out the first sentence and ask students if *must* is stressed or unstressed (*unstressed*).

Stronger classes: Students read through the instructions. Make sure they remember to circle *must* if it is weak and underline *must* if it is stressed. Play the recording for students to circle and underline *must* as appropriate.

Weaker classes: Play the recording twice. The first time, ask them only to listen and circle weak *must*. Play it a second time and ask them to underline *must* when it is stressed.

Check answers, playing and pausing the recording again as necessary.

TAPESCRIPT/ANSWERS
1 I (must) go now, it's late.
2 You must see that film, it's great!
3 You must do your homework!
4 I (must) start doing some exercise!

b and **c** ▶ CD2 T13 Students read through the questions. Elicit the answers, saying the sentences yourself for students to hear them again, if necessary. Play the recording again, pausing for students to repeat each sentence.

> **Answers**
> Sentences 2 and 3. Sentence 2 is a strong recommendation and sentence 3 is personal obligation.
> The 't' in *must* isn't pronounced when *must* is weak.

Unit 10 Exercise 3
Sentence stress: rhythm

a ▶ CD2 T16 Students turn to page 111 and read through sentences 1 to 4. Go through the example as a class, either reading it out yourself or playing and pausing the recording. Students underline the stressed syllables in the other sentences. Students can compare answers in pairs. Play the recording, pausing after each sentence for students to check or change their answers. Play the recording again if necessary to clarify any problems.

TAPESCRIPT/ANSWERS
1 How long has she been playing the violin?
2 I haven't been learning English very long.
3 I've been waiting for you for ages.
4 How long have we been walking?

b ▶ CD2 T16 Play the recording again, pausing after each sentence for students to repeat.

Unit 11 Exercise 5
/z/ or /s/ in *used*

a ▶ CD2 T24 Students turn to page 111 and read through the instructions and sentences 1 to 4. Check any problems. Explain that the sentences focus on the verb *used to* and *used*. Write the first sentence on the board. Play the recording, pausing it after the first sentence and go through this as an example. Ask a student to come out and circle or underline the sound in *used*. Make sure students understand the difference in the sound of each verb at this point. Play the recording again while students listen and complete the exercise.

Weaker classes: It may help students to play the recording twice, first to listen for the /z/ sound and circle it, then a second time to listen for the /s/ sound and underline it. Students can compare answers in pairs. Do not give answers at this point.

b ▶ CD2 T24 Play the recording, pausing it as necessary for students to check their answers. The 'd' in *used* is silent in these examples because the following word starts with a consonant (the 'd' in *used* is pronounced if the following word starts with a vowel – as in *I used a lot of water*).

TAPESCRIPT/ANSWERS
1 I (used) the dictionary.
2 I used to watch a lot of videos.
3 Who (used) the computer?
4 John used to live in London.

c ▶ CD2 T24 Play the recording again, pausing after each sentence for students to repeat. If students are still having problems with the pronunciation, drill a few more times as a class.

Unit 12 Exercise 3
'd

a ▶ CD2 T29 Students turn to page 111 and read through sentences 1 to 4. Play the recording, pausing after the first sentence and go through this as an example. Play the recording again for students to listen and complete the exercise. Remind them to circle the word they hear. Check answers, playing and pausing the recording again as necessary.

TAPESCRIPT/ANSWERS
1 I (read) a book.
2 I ('d go) for a walk.
3 I ('d close) the window.
4 I (talk) to the teacher about it.

b ▶ CD2 T30   Students read through sentences 1 to 4. Play the recording, pausing after each sentence for students to repeat.

TAPESCRIPT

1 I'd go to the doctor.
2 I'd study harder.
3 I'd look on the Internet.
4 I'd go to the library.

Unit 13 Exercise 3
✱ *had* and *'d*

a ▶ CD2 T36   Students turn to page 111 and read through the instructions. Play the recording, pausing it after the first sentence and go through this as an example. Make sure students know they must circle the weak forms and underline the strong forms. Play the rest of the recording while students listen and complete the exercise.

Weaker classes: Students may find it useful to listen once for the weak forms and a second time for the stressed forms. Do not give answers at this point.

TAPESCRIPT/ANSWERS

1 I <u>had</u> a strange dream last night.
2 It was like a dream that (had) come true.
3 My dad <u>had</u> no time to help me.
4 Other explorers (had) looked for the city, but they <u>hadn't</u> found it.

b ▶ CD2 T36   Students read the question. Elicit that when *had* is in the past simple, it is stressed. Play the recording again for students to listen and check their answers. Play the recording again, pausing after each sentence for students to repeat.

Unit 14 Exercise 7
✱ *would ('d) have / wouldn't have*

a ▶ CD3 T5   Students turn to page 111 and read through sentences 1 to 4. Play the recording, pausing it after the first sentence for students to hear the pronunciation of the underlined part clearly. Elicit the answer to the question (*have* is shortened to /ə/ in third conditional sentences because it is a weak form).

TAPESCRIPT

1 <u>I'd have</u> been OK.
2 My glasses <u>wouldn't have</u> broken.
3 I <u>wouldn't have</u> been late.
4 <u>We'd have</u> seen the film.

b ▶ CD3 T5   Play the recording again, pausing after each sentence for students to repeat. Make sure students are using the same rhythm. If students are still having problems, drill the sentences as a class.

PRONUNCIATION   119

Get it right! key

Unit 1 Phrases with *get*
Students' answers

Unit 1 Past simple
1 gave; said   2 took   3 think   4 enjoyed   5 wore

Unit 2
1 quickly   2 wonderful   3 easy   4 usually
5 easily   6 finally

Unit 4
1 I haven't found a good website yet for our school project.
2 I have already seen them in concert.
3 He hasn't been abroad yet.
4 John's already gone out.

Unit 5
1 They let her come home after midnight but she isn't allowed to invite friends to stay the night.
2 They let her use the computer and internet but she isn't allowed to use the telephone for international calls.
3 They let her swim in the swimming pool but she isn't allowed to keep food in her room.

Unit 6
1 made   2 have   3 make   4 go   5 made
6 make   7 done   8 making   9 Do

Unit 7
[a] 1 My mum bought me a new guitar.
2 I'm going to the beach with my friends.
3 This is an interesting book – why don't you read it?
4 I hope to see a lot of new places like the British Museum when I'm in London.

[b] 1 No 'the'
2 Add 'the' before 'dolphins'
3 No 'the'
4 'an'
5 No 'the'

Unit 9
[a] 1 someone   2 anything   3 never   4 Everyone
5 anything   6 nobody   7 ever

[b] Students' answers

Unit 10
1 has finished
2 has been making
3 have learnt
4 has been studying
5 has won

Unit 11
2 surgeon   3 sore throat   4 backache
5 antiseptic   6 temperature   7 crutches
8 wheelchair   9 bandage   10 headache

Unit 12
1 No preposition   2 on   3 in   4 on

Unit 13
1 had already been   2 was   3 had snowed
4 told us   5 got   6 had given   7 ate   8 were
9 had put   10 sent

Unit 14
[a] 1 b   2 a   3 b
[b] 1 tell   2 explained (or said)   3 told   4 said
5 say   6 explained

Project 1
A group presentation

Divide the class into groups of three or four. Read through the instructions with the class.

Exercise 1c could be set as a research task, giving students more time to research their invention.

1 Do your research

a Students read the instructions and look at the pictures. Give them a few minutes to choose their invention or to think of their own idea.

b Students read through the instructions and the model on the page. Each group should appoint someone to take notes at this stage.

c Read the instructions. Students should brainstorm ideas for resources: names of magazines, newspapers, books they have heard of, website addresses, or people that could recommend these resources (librarians, parents, teachers etc.).

If you set this as a homework research task, ask students to share their information and visuals with the rest of the group. Alternatively, give students time to search the Internet or look up the invention in an encyclopaedia and to find some pictures.

2 Prepare the presentation

a Students work on this in class. They will need to go through all the information they have collected, and decide what they are going to use, and how. Tell them that the presentation should be a minimum of two minutes and a maximum of ten minutes.

If you have time, a presentation can take the form of a large poster, with handwritten or printed text, pictures, photos, drawings or real objects. Students can then use the poster as a background for the spoken presentation.

b Group members decide who is going to talk and what they are going to talk about. Check that everyone has a speaking role, no matter how small.

c Give groups time to decide on a way to present their information. They will need to practise the presentation. They can do this in their groups in class, or, if this is too noisy, you could ask certain groups to work outside the classroom (if possible). Monitor and check students are using the correct language and pronunciation and support them as necessary.

d Students should make their presentations in the next lesson, voting for the best presentation.

Project 2
A poster presentation

Divide the class into groups of three or four.

1 Do your research

a Read through the instructions as a class and look at the photos.

Each group decides which type of house they are going to write about. Give them a few minutes to do this and monitor the discussions, making sure each student has a chance to voice their opinion.

b Students read through the instructions and think about the questions they may want to answer. They should brainstorm ideas for resources: names of magazines, newspapers, books they have heard of, website addresses, or people that could recommend these resources (librarians, parents, teachers etc.).

Give students time to search the Internet or look in an encyclopaedia to find some pictures or set this as a homework research task.

c Students read through the instructions. Encourage groups to think about the information they want to include and why they find it interesting. They should make notes at this point on the different types of houses they have chosen.

2 Make the poster

a This part of the project can be set for homework. As a class, brainstorm ideas for finding visuals, website addresses, magazines, comics, etc. Students should bring in their visuals to the next lesson.

b Students look at the pictures the group has collected and select a few to illustrate their poster. The groups must agree on the visuals. Students work in their groups and write short texts about the houses they are going to include on their poster. This should be done on rough paper. When students are satisfied that their texts are written correctly and grammatically, they can transfer them to the poster.

c Supply each group with a large sheet of paper, sticky tape or glue, for them to make their posters. They should write the title at the top. Make sure they leave space for writing at the bottom.

d Students now write their personal opinions of the houses they chose on their posters. Students can check their texts in their groups before deciding on final versions and sticking them on to their poster.

PROJECTS

e Each group should prepare a short presentation to explain their poster to the rest of the class. Encourage other groups to ask questions about posters. Posters can then be displayed on the classroom walls and students can vote for the best poster and presentation.

Project 3
A class survey

1 Do the survey

You may find it useful to take in some magazine questionnaires with you for this lesson. You may find it useful to make copies of the questionnaires before students do Exercise 1b.

a Read through the instructions with the class. Go through the example with them, drawing their attention to the different types of questions. Remind them to use different forms of questions to make their survey more interesting.

b Students read through the model questionnaire (or show them some examples from magazines if you have brought them in). Students then prepare their own questions. Remind them to think about various possibilities for the answers to their questions.

Weaker classes: They can use the first three questions from the model questionnaire and then add three questions of their own.

Monitor and check that each member of the group is noting down the questions, since they will all need to ask the questions in Exercise 1c.

c Students ask the others in their group the questions and note down their answers. Then students circulate round the class asking as many students as they can, noting down their answers. Monitor and check students are using the correct question forms and intonation and pronunciation. Note down any problems to discuss at the end of the lesson.

2 Write up the results

a Students regroup in their original questionnaire group (from Exercise 1) and discuss their answers. They can work out how many people they interviewed and what percentage answered in the same way. Monitor and help as necessary.

b Read through the example with the class and show how it relates to the example question in Exercise 1b. Using their own information from Exercise 2, students now write sentences to describe their results. Make sure each student in the group completes this task. Monitor and help as necessary. Ask students to feed back to the rest of the class. Were there any interesting results? If so, discuss these further as a class.

Students can transfer all their sentences onto a poster and add illustrations if they want.

Project 4
Designing a website

Divide the class into small groups of three or four.

1 Prepare your website

a Students read the instructions and questions. They then look at the pictures and read the web page and answer the questions. Check answers.

> **Answers**
> 1 Four students.
> 2 The name of the school, number of students, subjects, sports activities, clubs and teachers.

b **Stronger classes:** Using the web page as a model, give students time to think about their own school and the kind of information they want to include on their website.

Weaker classes: You can write the following question prompts on the board:
Name of school?   Sports?
When opened?   Clubs?
How many pupils? Teachers?
Which subjects?

Encourage students to note down the information for each prompt in their groups.

c Students read the instructions and read the web page again to find out the links.

d Students think about the kind of photos they would like to include. Encourage them to think about how the pictures will link with the texts.

2 Make your website

a Using the model on page 125, students write a rough version of their own home page with the information they discussed in Exercise 1b. Encourage them to think about unique qualities of their school. Remind them to write the copy for their link pages, using the notes they made in Exercise 1c.

Once students are happy with their draft versions, they can transfer the information onto their large sheets of paper.

b Display the web pages around the class where students can read each other's work. Students could vote for the best website.

Workbook key

Welcome section

A

1 2 has 3 's getting 4 's wishing 5 washes 6 's singing 7 likes

2

E	P	L	A	Y	I	N	G	R	I
N	R	I	N	N	O	N	O	U	N
R	E	S	W	I	M	M	I	N	G
E	L	T	I	R	R	A	N	I	N
A	Y	E	M	B	U	T	G	N	I
D	A	N	C	I	N	G	L	G	T
I	I	I	G	N	R	O	S	N	
N	E	N	O	T	I	N	G	I	I
G	N	G	S	A	N	T	N	N	A
P	L	A	I	N	G	O	I	N	P

3 2 pilot 3 shop assistant 4 firefighter 5 lawyer 6 vet 7 architect 8 flight attendant 9 teacher 10 doctor

B

1 2 much 3 many 4 many 5 much 6 much

2 In any order
2 There aren't any bananas.
3 There is some milk.
4 There isn't any coffee.
5 There aren't any tomatoes.
6 There are some apples.
7 There isn't any tea.
8 There is some bread.

3 2 smallest 3 better 4 most 5 highest 6 bigger 7 best 8 worse

4 2 up 3 out 4 off 5 out 6 up

C

1 2 'll rain tomorrow 3 won't go swimming 4 won't go to Italy

2 2 well 3 happy 4 quickly 5 badly 6 bad 7 carefully 8 honestly

3 2 's going to read 3 's going to go 4 are going to

4 2 in two years' time 3 next month 4 the day after tomorrow 5 in two hours' time 6 the week after next

D

1 2 I'll buy a bike if my parents give me money for my birthday.
3 If we don't play well, we won't win the game.
4 If you listen to music all day, you won't pass your exams.

2 2 cool 3 fantastic 4 dull

3 2 miserable 3 polite 4 relaxed 5 friendly 6 disorganised 7 lazy 8 honest

4 2 've never slept 3 Have [you] ever been 4 've never been 5 's never spent 6 Have [you] ever eaten 7 've never tried

1 Great idea!

1 a Rubber – produce toys – chewing gum
Mice – supply of potatoes – mouse trap
After lunch – mountain of dishes – dishwasher
Summer – ice skates – roller skates

b 2 chewing gum 3 roller skates 4 windscreen wipers 5 mouse trap

2 a 2 was dancing 3 were sitting 4 was drawing 5 were laughing 6 were kissing 7 was trying

b 2 weren't cooking 3 wasn't reading 4 wasn't having a shower 5 wasn't sleeping 6 weren't eating

c 2 eating a sandwich
3 Was Mike looking out of the window? Yes, he was.
4 Were my parents cooking dinner? No, they weren't. They were talking.
5 Was I watching TV? Yes, I was.
6 Were my grandparents eating dinner? No, they weren't. They were sleeping.

d 2 were you playing 3 were they going 4 were you talking 5 was he holding 6 was she waiting

3 a 2 get angry 3 got / confused 4 got wet 5 got home 6 get dry

b 2 get together 3 gets a lot of pleasure 4 got sick 5 get a chance 6 got a phone call

4 a 2 was having / rang 3 was watching / ate 4 stole / was swimming 5 fell / was playing 6 was sunbathing / jumped

b 2 We were listening to music when the lights went off.

WORKBOOK KEY 123

The lights went off when we were listening to music.
3 I was running on the beach when I lost my keys.
I lost my keys while I was running on the beach.
4 I was talking to my friend when somebody stole my bag.
Somebody stole my bag while I was talking to my friend.
5 You were taking the dog for a walk when Danny called.
Danny called while you were taking the dog for a walk.
6 I was getting ready for the beach when it started to rain.
It started to rain while I was getting ready for the beach.

C Possible answers:
2 my friends were having a fight.
3 my father told a story.
4 my friend phoned me
5 I fell asleep
6 the sun was shining

5 ▶ CD3 T8 TAPESCRIPT/ANSWERS
3 A: She was <u>sleeping</u>.
  B: No, she <u>wasn't</u>! She was <u>reading</u>.
4 A: They were <u>kissing</u>.
  B: No, they <u>weren't</u>. They were <u>dancing</u>.
5 A: We were <u>doing</u> our <u>homework</u>.
  B: No, you <u>weren't</u>. You were <u>playing games</u>.
6 A: I wasn't <u>writing</u> a <u>letter</u>.
  B: Yes, you <u>were</u>!

6 1 paper rolls 2 radio 3 popular
4 wax cylinders 5 records 6 recordings
7 disks 8 steel needle 9 invented

7 1 a wax cylinder 2 vinyl records
3 a gramophone

8 **a** 1 T 2 F 3 N
   b 2 F 3 T 4 F 5 T

9 2 a 3 c 4 a

▶ CD3 T9 TAPESCRIPT

1
Boy: So, the Menches brothers ...
Girl: What, the people who say they invented the hamburger?
Boy: Yes. Well, they also say that once they were working at a fair, selling ice cream, and at that time people ate ice cream from dishes. Anyway, it was so busy that they didn't have any more dishes, so Charles, one of the brothers, noticed a man who was selling this kind of sweet pastry, he tasted it, then got the idea of rolling it into the shape of a cone! He bought everything the man had.
Girl: So that's how they invented the ice cream cone!

2
Girl: I read another story on the internet about 'Old Dave', another guy who said he invented the hamburger.
Boy: So what was that about?
Girl: Well, he said that he was selling chips with his hamburgers, except they didn't have a name for them then.
Boy: Americans call them French fries, don't they?
Girl: Well, yes, that's the point. A journalist asked Dave where he got the idea for his potatoes from, and he said 'Paris', meaning Paris, Texas. That's where he was from, you see.
Boy: And the journalist thought he meant Paris, France?
Girl: Exactly. So people started calling them French fries.
Boy: That can't be true! No way!

3
Girl: It's interesting, isn't it, how food was invented?
Boy: Yes – and what about this one? In about 1750 – you know, hundreds of years ago – an important man in England was really very busy, so busy that he didn't have time for lunch, and he asked his cook just to put some meat between two pieces of bread! And so we got ...
Girl: Sandwiches?
Boy: That's right.
Girl: But why that name?
Boy: Because the man in England lived in a town called Sandwich.
Girl: You're joking!
Boy: No, I'm not – it's true!

4
Girl: And did you ever hear about Thomas Adams?
Boy: No. What about him?
Girl: Well, he had some stuff called 'chicle' – a bit like rubber, you know? From trees in Mexico. And he tried to make car tyres with it, and he tried to make rubber shoes with it, but nothing worked.
Boy: What has this got to do with food?
Girl: Well, one day, he was thinking, and he put a piece of this 'chicle' in his mouth – and he started chewing it, and he liked it!
Boy: Oh, no! Don't tell me! Chewing gum?
Girl: That's right. He invented chewing gum! He started selling it in 1871.

Unit check

1 1 didn't hear 2 get 3 got to school
4 got a horrible surprise 5 got nervous
6 didn't get 7 was shining 8 was getting
9 got wet

2 2 b 3 c 4 a 5 a 6 a 7 a 8 a 9 c

3 2 remote control 3 windscreen wipers
4 engine 5 invented 6 got to 7 idea
8 a chance 9 surprise

2 He ran faster

1 2 slower 3 shorter 4 best 5 more than

2 a) 2 worst 3 the oldest 4 much tidier
5 older 6 the cleverest

b) 2 the happiest 3 the tallest 4 better
5 the most expensive 6 the most successful

c) 2 Today is a bit colder than yesterday.
3 A Ferrari is much faster than a Fiat.
4 Mrs James is far younger than Mr James.

3 a) 2 quiet 3 fast 5 boring 6 cold
7 beautiful 9 tidy Mystery word: difficult

b) easy

4 a) 2 e 3 a 4 b 5 f 6 c

b) 2 is not as tall as his brother
3 is not as expensive as the PC
4 is not as thin as the dog
5 is not as good as Liverpool
6 is as cold as yesterday

5 a) 2 slowly 3 easily 4 happily 5 fast
6 badly 7 well 8 hard

b) 2 fast 3 drives slowly 4 write clearly
5 types quickly 6 it well / easily

c)
	Paul	David	Fred	Richard
Height	1.7m	1.5m	1.6m	1.8m
Money in bank	£50	£200	£100	£200
Grade in French test	F	B	A	C
Position in school Olympics 100m	4th	1st	2nd	3rd

6 a) ▶ CD3 T10 TAPESCRIPT/ANSWERS
2 as black as night 3 as quick as a flash
4 as strong as an ox 5 as busy as a bee
6 as white as snow

b) Students' own answers

7 2 we're talking about 3 guess what
4 that's not the point 5 that sort of thing
6 at the end of the day

8 2 a 3 g 4 b 5 h 6 c 7 f 8 e

9 a) Students' own answers

b) 1 A 2 C 3 D 4 F 5 E 6 B

10 2 a 3 b

▶ CD3 T11 TAPESCRIPT

Boy 1: So I guess you had a great time eh, Phil?
Boy 2: Well yes – I mean, the World Cup Final, Italy and France – brilliant! My dad and I really enjoyed it. In that wonderful new stadium – fantastic.
Boy 1: What did you enjoy most?
Boy 2: Well, you know, it wasn't the most exciting match ever, to be honest – but at the very end there were penalties, you know, to decide the winner, and wow, that was so exciting! So I guess that was the best bit.
Boy 1: What did you do when the match finished?
Boy 2: Well, we decided to stay a bit, you know, we saw the Italians getting the Cup and we watched the fans celebrating, so in the end, we didn't leave the ground until about an hour after the match.
Boy 1: And what did you do afterwards?
Boy 2: Well, my dad and I were just really, really hungry! So we went back into the city and we found an Italian restaurant to have some pizza …
Boy 1: An Italian restaurant!!??
Boy 2: Yes – it was full of Italians, singing and celebrating, it was just brilliant!
Boy 1: That sounds great.
Boy 2: It was … and then the next morning we …

11 a) The second one – there's more description.
1 It was a fantastic experience / thousands of people / couldn't wait to get to our seats
2 huge, modern; happy; excitedly
Fantastic; excited; huge; modern; early; happy; excitedly
3 so; and; and
4 thousands of people; we arrived at the huge, modern stadium.

b) Possible answers
2 My alarm clock didn't ring so I was late for work.
3 The meal was incredibly nice.
4 My favourite restaurant is Italian. It's the best restaurant in town.

WORKBOOK KEY 125

Unit check

1 1 difficult 2 quiet 3 tidy 4 near 5 easy
6 boring 7 new 8 young

2 2 c 3 a 4 a 5 c 6 b 7 a 8 c 9 a

3 2 best 3 easy 4 as fast 5 nil 6 referee
7 drew 8 noisy 9 most interesting 10 messy

3 Our world

1 2 a 3 f 4 b 5 c 6 e

2 [a] 2 F 3 A 4 B 5 E 6 D
[b] 2 P 3 C 4 P 5 C 6 P 7 P
[c] 2 a 3 b 4 d 5 c 6 e 7 f
[d] 2 might go 3 might not do 4 'll be
5 might not take 6 might have
7 won't do 8 'll be

3 [a] 2 fumes 3 pollution 4 atmosphere
5 power station 6 recycling 7 rubbish
8 litter
[b] 2 f 3 b 4 a 5 g 6 d 7 e
[c] 1 forests 2 fumes 3 pollution
4 warming 5 litter 6 picking 7 clean
8 rubbish 9 recycle

4 [a] 1 cut down 2 will rise 3 goes up
4 will start 5 won't get 6 dies 7 will be
[b] 2 Will you buy me a present if I'm good?
3 I'll give James your message if I see him.
4 Will they arrive late if it rains?
5 What will you do if he doesn't phone?
6 My sister will lend me her mobile if I ask her.
7 If you haven't got any money, I'll give you some.
[c] 2 Unless 3 if 4 If 5 if 6 unless
[d] Students' own answers

5 ▶ CD3 T12 TAPESCRIPT/ANSWERS
2 They want to go to bed.
3 I won't be here.
4 So you want to play squash?
5 I think you might be right.
6 You said you're my teacher.

6 1 use one per cent
2 we cannot reach
3 polar ice caps
4 needs to be moist
5 have access to
6 called evaporation

7 [b] Noun / environmental
[c] 1 pollution 2 pollute 3 energetic
4 powerful 5 waste 6 wasteful
7 increase 8 warmth 9 warm
10 recycling 11 recycle

8 2 ✓ 3 ✓ 4 ✗ 5 ✗ 6 ✓

▶ CD3 T13 TAPESCRIPT

Aunt June: So what's your school like, Mike? I mean, I know you like sports – has the school got good facilities?

Mike: Oh, yeah. There's a really good gym, and really big sports fields. The sports facilities are great!

Aunt June: Do you have lunch at school?

Mike: Yes, I do – and actually, the food is pretty good. It's the usual thing, you know: hamburgers, pizzas, chips, that kind of thing, but I like it!

Aunt June: OK, good. But tell me about the teachers.

Mike: Aha, the teachers! Well, you know, you can't have a school without teachers! And the teachers at our school, they're OK. I mean, some are better than others, of course, but most of the teachers are nice.

Aunt June: Good!

Mike: But the problem is, I think the lessons are too short. All the lessons are 45 minutes. Well, sometimes we get double lessons, an hour and a half, but 45 minutes really is too short, I think.

Aunt June: That's interesting! Not many students at school complain about the lessons being too short! What else don't you like?

Mike: Hmm. Well, I think the uniform's awful! Green and black! It's horrible. And I hate wearing ties – and of course we have to wear a green and black tie.

Aunt June: And I'm sure you hate the school rules too!

Mike: Actually, no! The rules are OK. You know, the usual things: no running in corridors, no mobile phones in the classroom, things like that. But I think the rules are OK.

Aunt June: Wow! So it seems like it's not a bad school.

9 [a] 1 the lessons, the facilities and the meals
2 write an article for the school website saying what is wrong with the school and what they can do to improve it.
3 100 euros
[b] Students' own answer

Writing tip

a 2 4 1 6 3 5

b first of all; secondly; finally; for instance; to sum up

Unit check

1 1 fumes 2 pollute 3 will 4 may not
5 renewable energy 6 atmosphere 7 litter
8 waste 9 recycle

2 2 b 3 c 4 c 5 c 6 b 7 b 8 a 9 b

3 2 pollutes 3 cutting down 4 clean up
5 power station 6 waste 7 sanitation
8 rubbish 9 environment

4 Holiday or vacation?

1 2 a 3 c 4 b 5 c 6 c

2 **a** 2 aren't we 3 can't she 4 didn't they
5 doesn't he 6 can she 7 haven't they

b 3 ✓ 4 ✗ doesn't he? 5 ✗ didn't you?
6 ✓ 7 ✗ hasn't she? 8 ✗ should they?

c 2 didn't you 3 aren't you 4 won't you
5 isn't he 6 can't he 7 is it
8 shouldn't you

3 **a** ▶ CD3 T14 TAPESCRIPT/ANSWERS
3 doesn't she 4 do they 5 can't I
6 won't you

b 3 U 4 U 5 D 6 U

4 **a** 2 lift – elevator 3 trousers – pants
4 underground – subway
5 flat – apartment 6 rubbish – garbage

b 2 elevator 3 underground 4 vacation
5 trousers 6 sidewalk

c 2 fall – autumn 3 drapes – curtains
4 hood – bonnet 5 trunk – boot
6 line – queue

5 **a** 1 been 2 began 3 begun 4 come
5 drank 6 ate 7 gone 8 knew
9 known 10 seen 11 wrote 12 written

b 2 F 3 A 4 D 5 B 6 E

c 2 yet 3 already 4 yet 5 yet 6 already
7 yet 8 yet

d 2 Has Maria already gone to Sally's house?
Yes, but she hasn't come back yet.
3 I have already bought the new Killers CD.
Have you listened to it yet? / Have you already listened to it?
4 Have you already gone to sleep? / Have you gone to sleep yet?
No, and you have already asked me three times.

6 **a** 2 I've just phoned Jenny.
3 We've just arrived.
4 My parents have just gone out.
5 The film has just finished.

b 2 She's just bought an ice cream but she hasn't eaten it yet.
3 He's just written a letter but he hasn't posted it yet.
4 She's just bought a CD but she hasn't listened to it yet.

7 2 Have a look 3 in the middle of 4 the kind f thing 5 no wonder 6 you're not supposed to

9 **a** 2 ✓ 4 ✓ 6 ✓ 7 ✓

▶ CD3 T15 TAPESCRIPT

Josh: ... and American people are really friendly, very nice – only we had a few problems understanding them sometimes!

Sally: Really? Why? Because they use different words?

Josh: Well, sometimes – like, for example, we went to a restaurant the first night in New York, and at the end my dad asked for the bill and the waiter looked at him and said, 'Oh, you mean the check. OK, sir'!

Sally: Uh huh.

Josh: And of course in the hotels you see signs for elevators, not lifts, and in the bathrooms and toilets there are signs that ask you to turn off the faucets.

Sally: Faucets?

Josh: Yeah, you know, what we call taps in Britain.

Sally: Really? I didn't know that one.

Josh: Yeah, and you know we rented a car for a few days? Well, when we went to fill the car with petrol, my mum asked for 'petrol' and of course the guy didn't understand.

Sally: They call it 'gas', don't they?

Josh: That's right. And then of course there are things like trucks.

Sally: What we here in Britain call 'lorries', yeah?

Josh: Yeah, but the American ones are huge: they're about twenty metres long and have got twenty wheels or something!

Sally: And Americans certainly do pronounce things differently, too, don't they ...

b ▶ CD3 T16 TAPESCRIPT/ANSWERS
2 c 3 e 4 b 5 a

WORKBOOK KEY 127

10 Students' own answers

Unit check

1 1 popular 2 Have you heard 3 yet
4 apartment 5 already 6 subway
7 have a look 8 garbage 9 the kind of thing

2 2 b 3 c 4 c 5 a 6 a 7 a 8 a 9 c

3

V	O	T	R	U	C	K	A	C	v	E
M	C	J	G	R	W	Q	H	O	G	L
K	A	X	A	O	W	K	T	O	R	E
Y	N	W	R	U	S	K	Q	K	O	V
M	D	Q	B	B	G	L	B	I	T	A
Z	Y	H	A	D	K	A	Y	E	A	T
N	E	J	G	P	A	N	T	S	V	O
J	T	S	E	A	U	E	N	V	E	R
T	S	I	D	E	W	A	L	K	F	D
G	F	R	F	N	R	D	D	B	L	A
S	S	U	B	W	A	Y	S	Y	E	P
A	P	A	R	T	M	E	N	T	R	A

5 Growing up

1 2 a 3 d 4 b 5 c 6 e

2 a 2 is grown 3 is visited 4 's written
5 are made 6 are visited 7 are grown

b 2 e 3 b 4 f 5 a 6 c

c 2 Foreign money is changed here.
3 Colour films are developed here.
4 Fresh food is served here.
5 Cameras are repaired here.
6 English lessons are given here.

d 2 is sold every day
3 are designed in that company
4 are made in grammar exercises
5 A lot of new houses are built every year.
6 Football is often played on Saturdays.

3 a 2 child 3 pensioner 4 baby 5 toddler
6 adult

b 2 baby 3 child 4 teenager 5 pensioner
6 toddler

c 2 act your age 3 getting on 4 youth
5 Adulthood 6 look her age

4 a 2 I'm not allowed to watch TV until 11.30.
3 You're not allowed to cycle here.
4 The teacher doesn't let us leave early.
5 Our parents don't let us play football
in the garden.
6 My brother doesn't let me use his computer.

b 2 're not allowed to 3 're allowed to
4 're not allowed to 5 'm allowed to
6 're not allowed to

c 2 We're allowed to wear jeans to school.
3 We're not allowed to run in the school
corridor.
4 My sister lets our cat sleep on her bed.
5 My parents let me put posters on my wall.
6 Teenagers aren't allowed to go into that club.

5 a ▶ CD3 T17 TAPESCRIPT/ANSWERS
Know: show; low; throw; go
Now: sound; loud; round; shout; town; house;
down; allowed

b ▶ CD3 T18 TAPESCRIPT
(See page 33 of the Workbook.)

6 2 mustn't 3 can 4 can 5 aren't 6 are

7 /maʊs/; /ðəʊ/; /streɪt/; /kəʊm/

8 a To invite her to his 16th birthday party.
b No, she can't.
c 2 F 3 T 4 T 5 F 6 T

9 Students' own answers

Unit check

1 1 baby 2 given 3 toddler 4 child 5 let
6 adult 7 allowed to 8 get married
9 pensioner

2 2 a 3 a 4 b 5 b 6 a 7 c 8 a 9 b

3 2 come of age 3 childhood 4 at least
5 act your age 6 youth 7 underage
8 grounded 9 until

6 Have fun!

1 2 laugh 3 charity 4 need 5 has helped
6 travelled

2 a 2 a ✓; b ✗ 3 a ✗; b ✓ 4 a ✓; b ✗
5 a ✓; b ✗ 6 a ✓; b ✗

b 2 has been 3 has had 4 have told
5 have helped 6 has asked
7 have arranged

c 2 How long have you had
3 How long has she been
4 How long has he worked
5 How long have they been

d 1 has lived 2 loves 3 is 4 plays
5 hasn't played 6 want 7 has got 8 hope

WORKBOOK KEY

3 **a** 2 since; for 3 since; for 4 for; since
5 since; for 6 for; since

b 2 They have lived in this house since 2006.
They have lived in this house for X years.
3 I've been ill since Tuesday.
I've been ill for four days.
4 My aunt has had her car since 2008.
My aunt has had her car for X years.
5 We've had this computer since 2007.
We've had this computer for X years.

c 2 hasn't cut / for 3 hasn't phoned / since
4 haven't played / for 5 haven't been / since 6 haven't seen / for

d Students' own answers

4 **a** ▶ CD3 T19 TAPESCRIPT/ANSWERS
2 How long has he been there?
3 My parents have bought a new car.
4 James has gone home.

b ▶ CD3 T20 TAPESCRIPT/ANSWERS
2 We've lived here for a long time.
3 I've had this bike for three months.
4 We haven't eaten for two hours.

5 2 make 3 've made 4 made 5 had
6 making 7 made 8 made

6 1 What's the point of 2 as long as
3 come on 4 in other words 5 Know what

7 **b** has been interested; has already written; has been

8 2 a 3 b 4 a 5 c

Unit check

1 1 make me 2 for 3 makes fun 4 fun
5 time 6 made fools 7 funny faces
8 haven't 9 since

2 2 c 3 b 4 a 5 a 6 b 7 a 8 c 9 a

3 2 make 3 take 4 made 5 took 6 making
7 make 8 makes 9 takes

7 Disaster!

1 2 a 3 d 4 e 5 b

2 **a** 2 broken 3 sent 4 spoken 5 lost
6 given

b 2 was killed 3 was stolen 4 was found
5 wasn't invented 6 were sold

c 1 are broken 2 are damaged 3 was hit
4 were damaged 5 was destroyed
6 were killed 7 were introduced
8 are built

d 2 100,000 soldiers were killed in the war.
3 The door was left open last night.
4 All the books were printed on time.
5 The main railway station was closed yesterday.
6 All my money was stolen.
7 My suitcase was taken to my room.

e 1 lived 2 appeared 3 was pushed
4 was given 5 were killed
6 was produced 7 travelled 8 made
9 was heard 10 was thrown 11 produced

3 ▶ CD3 T21 TAPESCRIPT/ANSWERS
2 I wrote the wrong thing. 3 Listen to the answers. 4 They're climbing up a tall building.
5 They built a castle in the mountains.

4 **a** 2 hurricane 3 earthquake 4 floods
5 rescue 6 volcano 7 nuclear 8 killed
9 locust 10 tsunami 11 lost

b 2 on fire 3 homeless 4 catch fire
5 put out 6 starving 7 collapse
8 cracked

5 **a** 2 an 3 an 4 an 5 a 6 an / a
b 1 (–) no article 2 a 3 The 4 a 5 the
6 the

6 **a** 2 F 3 T 4 T 5 F 6 T 7 T
b 2 tiny 3 rough 4 threaten 5 Rising
6 source 7 reduce 8 refused

7 Students' own answers

8 2 Japan; 1710; 200,000
3 Portugal; 1755; 80,000
4 Ecuador; 1797; 40,000
5 China; 1556; 800,000

▶ CD3 T22 TAPESCRIPT

Interviewer: Good afternoon, Doctor Harris, thank you for coming on our programme.

Dr Harris: Good afternoon.

Interviewer: So, what do we know about terrible earthquakes in history?

Dr Harris: Well, we know that there were earthquakes before now – I mean, before our times – but of course we don't know exactly how big they were and how many people died.

Interviewer: But do we know about some of them?

Dr Harris: Well, we have a good idea. For example, there was an earthquake in Sicily, in southern Italy, in 1693. We think 60,000 people died. Then in about 1710 – er, we don't know for sure – in Japan, there was a city called Edo, where Tokyo now is, and ... erm ... we believe that 200,000 people or so were killed.

Interviewer: That's incredible. 200,000?

Dr Harris: Yes, that's right. Erm ... other great earthquakes ... erm ... well, the city of Lisbon, in Portugal, erm, in 1755, it was hit very badly, erm, about 80,000 people died. And in 1797, in Quito, Ecuador, over 40,000 people were killed.

Interviewer: So the one in Japan was the most terrible ever?

Dr Harris: Well, no. There was an earthquake in 1556, in China, in an area called Shaanxi ... erm ... There are records, you know. China's a very advanced civilisation, and ... erm ... we *think* that the number of people who were killed was about 800,000.

Interviewer: Good heavens! 800,000!!

Dr Harris: Yes indeed. It was probably the worst ever natural disaster to ....

9 a 2 He was 84 years old. 3 He lives in Mount St Helens in Washington. 4 The mountain exploded.

b Students' own answers

Unit check

1 1 killed 2 earthquakes 3 hurricanes 4 the 5 tsunami 6 floods 7 lose 8 volcano 9 destroy

2 2 c 3 c 4 a 5 b 6 c 7 a 8 b 9 c

3 2 emission 3 source 4 rough 5 hit 6 damaged 7 destroyed 8 disasters 9 damage

8 Ways of living

1 6; 2; 1; 8; 4; 7; 5; 3

2 a 2 There's too much noise in here.
3 I think we get too many tests at school.
4 Jack was sick because he ate too much ice cream yesterday.
5 I put too much sugar in my coffee.
6 You always ask me too many questions.

b 2 too many; not enough
3 too much; not enough
4 too many; not enough
5 too many; n't enough

3 a ▶ CD3 T23 TAPESCRIPT/ANSWERS
/aʊ/ out; /ʊ/ could; /ə/ famous

b ▶ CD3 T24 TAPESCRIPT
(See page 49 of the Workbook.)

4 a 1 garage 2 window 3 chimney 4 TV aerial 5 fence 6 door 7 garden

b Mystery word: bungalow 2 housing 3 chimney 4 garden 5 stairs 6 floor 7 cottage 8 window

c 1 central heating 2 basement 3 attic 4 roof 5 balcony 6 move house 7 share

5 a 2 Qinhai 3 tents 4 arm clothes 5 send Angie a postcard

b 3 B 4 A 5 A 6 B 7 B 8 A

c 2 E 3 B 4 A 5 F 6 D

d 2 'll 3 's going to 4 're going to 5 'll 6 'll 7 'll

6 a 2 If you say so 3 It's up to you 4 There's no point in arguing 5 There's nothing wrong with it 6 They're all over the place

b 2 There's nothing wrong with it.
3 They're all over the place.
4 There's no point in arguing.
5 It's up to you. 6 If you say so.

7 b 3 N 4 V 5 V 6 N 7 N 8 V 9 N 10 V

8 2 F 3 T 4 T 5 F 6 F 7 T

Unit check

1 1 semi-detached 2 garage 3 garden 4 too much 5 floor 6 chimney 7 housing 8 detached 9 enough

2 2 b 3 a 4 b 5 b 6 a 7 c 8 b 9 a

3 2 gate 3 balcony 4 caravan 5 bungalows 6 terraced 7 aerial 8 basement 9 attic

9 Your mind

1 2 2; 20 3 No one; everything; everyone 4 something; somebody 5 a small amount of; a small amount of

2 a 2 Some of them 3 somewhere 4 nowhere 5 everything 6 nothing 7 no one 8 none of them

130 WORKBOOK KEY

b 2 none of them 3 everywhere 4 Someone
5 none of them 6 nowhere

3 a 1 recognise 2 guess 3 imagine 4 believe
5 think 6 suppose 7 concentrate

b 2 visual 3 musical 4 mathematical
5 intrapersonal 6 verbal 7 naturalistic
8 interpersonal

c 2 knowledge 3 imagination 4 an estimate

4 a 2 must 3 mustn't 4 mustn't 5 mustn't
6 must 7 must

b 1 b You mustn't eat it.
2 a She mustn't walk b She doesn't have to walk
3 a You mustn't look b You don't have to look
4 a I mustn't move b I don't have to move

c 2 mustn't 3 mustn't 4 doesn't have to
5 mustn't 6 don't have to

d 2 doesn't have to 3 don't have to
4 mustn't 5 mustn't 6 doesn't have to
7 mustn't

5 a ▶ CD3 T25 TAPESCRIPT
(See page 57 of the Workbook.)

b ▶ CD3 T26 TAPESCRIPT
(See page 57 of the Workbook.)

6 2 Because she didn't speak her first words until she was 22 months.
3 She has studied several languages (six examples in the text).
4 No, she calls herself scatterbrained.
5 By delaying things until the last minute.
6 Because it helped her to be a normal teen (she had to fail in order to learn).

Writing tip

1 then 2 After that 3 in the end
4 Finally 5 then

8 a A 4 B 2 C 1 D 5 E 3

▶ CD3 T27 TAPESCRIPT

Mack: ... Oh Jane, you look like you've had an awful day!
Jane: Oh, I have! It's been terrible!
Mack: Why? What happened?
Jane: Well, this morning I was walking to school and I was almost there, and suddenly I remembered that today's Friday.
Mack: So?
Jane: Well, Friday's the day we have swimming at school – and I remembered that my swimming costume was at home, so I had to run back to get it. Then, when I got home, I couldn't remember where my costume was. It took me about fifteen minutes to find it.
Mack: So you were late for school.
Jane: Yes. The teacher had a real go at me when I got there! And you know, after that, things got even worse!
Mack: Worse?
Jane: Yes! In the afternoon there was an English test, and I wasn't prepared for it.
Mack: Why not?
Jane: Well, to be honest, I didn't remember that we had a test! Well, in the end it was OK – I *think* – I mean, I think I didn't do too badly.
Mack: Well, never mind. Anyway, I've got to go, but I'll see you at Tony's birthday party tonight, OK?
Jane: What? Oh, no! Tony's birthday! And I haven't bought him a present!
Mack: Oh, dear – you *have* got a bad memory!

b after that, in the end, suddenly

Unit check

1 1 remember 2 some of them 3 someone
4 imagine 5 forget 6 memorise
7 bad memory 8 remembers 9 remind

2 2 a 3 a 4 a 5 c 6 a 7 c 8 a 9 b

3 2 accepted 3 scatter brained 4 failing at
5 several 6 failures 7 last minute 8 baby talk
9 hangs out

10 Music makers

1 1 leader 2 percussionists 3 albums 4 area
5 violence 6 complex 7 tin cans
8 neighbourhood

2 a B 5 C 1 D 6 E 4 F 2

b 2 Have been trying 3 has been raining
4 have been tidying up 5 have been using
6 have you been doing; has been running

c 2 I have been working really hard.
3 The sun has been shining all day.
4 She hasn't been studying hard enough.
5 Have you been eating all morning?
6 Have you been waiting long?
7 Has he been cleaning his car?

3 a B 1 C 6 D 2 E 5 F 3

b 2 a ✗ b ✓ 3 a ✓ b ✗ 4 a ✗ b ✓
5 a ✓ b ✗ 6 a ✗ b ✓

WORKBOOK KEY 131

c 2 has wanted   3 have forgotten
   4 have done   5 has been talking
   6 has written   7 has been using
   8 have been tidying

d 1 21   2 has he lived   3 40   4 has he made
   5 30   6 has he been   7 has he worked /
   has he been working

4 ▶ CD3 T28 TAPESCRIPT/ANSWERS
1 B: I've been <u>waiting</u> for <u>three hours</u>!
2 A: <u>Where's</u> she been <u>living</u>?
   B: She's been <u>living</u> in <u>London</u>.
3 A: <u>What's</u> he been <u>doing</u>?
   B: He's been <u>looking</u> for a new <u>flat</u>.

5
a 2 rock   3 hip-hop   4 classical
   5 jazz /reggae

b 2 clarinet   3 violin   4 saxophone
   5 trumpet   6 flute   7 drums   8 guitar
   9 keyboards

c 2 MP3   3 to live   4 stereo   5 singles

d 2 an orchestra   3 conductor
   4 recording studio   5 a choir
   6 an open air concert

6
2 loads of   3 check it out   4 I'm just saying that
5 What do you mean   6 got nothing to do with

7
2 b   3 e   4 a   5 d

8
b 3   c 2   d 4

Unit check

1 1 has been collecting   2 has collected   3 singer
   4 listen   5 have been playing   6 plays   7 drums
   8 jazz   9 saxophone

2 2 c   3 c   4 b   5 b   6 b   7 c   8 c   9 b

3 2 violin   3 synthesizer   4 trumpet   5 piano
   6 keyboards   7 clarinet   8 flute   9 guitar

11 A visit to the doctor's

1
a 2 hospital   3 painful   4 health   5 patients
   6 injection; antiseptic   7 tablet   8 treat
   9 hurts   10 epidemic

b 2 a   3 f   4 b   5 c   6 e

c 2 hurt   3 temperature   4 stomach ache
   5 sore   6 pain   7 surgeon   8 vaccination

2
a 2 who   3 who   4 where   5 who   6 who
   7 where

b 2 where   3 that/which   4 which/that
   5 who   6 which/that   7 where   8 who

c 2 Andalusia is a place in Spain where you can
     spend a holiday in a cave.
   3 Lyon is a city in France in which a free
     bicycle scheme started many years ago.
   4 Evaporation is a process which puts water
     back into the atmosphere.
   5 Crocodile nests are huts which are used in
     a ceremony in Papua New Guinea.
   6 Pompeii is the city which was destroyed in
     the year 79 AD.

3
a 2 We used to go to the park.
   3 That shop used to be very cheap.
   4 Did your father use to play the guitar in
     a band?
   5 My brother didn't use to enjoy Maths.

b 2 used to like; eat
   3 used to play; don't play
   4 used to be; is
   5 didn't use to go; go
   6 loves; used to hate
   7 didn't use to read; read
   8 Did use to go; stay up

c 2 to bed early, but now she goes to bed late.
   3 used to play on the computer, but now she
     reads books.
   4 She used to play tennis, but now she plays
     football.
   5 She used to hate dancing, but now she loves
     dancing.
   6 She used to love Maths, but now she hates
     it.

d Students' own answers

4
a ▶ CD3 T29 TAPESCRIPT/ANSWERS
   2(used)   3 used   4(used)   5(use)   6 use

5
4; 11; 5; 9; 1; 6; 2; 10; 3; 8; 7

7
2 c   3 a   4 a   5 c   6 b

▶ CD3 T30 TAPESCRIPT
1
Speaker 1: Oh, I'm really sorry I'm late. I missed the
  bus to the airport and I had to take a taxi.
Speaker 2: Oh, don't worry. The plane's delayed
  anyway. Look, why don't we go and have a drink
  before we check in for our flight?
Speaker 1: Oh! Good idea.

2
Speaker 3: Got a pen you can lend me?
Speaker 4: You know, it's strange – you've never
  got a pen! Can't you afford them?
Speaker 3: Ha, ha. Come on, just lend me a pen, OK?

132 WORKBOOK KEY

3

Speaker 1: Hello. Can I help you with anything?

Speaker 2: Erm ... yes, I saw in an article that I was reading that it's possible to buy trainers for children – with little lights in them.

Speaker 1: Yes, that's right, but I'm afraid we haven't got any at the moment. We should have more next week.

4

Speaker 2: Excuse me. I'm looking for a shop called 'Fun Reading'.

Speaker 1: Oh, yes. Is that the place where you can get children's books?

Speaker 2: That's the one. I want to get something for my daughter to take to school.

Speaker 1: Well, I think it's in Baker Street – that's just over there ...

5

Speaker 2: Well, not long now and we'll be at the airport. Are you OK in the back there, Jenny?

Speaker 4: Ooh, not really, Dad, no. Do you think we can stop for a minute?

Speaker 2: OK – we've got plenty of time. Let's stop and get something to eat.

6

Speaker 2: Annie, are you daydreaming again?

Speaker 4: You sound just like my teacher!

Speaker 2: Well, I'm sure your friends don't sit around all day looking out of the window. Haven't you got homework to do?

8 **b** 2 South Africa and USA   3 1967
4 Louis Washkansky   5 18 months
6 He led a normal life.

Unit check

1 1 ended up with   2 who   3 temperature
4 sore throat   5 pain   6 that   7 hurts
8 ambulance   9 treat

2 2 c   3 a   4 c   5 c   6 a   7 b   8 b   9 b

3 2 epidemic   3 vaccination   4 surgeon
5 patients   6 antiseptic   7 injection
8 stomach   9 chest

12 If I had ...

1 2 **blogs** videos   3 **hates** likes   4 **designs** files
5 **websites** podcasts   6 **computer programmer** web designer

2 **a** B 6   C 5   D 2   E 4   F 1

b 2 had; 'd go   3 didn't have; would smell
4 'd like; were   5 'd buy; weren't
6 'd go; didn't

c 2 left; would have   3 knew; would tell
4 would be; knew   5 didn't have; would read
6 didn't eat; would be

d 2 If I had a computer, I would send emails.
3 If I didn't like music, I wouldn't spend all my money on CDs.
4 If I were a good player, I would be in the school team.
5 If I didn't do a lot of exercise, I wouldn't be very fit.
6 If he didn't speak good English, he wouldn't watch American TV programmes.

e Students' own answers

f 2 e   3 a   4 b   5 f   6 c

g 2 If I were you, I'd go to bed.
3 If I were you, I would eat something.
4 If I were you, I'd talk to your parents.
5 If I were you, I'd count sheep.
6 If I were you, I'd talk to your teacher.

3 **a** 1 surf   2 screen   3 keyboard   4 printer
5 touch pad   6 run   7 download
8 password   9 hard disk   10 saved
11 USB stick   12 crashed

b 2 adaptor   3 search engine   4 off line
5 drives   6 power lead

c 2 extension lead   3 lightbulb   4 socket
5 battery charger   6 button   7 wire
8 battery   Mystery word: internet

4 **a** ▶ CD3 T31   TAPESCRIPT/ANSWERS
2 They eat   3 I'd ask   4 We'd love
5 They listen   6 We'd have

5 **a** 2 shame   3 good   4 same   5 worth
6 show

b 1 It's not good   2 it just goes to show
3 It's not worth it   4 Looks like
5 It's a shame

7 2 a   3 b   4 b   5 a   6 c   7 c   8 d   9 a   10 d

Unit check

1 1 printer   2 screen   3 logs on   4 Net
5 search   6 downloads   7 crashes   8 had
9 didn't

2 2 c   3 b   4 c   5 a   6 b   7 a   8 b   9 a

3 2 USB slots   3 search engine   4 USB stick
5 power lead   6 provider   7 adaptor
8 keyboard   9 browser

WORKBOOK KEY   133

13 Lost worlds

1 a A 2 B 3 C 1 D 7 E 6 F 5 G 8 H 4

b 2 f 3 d 4 a 5 h 6 g 7 e 8 b

c 2 had left 3 hadn't studied 4 had visited
5 had eaten 6 had lost 7 had shut
8 had seen

d 2 was; had broken / broke
3 didn't buy; spent 4 wasn't; hadn't invited
5 forgot; went 6 looked; had put

e 1 didn't give 2 was 3 became 4 allowed
5 had been 6 continued 7 won
8 had worked 9 became 10 hadn't been

2 a ▶ CD3 T32 TAPESCRIPT/ANSWERS
2 had 3 (had) 4 (had), had 5 had 6 (had)

3 a 2 inventor 3 journalist 4 cyclist
5 explorer 6 receptionist 7 teacher
8 juggler 9 plumber 10 decorator

b 2 explorer 3 driver 4 tourist
5 astronomer 6 manager 7 journalist
8 receptionist 9 decorator
10 archaeologist

4 2 El Dorado 3 Shambhala 4 El Dorado
5 Atlantis 6 El Dorado

5 b 2 adjective 3 noun 4 noun 5 adjective
6 adjective 7 adjective 8 noun

c -ation: information; communication; combination
-ist: archaeologist; artist; tourist; violinist
-er/-or: climber; decorator; painter; swimmer

6 2 B 3 A 4 C

▶ CD3 T33 TAPESCRIPT

Greg: ... Oh yes, it was brilliant, we flew from London to Lima in Peru, my dad and I, and then we flew to another city called Cuzco, a really old place up in the Andes mountains. We stayed in a small hotel overnight – it was cold, too! And the next morning, really early, you know, about half past six, we went to the train station and took the train.

Friend: Were there many people on the train?

Greg: Oh, yeah. All tourists like us – lots of Americans. A lot of them were quite old as well. It was really full, though. Every seat was taken. But it was a really exciting journey!

Friend: Why? What happened?

Greg: Well, we'd been on the train for about three hours, I think – yeah, it was about half past nine – and the train was going really slowly round a bend, and suddenly there was like a thump noise, and the train stopped, and I could see that the first part of the train was leaning over!

Friend: Wow!

Greg: Yeah, you see, it had rained a lot the night before, and some mud had come down from the mountains and was on the tracks, where the train goes ... and the wheels of the first part of the train slipped on the mud and came off!

Friend: Wow! Was anybody hurt?

Greg: No – I mean, two or three people fell over and I think one elderly lady hurt her arm, but that was all ... luckily!

Friend: So what did you all do?

Greg: Well, we heard someone say that it was only five kilometres to Machu Picchu, so my dad and I, and some other people too, we just started walking in a group along the tracks. It was a really hot day, but it was a beautiful walk beside a river, and it took us about two hours, but then we got to another place and took a bus up to Machu Picchu!

Friend: And what was it like?

Greg: Oh wow, it's a fantastic place! ...

Unit check

1 1 journalist 2 receptionist 3 owner
4 decorator 5 teacher 6 traveller
7 explorer 8 artist 9 cyclist

2 2 c 3 c 4 a 5 b 6 c 7 b 8 c 9 c

3 2 traveller 3 collector 4 farmer 5 juggler
6 archaeologist 7 presenter 8 inventor
9 winner

14 A stroke of luck

1 a 1 came off 2 broken 3 fell out 4 landed
5 bought 6 act 7 fly 8 had gone

b 2 f 3 a 4 e 5 c 6 b

134 WORKBOOK KEY

2

a

DIRECT SPEECH	REPORTED SPEECH
Present perfect	Past perfect They had never been to London.
Past simple	Past perfect They said they had arrived the week before.
am/is/are going to	Was going to He said his uncle was going to live in Paris.
can/can't	Could/couldn't She said she couldn't come on Saturday.
will/won't	Would/wouldn't He said he would go the following week.

b 1 would be   2 had never been   3 had stolen
4 was   5 didn't have   6 didn't want
7 was trying   8 was going   9 could take

c Claudia, Sandra and Josh like the park. Mitsuko doesn't like it.

▶ CD3 T34   TAPESCRIPT

Sandra: Hi. My name's Sandra. This is Claudia.
Claudia: Hi.
Sandra: We arrived here at two o'clock.
Claudia: Yeah, that's right. Some of the rides here are very good!
Sandra: Yeah, very good! But you know, the queues are *very* long!
Claudia: Yeah – and we think it's very expensive here, too. Bye!
Josh: Hello! My name's Josh, and … erm … I think this is a great place! Erm … all the rides are cool, but my favourite is The Elevator. I've been on it three times already, and I'm going again!
Mitsuko: Hi. I'm Mitsuko. Erm … I don't like the park very much! Erm … you know, some of the rides are very scary, and I can't go on them! So … erm … I won't come here again.

d 1 two o'clock   2 were very good
3 were very long   4 thought   5 was
6 was a great   7 were cool   8 favourite was
9 he'd been on it   10 was going
11 didn't like   12 some of the rides were
13 couldn't go   14 wouldn't go

3

a [word search grid]

b 2 invitation   3 management   4 information
5 calculation   6 cancellation   7 equipment

4
2 pot luck   3 fingers crossed   4 all the luck
5 by chance   6 bad luck / superstitious
7 touch wood

5
2 to the questions he wouldn't have got all the answers wrong.
3 got all the answers wrong the other kids wouldn't have laughed at him.
4 have felt really miserable if the other kids hadn't laughed at him.
5 If he hadn't felt really miserable, he wouldn't have eaten a huge lunch.
6 If he hadn't eaten a huge lunch, he wouldn't have been sick later on.

6
a ▶ CD3 T35   TAPESCRIPT
(See page 87 of the Workbook.)

b ▶ CD3 T36   TAPESCRIPT
(See page 87 of the Workbook.)

7
1 It's just that   2 what's going on   3 was like
4 it's a bit like   5 surely

9
b 2 T   3 N   4 F   5 F   6 T   7 N   8 N

Writing tip
1 First of all   2 but   3 Secondly   4 because
5 I think   6 Finally   7 In my opinion

Unit check

1 1 management   2 equipment   3 entertainment
4 improvements   5 communication
6 calculations   7 education

2 2 a   3 a   4 c   5 c   6 a   7 a   8 c   9 a
10 a

3 2 reservation   3 payment   4 invitation
5 reaction   6 accommodation   7 cancellation
8 information   9 treatment   10 calculation

1 Present simple

Write the opposite.

0 We don't know your sister.
    We know your sister.

1 He doesn't study in London.
    ....

2 They live in a small house.
    ....

3 I enjoy my French lessons.
    ....

4 You don't understand German very well.
    ....

5 She teaches English.
    ....

[ ]5

2 Present simple

Complete the questions using the verbs in brackets.

0 _Does_ Mary _play_ the guitar? (play)

1 .... you .... listening to classical music? (enjoy)

2 .... John .... a fast car? (have)

3 .... they .... who I am? (know)

4 .... your brother .... tennis well? (play)

5 .... your parents .... living in New York? (like)

[ ]5

3 Present simple or present continuous?

Circle the correct answer.

0 We (don't know) / aren't knowing the answer.

1 Maria *usually walks / is usually walking* to school.

2 I *listen / am listening* to music at the moment. Please be quiet!

3 My father *teaches / is teaching* English.

4 We *go / are going* on holiday twice a year.

5 I *want / am wanting* to buy a new dictionary.

[ ]5

Name ....

Class .... Date ....

4 Hobbies and interests

Put the letters into the correct order to make hobbies and interests.

0 ptorcume smage   _computer games_
1 dagiren   ....
2 miwginsm   ....
3 giptanin   ....
4 angdinc   ....
5 aminec   ....

[ ]5

5 have to / don't have to

Complete the sentences with the correct form of *have to / don't have to*.

0 You _don't have to_ finish your meal if you aren't hungry.

1 I .... wait two hours for the bus yesterday.

2 .... you .... leave now? Yes, I do.

3 I .... study very hard if I want to pass my exams.

4 John .... study hard because he's good at everything.

5 .... your mother .... cook for you every day?

[ ]5

6 Jobs

Complete the sentences with the names of jobs.

0 A _nurse_ helps a doctor with his/her patients.

1 A .... flies an aeroplane.

2 A .... looks after your teeth.

3 A .... works in a school and educates his/her pupils.

4 A .... looks after sick animals.

5 A .... works in a shop and sells you things.

[ ]5

ENTRY TEST B

1 Past simple: regular and irregular verbs

Complete the sentences with the correct form of the verbs in the past.

0 He __waited__ for her outside the cinema. (wait)
1 Where _____ your sister yesterday? (be)
2 They _____ vegetable soup for lunch. (make)
3 _____ your team _____ ? No, I'm afraid not. (win)
4 Gerry _____ home at ten. (leave)
5 We really _____ the film last night. (enjoy)

[5]

2 Countable and uncountable nouns

Complete the sentences using *a, an, some, much* or *many*.

0 I'd like __some__ tea please.
1 Quick! We don't have _____ time.
2 She doesn't have _____ friends, does she?
3 Would you like _____ apple?
4 There's _____ bread on the table.
5 I'll just have _____ glass of water thanks.

[5]

3 Food and drink

Which is the odd one out? Circle the correct answer.

0 apples grapes (carrots)
1 oranges onions carrots
2 beef fish chicken
3 burger pizza salad
4 potatoes onions milk
5 tomatoes pasta rice

[5]

4 *some* and *any*

Complete the sentences with *some* or *any*.

0 Do you have __any__ money with you?
1 I've got _____ very good friends.
2 Are there _____ tomatoes in the fridge?
3 He hasn't got _____ time today, but he's free tomorrow.
4 There's _____ bread on the table, isn't there?
5 I don't want _____ presents for my birthday.

[5]

5 Comparative and superlative adjectives

Complete the sentences with the correct form of the adjectives.

0 English grammar is __easier than__ German grammar. (easy)
1 She must be _____ person in the class. (happy)
2 London is _____ Madrid. (big)
3 Jack is _____ boy I know. (intelligent)
4 What's _____ thing you've ever done? (bad)
5 Paul is _____ me at playing football. (good)

[5]

6 Multi-word verbs

Complete the sentences. Use the correct form of the multi-word verbs from the box.

> ~~climb up~~ pick up put on
> get in take off get out

0 Look at that boy! He __'s climbing up__ the tree.
1 Don't leave your clothes on the floor. _____ them _____ now!
2 Come on, _____ . You'll get wet if you stay out in the rain.
3 When I got home, I _____ my coat and sat down.
4 _____ a thick pullover. It's very cold today.
5 I never want to see you again! _____ !

[5]

ENTRY TEST C

Name ....
Class .... Date ....

1 will / won't

Complete the sentences with *will* or *won't*.

0 Don't worry. It ___won't___ rain, I'm sure.
1 I .... phone you at six.
2 You .... be fine. You're good at Maths.
3 I'm sure the test .... be very difficult. Our teacher is so nice!
4 The swimming pool .... be crowded as it's so hot today.
5 My brother .... help you later as he's not working.

[5]

2 too + adjective

Complete the sentences with *too* and an appropriate adjective.

0 I can't do this exercise. It's ___too difficult___.
1 I won't buy that new CD. It's .... and I haven't got any money.
2 I couldn't stay awake yesterday evening. I was ....
3 They didn't swim in the sea today as the water was ....
4 You have to be over 18 to see this film. You're ....
5 You can't phone your mother now. It's midnight. It's .... !

[5]

3 Adverbs

(Circle) the correct adverb in each sentence.

0 Barbara speaks very (quietly) / *fast*. It's difficult to hear her.
1 Max always arrives *late / lately*. It's very rude.
2 Don't drive so *fastly / fast*. It's dangerous!
3 Maria sings *goodly / well*. I love her voice.
4 If you study *hard / hardly*, you'll pass your exams.
5 My mothers walks *slow / slowly* now as she's quite old.

[5]

4 Expressions to talk about the future

The underlined words are incorrect. Write the correct sentences.

0 I think I'm getting married one day.
   ___I think I'll get married one day.___
1 I hope for find the man of my dreams.
   ....
2 Maybe I live abroad for a couple of years.
   ....
3 I'm doubting I'll go to university.
   ....
4 I think I'm learning to drive one day.
   ....
5 I don't think I have any children in the future.
   ....

[5]

5 Future time expressions

(Circle) the correct time expression.

0 What are you doing (*this*) / *today* evening?
1 Today is Monday. The *next day / day after tomorrow* is Wednesday.
2 I'm going to see my uncle *last weekend / next weekend*.
3 Mum's going out *after an hour / in an hour*.
4 It's June. I'm going on holiday *next month / the next month*.
5 They're going to get married *in three weeks' time / in three week's time*.

[5]

138

Name _____
Class _____ Date _____

1 First conditional

Complete the sentences with the correct form of the verbs.

0 If I __see__ (see) Giberto, I __'ll tell__ (tell) him your news.
1 You _____ (be) cold if you _____ (go) out without a coat.
2 If it _____ (rain) later, we _____ (not have) a picnic.
3 If you _____ (not have) enough money, I _____ (lend) you some.
4 The teacher _____ (be) really angry if you _____ (be) late again.
5 If I _____ (get) good marks, my mum _____ (buy) me a present. ☐ 5

2 Adjectives for feelings and opinions

(Circle) the correct adjective in each sentence.

0 Our History lessons are always so (boring) / bored.
1 The film was really exciting / excited, wasn't it?
2 I'm so tired / tiring all the time. I must be ill.
3 Great dress, Kitty! You look really awful / cool!
4 His uncle died in the crash. How dreadful / interesting!
5 I hate that new building. I find it so attractive / ugly. ☐ 5

3 should/shouldn't

Complete the sentences. Use should or shouldn't with a verb from the box.

| go believe try stop eat study |

0 Young children __should go__ to bed early.
1 You _____ so much fatty food.
2 We _____ harder if we want to do well in the exam.
3 My father _____ smoking. It's so bad for him.
4 I _____ to be tidier.
5 You _____ everything you read in the newspapers! ☐ 5

4 Present perfect with ever/never

Put the words in the correct order to make sentences.

0 never / swum / I / in / sea / the / have
   __I have never swum in the sea.__
1 in / flown / has / sister / never / my / a / plane
   _____ .
2 Indian / you / ever / food / have / tried
   _____ ?
3 people / they / any / have / met / Scottish / never
   _____ .
4 never / we / to / have / States / the / been
   _____ .
5 parents / your / your / friend / ever / best / met / have
   _____ ? ☐ 5

5 Personality adjectives

Complete the sentences with a suitable adjective. The first letter will help you.

0 The English are very __polite.__ They say please and thank you a lot.
1 My sister is very h_____ . She always tells the truth.
2 Marco is so l_____ . He never does any work.
3 Our neighbours are very u_____ . They don't even say hello.
4 My mother's never m_____ . She's cheerful all the time.
5 I can't find anything. I'm so d_____ ! ☐ 5

Entry Test A

1
1 He studies in London.
2 They don't live in a small house.
3 I don't enjoy my French lessons.
4 You understand German very well.
5 She doesn't teach English.

2
1 Do you enjoy listening to classical music?
2 Does John have a fast car?
3 Do they know who I am?
4 Does your brother play tennis well?
5 Do your parents like living in New York?

3
1 usually walks   2 am listening   3 teaches
4 go   5 want

4
1 reading   2 swimming   3 painting
4 dancing   5 cinema

5
1 had to   2 Do ... have to   3 have to
4 doesn't have to   5 Does ... have to

6
1 pilot   2 dentist   3 teacher   4 vet
5 shop assistant

Entry Test B

1
1 was   2 made   3 Did ... win   4 left
5 enjoyed

2
1 much   2 many   3 an   4 some   5 a

3
1 oranges   2 fish   3 salad   4 milk
5 tomatoes

4
1 some   2 any   3 any   4 some   5 any

5
1 the happiest   2 bigger than   3 the most intelligent   4 the worst   5 better than

6
1 Pick ... up   2 get in   3 took off
4 Put on   5 Get out

Entry Test C

1
1 will/'ll   2 will/'ll   3 won't   4 will
5 will

2
1 too expensive   2 too tired   3 too cold/rough   4 too young   5 too late

3
1 late   2 fast   3 well   4 hard   5 slowly

4
1 I hope I'll find the man of my dreams.
2 Maybe I'll live abroad for a couple of years.
3 I doubt I'll go to university.
4 I think I'll learn to drive one day.
5 I don't think I'll have any children in the future.

5
1 day after tomorrow   2 next weekend
3 in an hour   4 next month   5 in three weeks' time

Entry Test D

1
1 will/'ll be ... go   2 rains ... won't have
3 don't have ... will/'ll lend   4 will be ... are
5 get ... will/'ll buy

2
1 exciting   2 tired   3 cool   4 dreadful
5 ugly

3
1 shouldn't eat   2 should study   3 should stop   4 should try   5 shouldn't believe

4
1 My sister has never flown in a plane.
2 Have you ever tried Indian food?
3 They have never met any Scottish people.
4 We have never been to the States.
5 Have your parents ever met your best friend?

5
1 honest   2 lazy   3 unfriendly
4 miserable   5 disorganised

Teaching notes for communication activity and grammar practice

Unit 1
Communication activity
Areas practised

Past continuous; House vocabulary

- Divide the class into student A and B pairs. Copy and cut up one sheet for each pair.
- Explain that students must ask and answer using the past continuous tense to find out what the people missing from their picture were doing. Ask a stronger pair to demonstrate.

  A: *What was Josh doing last night?*

  B: *He was playing with his toys.*

- Explain to students that they must write the answer on their half of the picture under the relevant names.
- Students now complete the exercise.

Grammar practice key

2 Mrs Brown was reading a book in her room.
3 Julie Brown was sunbathing on the balcony.
4 Tom and Barry Brown were talking to the local girls.
5 Grandmother Brown was sleeping on the beach.
6 Marc Brown was talking on his mobile phone.
7 Grandfather Brown was listening to the radio.
8 Ellie Brown was sitting in a café.
9 Anita and Roberto Brown were waiting at the airport.

2
2 Where was she going when she fell?
3 Who were you talking to when I arrived?
4 What were they watching when the television stopped working?
5 Where were they going when they heard the news?
6 Who were you working for when you lost your job?
7 What was he doing when he broke his leg?
8 Where were you travelling to when you lost your passport?
9 Who were we visiting when the train was late?

3
2 It was raining when I looked out of the window just now.
3 My uncle arrived while my parents were watching television.
4 We were walking to school when we saw the bus.
5 Carlo was writing an email when the computer crashed.
6 It started to rain while we were walking to the park.
7 Our dog was running in the park when he saw a cat.
8 I was going to bed when I heard a noise downstairs.
9 While we were listening to the radio, the doctor arrived.

4
2 saw 3 stopped 4 saw 5 were shouting
6 was crying 7 was 8 didn't have 9 arrived

Unit 2
Communication activity
Areas practised

Comparative and superlative adjectives: *as ... as, much / far / a lot ... than*; Revision of present and past simple of the verb *be*

- Divide the class into groups of four. Copy one game for each group. You will also need some dice and counters.
- Students throw the dice and move the number of spaces on the board. They must then make two correct sentences using the prompts on the square they land on. One sentence must use a superlative or comparative with *as ... as* or *much / far / a lot ... than*.

  Example: I think dogs are a lot messier than cats. / Dogs aren't as tidy as cats.

- The other students in the group must decide if the sentences are grammatically correct and make sense. If so, the next person has a turn and the game continues. If the sentences are wrong, the student must correct them and move back one square.
- The first to reach the finish is the winner.

141

Grammar practice key

1
2 Mobile phones are cheaper than computers.
3 Alaska is colder than Rome.
4 Monkeys are more intelligent than frogs.
5 Skiing is more difficult than cycling.
6 Australia is bigger than Great Britain.
7 Computer games are more expensive than CDs.
8 Hollywood film stars are richer than nurses.
9 The Eiffel Tower is taller than Big Ben.

2
2 Who is the tallest person in your family?
3 Which is the most beautiful city in your country?
4 Which is the hottest place in the world?
5 Which is the worst programme on TV?
6 Who is the most boring person you know?
7 Who is the best actor or actress you know?
8 Which is the most famous building in your city?
9 Which is the easiest subject at school?

3
2 A frog isn't as intelligent as a monkey.
3 Whales aren't as dangerous as sharks.
4 Buses aren't as fast as planes.
5 English isn't as difficult as Chinese.
6 Rome isn't as hot as Cairo.
7 Edinburgh isn't as big as London.
8 Children aren't as tall as adults.
9 Digital cameras aren't as expensive as computers.

4
2 easily 3 quickly 4 badly 5 well
6 quietly 7 nervously 8 clearly 9 happily

Unit 3
Communication activity
Areas practised
First conditional; *unless* in first conditional sentences; Vocabulary: the environment; energy types; *I agree*; *I don't agree because …*; *I think …*

- Divide the class into student A and B pairs. Copy and cut up one set of sentences for each pair.
- Give out the cards to each pair in jumbled order.
- Students must fit the sentence halves together so they are grammatically correct and make sense. Once they have completed the activity, ask students to choose one statement.
- Students decide if they agree or disagree with their statement. Encourage them to give reasons and to use the vocabulary from this unit.
- Class feedback.

Grammar practice key

1
2 will 3 will 4 might 5 won't 6 will
7 may 8 will 9 will

2
2 work / 'll pass
3 take / won't
4 go / will you buy
5 don't have / will you do
6 fails / 'll leave
7 go / 'll have
8 studies / 'll become
9 buy / 'll drive

3
2 f 3 c 4 h 5 a 6 b 7 e
8 i 9 d

4
2 If 3 Unless 4 If 5 unless 6 unless
7 If 8 If 9 Unless

Unit 4
Communication activity
Areas practised
Present perfect: *already/yet* questions and short answers

- Divide the class into student A and B pairs. Copy and cut up one sheet for each pair.
- Ask a stronger pair to demonstrate the example, drawing students' attention to the use of *yet* and *already*.
- Students complete the activity.

Grammar practice key

1
2 don't they? 3 could you? 4 aren't you?
5 isn't he? 6 hasn't she? 7 aren't we?
8 do they? 9 is there?

2
2 already 3 yet 4 already 5 already
6 yet 7 yet 8 already 9 already

3
2 (✓)
3 (✗) We have just got back from our holiday in Germany.
4 (✓)
5 (✗) He's just gone back to school after the accident, hasn't he?
6 (✓)
7 (✓)
8 (✗) Have you finished that book yet? You've been reading it for months!
9 (✓)

4
2 Has Sarah worked in Africa?
3 Have Sam and Tom broken the table?
4 Have his parents heard the news?
5 Have they played football every day this week?
6 Has she been shopping with her best friend?
7 Have you read that book?
8 Has Anna taken lots of photographs?
9 Has he fallen asleep?

Unit 5

Communication activity

Area practised
Present simple passive

- Divide the class into student A and B pairs. Copy and cut up one sheet for each pair.
- Explain that they must complete the picture activity first, using the prompts under each picture. They will need notebooks for this. Remind them they must use the present simple passive tense.
- Once they have done this, students can check their answers by reading out their sentences to their partners.

Grammar practice key

1
2 The towels are changed every day.
3 That newspaper is sold every Monday.
4 The doors are opened at nine o'clock.
5 Your photo is taken at the entrance.
6 David is invited to Pat's party every year.
7 Bread is sold in the supermarket.
8 Elephants are killed for their tusks.
9 Lots of good films are directed by Steven Spielberg!

2
2 Are they prepared for the storm? Yes, they are.
3 Is champagne produced in France? Yes, it is.
4 Are doctors and dentists paid a lot? Yes, they are.
5 Are all credit cards accepted? No, they're not.
6 Are dogs allowed in this hotel? No, they're not.
7 Is this table made of wood? Yes, it is.
8 Is Spanish spoken here? No, it isn't.
9 Are stamps sold in the post office? Yes, they are.

3
2 (✗) Motorbikes are not often bought by women.
3 (✓)
4 (✓)
5 (✗) This game is played by lots of people.
6 (✗) Their shopping is delivered to their house.
7 (✓)
8 (✗) The washing is done every Wednesday.
9 (✗) The house is painted once a year.

4
2 She won't let him go to the concert.
3 His parents won't let him buy a new computer.
4 They are allowed to use the Internet.
5 Harry won't let his brother wear his hat.
6 Her parents won't let her have a party.
7 Dana's allowed to invite her friends.
8 Jamie isn't allowed to go out tonight.
9 I won't let you borrow my guitar.

Unit 6

Communication activity

Area practised
For/since + time expressions

- Divide the class into small groups of three or four. Copy and cut up one set of cards for each group.
- Appoint a dealer to deal the dominoes out face down.
- The student on the left of the dealer must turn their first domino over and place it in the centre of the table for everyone to see.
- The next student in the group must match one of their dominoes to one side of the first domino. For example, if the first student places a domino with *For / last week* and the next student has a domino with *Since / ten years*, they could match *Since* with *last week* or *For* with *ten years*. If the student has no matching domino, they must miss a turn.
- To make the game more challenging, the student who places a domino must make a correct sentence in the present perfect tense using the words on the dominoes.
- Students continue in this way until the first student with no dominoes left is the winner.

Grammar practice key

1
2 (✓)
3 (✗) John and Max have been skiing in Italy.
4 (✗) Lisa has broken her leg.
5 (✓)
6 (✗) She has bought a new dress.
7 (✗) The tree has grown enormously!
8 (✗) He has just made dinner.
9 (✓)

2
2 Have you ever broken your leg?
3 Have you ever met the king?
4 Have you ever climbed a mountain?
5 Have you ever read a book in English?
6 How many times have you been late for school?
7 How many times have you eaten pizza?
8 Have you ever been to Hong Kong?
9 Have you lived in the same place all your life?

3
2 They haven't just broken the window.
3 Hasn't he been in hospital for a long time?
4 He hasn't worked in the circus since he was five.
5 Haven't you heard their new song?
6 Jack hasn't taught Maths for eight years.
7 Elisabetta hasn't slept for 12 hours.
8 She hasn't just woken up.
9 Haven't you ever eaten fish?

4
2 for 3 since 4 for 5 since 6 for
7 since 8 since 9 for

Unit 7

Communication activity

Areas practised
Past simple passive; Natural disasters vocabulary

- Divide the class into student A and B pairs. Copy and cut up enough sheets for each pair.
- Give students a few minutes to prepare their questions. Monitor and help as necessary, making sure students are forming the past simple passive tense correctly.
- Students ask each other questions to complete the quizzes, checking the answers at the end of the quiz and adding up the scores. Make sure they take turns to ask and answer.

Grammar practice key

1
2 Where were the last Olympics held?
3 Where was the money found?
4 When was the painting stolen?
5 How many people were injured in the accident?
6 When was that photo taken?
7 Where was the shipwreck discovered?
8 When were those houses completed?
9 How many houses were damaged in the storm?

2
2 was given 3 was discovered 4 was filmed
5 are held 6 was given 7 is grown
8 were built 9 is exported

3
2 (✓)
3 (✗) *Hamlet* was written by William Shakespeare.
4 (✓)
5 (✗) My dad's car was stolen last week.
6 (✓)
7 (✗) Nothing was destroyed in the earthquake.
8 (✓)
9 (✗) John F. Kennedy was shot by Lee Harvey Oswald.

4
2 the 3 The 4 a 5 a 6 a 7 a 8 the
9 a 10 The

Unit 8

Communication activity

Areas practised
Too much / too many / not enough; Homes vocabulary

- Divide the class into student A and B pairs. Copy and cut up one sheet for each pair.
- Explain that on each card there is information about a house or some people. Students must match the houses and the people. As they discuss the choices, they should decide what the problems are with each house using *too much / too many / not enough / near / far*, etc. They then write the letter of the house they have chosen in the box next to the picture.
- Go through the first card with the class as an example.
  A: *I think house C is right for Anna and Jon.*
  B: *I don't think so, it's got too many rooms. What about house F?*
- Ask for feedback. Does everyone agree?

Suggested answers
1 B 2 D 3 E 4 A 5 F 6 C

144 TEACHING NOTES FOR COMMUNICATION ACTIVITY AND GRAMMAR PRACTICE

Grammar practice key

1
2 too much
3 too many / not enough
4 not enough
5 too many ... too much
6 not enough
7 too many
8 too much
9 too many

2
2 (✓)
3 (✗) too many cars
4 (✓)
5 (✗) too much pasta
6 (✓)
7 (✗) not enough time
8 (✗) too much sugar
9 (✓)

3
2 're going to stay
3 'll answer
4 'll cut
5 're going to have
6 's going to buy
7 'll have
8 'll open
9 're going to see

4
2 h 3 d 4 g 5 a 6 f 7 i 8 e 9 b

Unit 9

Communication activity

Areas practised
Must / mustn't / have to / don't have to

- Divide the class into student A and B pairs. Copy and cut up one sheet for each pair. Do not give the answers out at this point.
- Give students a few minutes to read the instructions and the quiz questions. Check any problems.
- Give out the answer sheets and ask students to check their answers. Ask for feedback.
- Students now work alone and think up some questions about the customs and laws in their own country. Monitor and check they are using *must / mustn't / have to / don't have to* appropriately.
- Students can then swap questions with their partner and answer them.
- Class feed back. Are there any interesting or amusing questions? Students could vote for the most interesting or amusing quiz.

Grammar practice key

1
2 some of them 3 none of them
4 All of them 5 none of them
6 some of them 7 all of them
8 None of them 9 some of them

2
2 everywhere 3 no one 4 all of them
5 Everywhere 6 nothing 7 someone
8 No one 9 nowhere

3
2 (✓)
3 (✗) Someone gave it to me ...
4 (✓)
5 (✗) Everywhere is full.
6 (✗) ... someone in the sports department ...
7 (✓)
8 (✗) ... everyone should see ...
9 (✗) No one remembered my birthday ...

4
2 mustn't 3 don't have to 4 must 5 must
6 must 7 don't have to 8 don't have to
9 mustn't

Unit 10

Communication activity

Areas practised
Present perfect simple and continuous

- Divide the class into student A and B pairs. Copy and cut up one sheet for each pair.
- Explain that students must write either the present perfect simple or the present perfect continuous form of the verbs in brackets. They will need notebooks for this. Then they must guess who they think the person is. Go through the first item as an example, if necessary.
- Monitor and check that students are using the tenses correctly and note down any repeated errors to go through as a class after the activity.
- Students read out their completed texts to their partner who corrects any mistakes and tells them if they have guessed correctly.

Grammar practice key

1
2 haven't been cooking ... 've only been cooking
3 have you been waiting

TEACHING NOTES FOR COMMUNICATION ACTIVITY AND GRAMMAR PRACTICE

4 hasn't been learning
5 've been travelling
6 have they been coming
7 's been talking
8 's been swimming
9 hasn't been working

2
2 Have you posted
3 've been waiting
4 Have you heard
5 've been searching
6 've watched
7 has your brother been tidying
8 Have you ever seen
9 's been practising

3
2 (✓)
3 (✗) ... have been married ...
4 (✓)
5 (✗) You've broken your leg ...
6 (✓)
7 (✗) I've had my new computer ...
8 (✗) Your brother's watched that DVD ...
9 (✓)

4
2 known
3 been doing ... been talking
4 found
5 been listening
6 visited
7 finished
8 had
9 been studying

Unit 11

Communication activity

Areas practised
Defining relative clauses; Medical (and other general) vocabulary

- Divide the class into student A and B pairs. Copy and cut up one sheet for each pair. If you have an odd number of students, have one group of three students and give two of the students the same crossword.
- Demonstrate the activity with a stronger pair. Explain that they listen to their partner's clues and write the missing words in their crossword. They must use defining relative clauses. For example:

A: *Number 1. This is someone who helps you when you have a problem with your teeth.*

- Make sure students are sitting opposite each other, or back to back, so they can't see each other's crossword. Give students time to complete the activity.
- Students can check their answers by looking at their partner's crossword.

Grammar practice key

2 I've got a pair of trousers which are too small.
3 The hotel where we stayed had a big gym.
4 Pippa has a friend who is a singer.
5 Please give me the pen which is on my desk.
6 I read a book which was very good.
7 I know somebody who can drive a bus.
8 There's the man who stole €10,000!
9 The city where Jane lives is called Cambridge.

2 Did Peter use to have long hair? No, he didn't.
3 Did Peter use to want to be a writer? Yes, he did.
4 Did Peter use to eat very much? No, he didn't.
5 Did Peter use to talk to everybody? Yes, he did.
6 Did Peter use to play with his friends? Yes, he did.
7 Did Peter use to like travelling by car? No, he didn't.
8 Did Peter use to stay at his grandmother's house? Yes, he did.
9 Did Peter use to drink coffee? No, he didn't.

3
2 (✗) Did you use to play football?
3 (✓)
4 (✗) We used to live in Liverpool.
5 (✗) They didn't use to like going to the gym.
6 (✓)
7 (✗) Did you use to watch Star Wars?
8 (✗) My sister used to smoke.
9 (✗) Danny and Eddie didn't use to sing.

2 Medicine didn't use to be as good.
3 She used to get stomach ache every weekend.
4 Vinny used to get a cold every winter.
5 My parents didn't use to go shopping very often.

146 TEACHING NOTES FOR COMMUNICATION ACTIVITY AND GRAMMAR PRACTICE

6 People didn't use to use computers.
7 He didn't use to work so hard.
8 Karen's eyes used to hurt when reading.
9 The doctor didn't use to live there.

Unit 12

Communication activity

Area practised
Second conditional

- Divide the class into student A and B pairs. Copy and cut up one sheet per pair.
- Ask a stronger pair to demonstrate the examples, making sure students understand that they must write out the second conditional sentences in full and then predict their partner's answers before asking questions. Tell them they mustn't read the analysis at the bottom of the page yet.
- Monitor and check that students are using the second conditional tense correctly and note down any repeated errors to go through as a class after the activity.
- Students then read their partner's analysis. Does their partner agree with it or not?

Grammar practice key

1
2 I would play tennis every day if I could.
3 If I went to bed early, I wouldn't be so tired.
4 You would take good photos if you had a good camera.
5 I would phone you if I had a mobile phone.
6 Lucy would let you drive if you asked her.
7 If I were rich, I would go on holiday now!
8 I would pass my exams if I studied.
9 He would see you if you turned the light on.

2
2 If Mary could swim, would she go every day?
3 Would she tell me if she knew the secret?
4 Would you tell him, if you were me?
5 Would you have more time if I came tomorrow?
6 Would you die if she didn't love you?
7 Would you go if you didn't have so much homework?
8 Would he be cold if he had a jacket?
9 Would Sam fix the computer if he could?

3
2 (✓)
3 (✗) … she would know …
4 (✗) Would you buy …

5 (✓)
6 (✓)
7 (✗) … if it wasn't Saturday.
8 (✗) If you saved your work …
9 (✗) Would you dance …

4
2 went … would change
3 wouldn't wash up … had
4 Would they travel … rained?
5 would take … had
6 Would Gregory work … won
7 would eat … didn't lose
8 ate … would be
9 read … would know

Unit 13

Communication activity

Area practised
Past perfect

- Copy and give out one sheet per student. Alternatively, this can be done in pairs.
- Explain that students must complete each sentence using the past perfect tense, using the pictures to help them.
- Students complete the activity. You can set a time limit if you prefer.
- If students worked individually, they can check answers in pairs. If students worked in pairs, then put pairs together to check answers.
- Check answers as a class.

Suggested answers
1 my friends had left. / it had closed.
2 that she had forgotten her passport.
3 he had lost his keys.
4 she had left her homework in her bedroom.
5 our parents had gone to bed.
6 she had changed since they were at school.
7 the film had started.
8 the programme had finished.

Grammar practice key

1
2 had taken   3 had fed   4 had scored
5 had reached   6 had stopped   7 had written
8 had won   9 had taught

2
2 Had Katie ever believed in aliens, until she saw one?
3 Had she ever travelled to India before?
4 Had Jack taken photos before they arrived?

5 Had Joe walked for ten kilometres?
6 Had Anna already left when Sue arrived?
7 Had he died before the doctor arrived?
8 Had the train left when you arrived?
9 Had she finished her homework by 11pm?

3
2 had learned … went
3 hadn't enjoyed … was
4 had collected … got
5 reached … had scored
6 was … had read
7 got … had made
8 promised … hadn't finished
9 forgot … hadn't written

4
2 (✗) were away
3 (✓)
4 (✓)
5 (✗) been to America
6 (✓)
7 (✓)
8 (✗) phoned
9 (✗) had taken

Unit 14

Communication activity

Area practised
Third conditional
You will need a dice for each group and some counters.

- Divide the class into groups of four. Copy and give out one game for each group.
- Students place their counters on the start square. The first student in the group rolls the dice and moves the number of squares shown on the dice.
- Once the student has moved to the relevant square, they read the prompt and then complete the third conditional sentence. The other members of the group must decide if the sentence is correct.
- If the sentence is correct, the student stays where they are; if the sentence is wrong, they move back to the start square. Alternatively, students can correct a wrong sentence and then move back one square.
- The first to reach the finish is the winner!

Grammar practice key

1
2 Mary told us it was her birthday.
3 David said we had to go to our English class.
4 Tom said they should drink lots of water.
5 Dad said I could go when I had finished.
6 Harry said a black cat had crossed his path that day.
7 My sister complained that I was always so lucky.
8 The director told them that he had made her a star.

2
2 She asked him if they were going to the cinema.
3 Tom asked what time they were leaving.
4 He asked me when I had gone to Africa.
5 Helen asked her when they went to bed.
6 The children asked their father what was for dinner.
7 He asked her if she was always so lucky.
8 Ana asked her where he had taken her on their first date.
9 She asked me where I had been.

3
2 (✓)
3 (✗) had gone
4 (✗) had borrowed
5 (✓)
6 (✗) have passed
7 (✓)
8 (✗) wouldn't have gone
9 (✗) had felt

4
2 If Sheila hadn't lost her keys, she could have got in.
3 If Paul hadn't seen a shooting star, he wouldn't have made a wish.
4 If Billy had studied, he wouldn't have failed the exam.
5 If Sam hadn't gone out, his camera wouldn't have been stolen.
6 If she had been in the play, she would have got a prize.
7 If he hadn't broken a mirror, he wouldn't have had seven years' bad luck.
8 If the director hadn't seen him, he wouldn't have made him a star.
9 If John hadn't been late, there would have been some dinner left.

Communication activity 1

Student A

What were the Kaotix family doing last night?

Living room
- Anna
- Josh
- Marco and Andrew

Bedroom
- Grandfather
- The cat

Student B

What were the Kaotix family doing last night?

Dining room
- Mum and Dad
- Molly

Kitchen
- Grandmother
- Frank
- The dog

PHOTOCOPIABLE © Cambridge University Press 2010 **Resources Unit 1** 149

Grammar practice 1

1 Write sentences about what the Brown family were doing on holiday this time last week. Use the prompts and the past continuous tense.

1 Mr Brown / drink / orange juice / at the swimming pool
   Mr Brown was drinking orange juice at the swimming pool.

2 Mrs Brown / read a book / in her room

3 Julie Brown / sunbathe / on the balcony

4 Tom and Barry Brown / talk / to the local girls

5 Grandmother Brown / sleep / on the beach

6 Marc Brown / talk / on his mobile phone

7 Grandfather Brown / listen / to the radio

8 Ellie Brown / sit / in a café

9 Anita and Roberto / wait / at the airport

2 Write the questions. Use the past continuous or past simple form of the verbs.

1 what / you / do / when / you / see / the accident?
   What were you doing when you saw the accident?

2 where / she / go / when / she / fell?

3 who / you / talk to / when / I / arrive?

4 what / they / watch / when / television / stop working?

5 where / they / go / when / they / hear / news?

6 who / you / work for / when / you / lose / job?

7 what / he / do / when / he / break / leg?

8 where / you / travel to / when / you / lose / your passport?

9 who / we / visit / when / train / be / late?

3 Complete the sentences. Use the past simple or past continuous form of the verbs and *when* or *while*.

1 I *was doing* (do) my homework *when* the phone *rang* (ring).

2 It _____ (rain) _____ I _____ (look) out of the window just now.

3 My uncle _____ (arrive) _____ my parents _____ (watch) television.

4 We _____ (walk) to school _____ we _____ (see) the bus.

5 Carlo _____ (write) an email _____ the computer _____ (crash).

6 It _____ (start) to rain _____ we _____ (walk) to the park.

7 Our dog _____ (run) in the park _____ he _____ (see) a cat.

8 I _____ (go) to bed _____ I _____ (hear) a noise downstairs.

9 _____ we _____ (listen) to the radio, the doctor _____ (arrive).

4 Complete the text. Use the past simple or past continuous form of the verbs.

I (1) *was driving* (drive) into town one day last week when I (2) _____ (see) a house on fire. I (3) _____ (stop) the car and (4) _____ (see) three people outside the house. They (5) _____ (shout) and one person (6) _____ (cry). There (7) _____ (be) a woman inside the house. I (8) _____ (not have) my mobile phone, but luckily a fire engine soon (9) _____ (arrive).

Communication activity 2

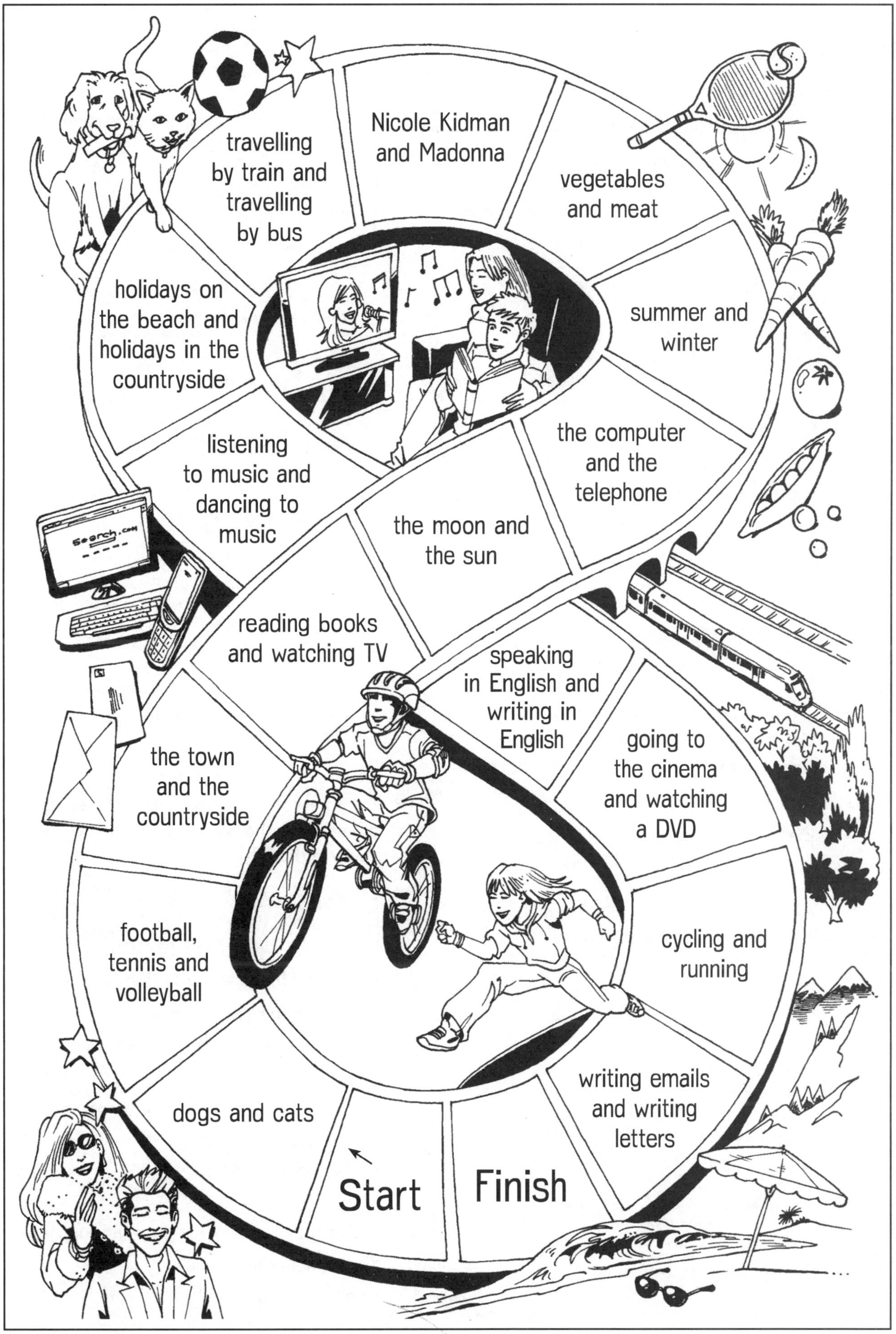

Grammar practice 2

1
Complete the sentences. Use the comparative form of the adjectives.

1 Mount Everest / Mount Fuji (high)
   Mount Everest is higher than Mount Fuji.
2 mobile phones / computers (cheap)
3 Alaska / Rome (cold)
4 monkeys / frogs (intelligent)
5 skiing / cycling (difficult)
6 Australia / Great Britain (big)
7 computer games / CDs (expensive)
8 Hollywood film stars / nurses (rich)
9 The Eiffel Tower / Big Ben (tall)

2
Write questions. Use *Which* or *Who* and the superlative form of the adjectives. Then answer the questions.

1 your subject / at school (good)
   Which is your best subject at school?
2 person / in your family (tall)
3 city / in your country (beautiful)
4 place / in the world (hot)
5 programme / TV (bad)
6 person / you know (boring)
7 actor or actress / you know (good)
8 building / in your city (famous)
9 subject / at school (easy)

3
Complete the sentences. Use *isn't/aren't as ... as* and the adjectives.

1 mouse / elephant (big)
   A mouse isn't as big as an elephant.
2 frog / monkey (intelligent)
3 whales / sharks (dangerous)
4 buses / planes (fast)
5 English / Chinese (difficult)
6 Rome / Cairo (hot)
7 Edinburgh / London (big)
8 children / adults (tall)
9 digital cameras / computers (expensive)

4
Complete the sentences with the correct adverb. Use the adjectives in the box to form the adverbs.

| quiet | fluent | bad | clear | happy |
| good | easy | nervous | quick | |

1 My best friend speaks English *fluently.*
2 I passed the History exam _____ .
3 I can't understand him. He talks too _____ .
4 The play was a disaster. The actors acted very _____ .
5 Liverpool played really _____ yesterday. They won 5–0.
6 She spoke so _____ no one could hear.
7 She moved her hands _____ .
8 Please speak more _____ .
9 The baby smiled _____ .

152 PHOTOCOPIABLE © Cambridge University Press 2010 Resources Unit 2

Communication activity 3

Part 1	Part 2
Unless we use more renewable energy,	there will be no more coal, oil or gas in future.
If people use more solar energy,	there will be less pollution.
Unless you study hard for the exam,	you won't pass.
What will you do	if the weather is nice this weekend?
If you fail your exam,	what will you do?
If pollution increases,	more plants and animals will die.
Unless more people cycle to work,	pollution will increase.
If there are more places for teenagers to go,	they won't cause problems in town centres.
If we don't drop litter,	we will have cleaner streets.
If temperatures continue to rise,	the ice at the poles will melt.
The problem of climate change won't go away	unless we do something about the causes.

Grammar practice 3

1 Circle the correct words.

1 Don't study Maths next year. You *might* / *might not* fail the exam again.
2 My parents are certain they *will* / *may* go to Majorca this summer.
3 I don't think they *will* / *might* win the next World Cup.
4 We're not sure what to do this weekend. We *might* / *will* go to a concert.
5 Alan is ill. I'm sure he *won't* / *might not* be at school today.
6 They're going to Kuala Lumpur. How *will* / *might* they get there?
7 I feel terrible. I think I *may* / *will* have a cold.
8 I'm sure there *will* / *might* not be more pollution in the future.
9 Take the car. The forecast said it *will* / *might not* rain later.

2 Complete the sentences. Use the correct form of the verbs.

1 If I ___go___ to university, I _'ll have to_ work hard. (go/have to)
2 If we _____ hard, we _____ our exams. (work/pass)
3 If you _____ an umbrella, it _____ ! (take/not rain)
4 If you _____ shopping today, what _____ you _____ ? (go/buy)
5 If you _____ any homework tonight, what _____ you _____ ? (not have/do)
6 If my brother _____ his exams again, he _____ school. (fail/leave)
7 If my parents _____ away this weekend, we _____ a party! (go/have)
8 If Ana _____ medicine, she _____ a doctor. (study/become)
9 If we _____ a new car, we _____ to the beach this weekend. (buy/drive)

3 Match the two parts of the sentences.

1 If I have homework,
2 If it rains at the weekend,
3 If my dad gives me money,
4 If my sister buys a new mobile phone,
5 If I see Ciara,
6 If we go to the pool now,
7 If my grandparents stay with us,
8 If I have a party,
9 If you go to the match,

a I'll tell her.
b it'll be very busy.
c I'll buy those new trainers.
d you'll get home late.
e they'll sleep in my bedroom.
f we won't go to the beach.
g I'll do it tonight.
h she'll use it all the time.
i lots of people will come.

4 *If* or *unless*? Circle the correct word.

1 *Unless* / *If* you work hard, you won't pass your exams.
2 *Unless* / *If* we don't hurry, we'll miss the start of the film.
3 *Unless* / *If* people do more recycling, there will be rubbish everywhere.
4 *Unless* / *If* you don't tell anyone, no one will know.
5 We'll come to the party *if* / *unless* we phone to say we can't.
6 You won't get there on time *unless* / *if* you drive.
7 *Unless* / *If* we don't have enough money, we won't go on holiday.
8 *Unless* / *If* my parents say no, I won't be able to come.
9 *Unless* / *If* Liverpool play better this year, they won't win the league.

Communication activity 4

Student A

You are going to stay with a family in London next week and you have to get ready. You have done some things already. There are other things you haven't done yet. Ask and answer to find out what your partner has already done and what your partner hasn't done yet. Student A starts.

- buy a guide book
- buy new trainers ✓
- find a big suitcase
- write to the family in London ✓
- borrow an MP3 player
- finish all school work ✓
- find the tickets

Ask student B about the following:

- buy a map of London
- buy an umbrella
- borrow a big suitcase
- send photos to the family in London
- find address book
- say goodbye to friends

A: *Have you bought a map of London yet?*
B: *Yes, I've already done that. / No, I haven't done that yet.*

Student B

You are going to stay with a family in London next week and you have to get ready. You have done some things already. There are other things you haven't done yet. Ask and answer to find out what your partner has already done and what your partner hasn't done yet. Student A starts.

- buy a map of London ✓
- buy an umbrella
- borrow a big suitcase ✓
- send photos to the family in London
- find address book
- say goodbye to friends ✓

Ask student A about the following:

- buy a guide book
- buy new trainers
- find a big suitcase
- write to the family in London
- borrow an MP3 player
- finish all school work
- find the tickets

B: *Have you bought a guide book yet?*
A: *Yes, I've already done that. / No, I haven't done that yet.*

Grammar practice 4

1 Circle the correct question tags.

1 Michael Jackson was American, *wasn't he* / *was he*?
2 The shops close soon, *do they* / *don't they*?
3 You couldn't give me some money, *could you* / *do you*?
4 You're the new English teacher, *don't you* / *aren't you*?
5 He's always late, *does he* / *isn't he*?
6 Your sister has taken my book, *hasn't she* / *isn't she*?
7 We're going to Spain next summer, *isn't it* / *aren't we*?
8 They don't live in America now, *don't they* / *do they*?
9 There's nobody in the shop, *is there* / *isn't there*?

2 *Already* or *yet*? Circle the correct word.

1 He hasn't finished his breakfast *already* / *yet.*
2 Sami and Harry have *already* / *yet* met.
3 Pietro and Paulo haven't done their English homework *already* / *yet*.
4 He's *already* / *yet* saved enough money to travel round the world.
5 He has *already* / *yet* finished reading his new book.
6 We haven't been to the new cinema *already* / *yet*.
7 Haven't they arrived *already* / *yet*?
8 It's only eight o'clock and she's *already* / *yet* gone to bed.
9 I've *already* / *yet* told you the answer!

3 Right (✓) or wrong (✗)? Correct the wrong sentences.

1 He hasn't finished his dinner yet, have he? ✗
   He hasn't finished his dinner yet, has he?
2 He has already been to Canada six times. ☐
   ....
3 We have yet got back from our holiday in Germany. ☐
   ....
4 Have you just made some coffee? ☐
   ....
5 He's just gone back to school after the accident, haven't he? ☐
   ....
6 You haven't bought another new car, have you? ☐
   ....
7 We've already seen this film three times. ☐
   ....
8 Have you finished that book just? You've been reading it for months! ☐
   ....
9 Have Suze and Alex finished their homework yet? ☐
   ....

4 Write the questions.

1 I have been to Australia.
   Have you been to Australia?
2 Sarah has worked in Africa.
   ....
3 Sam and Tom have broken the table.
   ....
4 His parents have heard the news.
   ....
5 They have played football every day this week.
   ....
6 She has been shopping with her best friend.
   ....
7 We have read that book.
   ....
8 Anna has taken lots of photographs.
   ....
9 He has fallen asleep.
   ....

Communication activity 5

Student A

Complete the sentences under each picture in the present simple passive tense. Write them in your notebooks. Then read out your completed sentences to student B. Were you correct?

1	2	3	4	5
			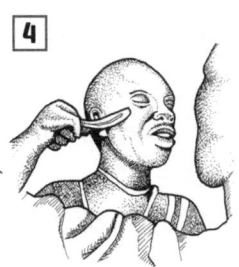	
A coming of age ceremony/hold/ Masai boys are 15 or 16 years old.	Headdresses/make/ the feathers of large birds.	Their heads/shave.	Their skin/paint/red.	Huts/call 'boma'/ build/the boys live together.

Now listen to student B and use the sentences below to check their answers.

1 A big festival is celebrated in Mexico on 1 and 2 November every year.
2 Food and drink is offered to dead relatives.
3 The names of dead relatives are written on skulls made of candy.
4 The candy skulls are eaten and sometimes wooden skull masks are worn.
5 The graves of relatives are decorated with candles and flowers.

Student B

Complete the sentences under each picture in the present simple passive tense. Write them in your notebooks.

1	2	3	4	5

A big festival/ celebrate/in Mexico on 1 and 2 November every year.	Food and drink/ offered/to dead relatives.	The names of dead relatives/write/ on skulls/make/of candy.	The candy skulls/eat/ sometimes wooden skull masks /wear.	The graves of relatives/ decorate/ with candles and flowers.

Now listen to student A and use the sentences below to check their answers.

1 A coming of age ceremony is held when Masai boys are 15 or 16 years old.
2 Headdresses are made from the feathers of large birds.
3 Their heads are shaved.
4 Their skin is painted red.
5 Huts called 'boma' are built, and the boys live together.

Then read out your completed sentences to student A. Were you correct?

Grammar practice 5

1 Write the sentences. Use the present simple passive tense.

1 She turns the lights off at midnight.
   The lights are turned off at midnight.
2 The hotel changes the towels every day.
3 He sells that newspaper every Monday.
4 They open the doors at nine o'clock.
5 The man takes your photo at the entrance.
6 Pat invites David to her party every year.
7 The supermarket sells bread.
8 People kill elephants for their tusks.
9 Steven Spielberg directs lots of good films!

2 Write the questions. Then answer the questions using the clues to help you.

1 She's invited to the party. (✓)
   Is she invited to the party? Yes, she is.
2 They're prepared for the storm. (✓)
3 Champagne is produced in France. (✓)
4 Doctors and dentists are paid a lot. (✓)
5 All credit cards are accepted. (✗)
6 Dogs are allowed in this hotel. (✗)
7 This table is made of wood. (✓)
8 Spanish is spoken here. (✗)
9 Stamps are sold in the post office. (✓)

3 Right (✓) or wrong (✗)? Correct the wrong sentences.

1 The Cup is usually won by United. ✓
2 Motorbikes are not often buyed by women.
3 Tulips are grown in Holland.
4 The computer is used by him and his family.
5 This game is playing by lots of people.
6 Their shopping delivered to their house.
7 The car is serviced every six months.
8 The washing is do every Wednesday.
9 The house is painting once a year.

4 Complete the sentences.

1 We / not allowed to / walk on grass
   We are not allowed to walk on the grass.
2 She / not let him / go to concert
3 His parents / not let him / buy new computer
4 They / allowed to / use the Internet
5 Harry / not let his brother / wear his hat
6 Her parents / not let her / have a party
7 Dana / allowed to / invite her friends
8 Jamie / not allowed to / go out tonight
9 I / not let you / borrow my guitar

Communication activity 6

For	last week	Since	ten years	For	I was 12
Since	an hour	For	yesterday	Since	ten o'clock
For	Since	Since	For	For	last January
Since	a week	For	three hours	Since	ten years
For	a long time	Since	last summer	For	a few months
Since	For	For	Since	Since	Since
For	For	Since	Since	For	an hour
Since	he was a baby	For	Since	For	a day

PHOTOCOPIABLE © Cambridge University Press 2010 Resources Unit 6

159

Grammar practice 6

1 Right (✓) or wrong (✗)? Correct the wrong sentences.

1 He has took hundreds of photos with the digital camera. ✗
   He has taken hundreds of photos with the digital camera.

2 I've eaten too much cake!

3 John and Max has been skiing in Italy.

4 Lisa has broke her leg.

5 They have flown to Paris.

6 She have bought a new dress.

7 The tree has growed enormously!

8 He has just make dinner.

9 We have been shopping all day!

2 Write the questions.

1 you ever / be / to Spain?
   Have you ever been to Spain?

2 you ever / break / your leg?

3 you ever / meet / the king?

4 you ever / climb / a mountain?

5 you ever / read / a book in English?

6 how many times / be / late for school?

7 how many times / eat / pizza?

8 you ever / be / to Hong Kong?

9 you / live / same place all your life?

3 Make the positive sentences and questions negative.

1 We have been swimming today.
   We haven't been swimming today.

2 They have just broken the window.

3 Has he been in hospital for a long time?

4 He has worked in the circus since he was five.

5 Have you heard their new song?

6 Jack has taught Maths for eight years.

7 Elisabetta has slept for 12 hours.

8 She has just woken up.

9 Have you ever eaten fish?

4 Complete the sentences with *for* or *since*.

1 It hasn't snowed here *since* December.

2 I haven't studied English _____ seven years.

3 She has played tennis _____ she was 11.

4 He hasn't visited the hospital _____ a long time.

5 The doctor hasn't seen his patients _____ six o'clock.

6 I haven't had so much fun _____ ages.

7 George has been a doctor _____ 2001.

8 Have you known Paula _____ last summer?

9 He has been in hospital _____ a week.

Communication activity 7

Student A

Work with a partner. Make questions in the past simple passive tense and ask your partner to choose one of the answers, a, b or c. Circle your partner's answers. Then check with the answers below. Add up your partner's score. How well did your partner do?

Now listen to your partner's questions and choose one of the answers. How well did you do?

Answers
1 1150 2 by a large fire (called 'The Great Fire of London') 3 1928 (by Alexander Fleming) 4 1465 5 1876 (by Alexander Graham Bell) 6 Paris 7 Germany 8 by a giant wave

General Knowledge quiz

1 When _____ the Leaning Tower of Pisa / build?
  a 1150 b 1350 c 1450

2 How _____ the city of London / destroy / 1666?
  a by a large flood b by a large fire
  c by an earthquake

3 When _____ penicillin / discover?
  a 1938 b 1828 c 1928

4 When _____ the first / music / print?
  a 1265 b 1465 c 1365

5 When _____ the telephone / invent?
  a 1901 b 1947 c 1876

6 Where _____ the first films / show / 1895?
  a Rome b Tokyo c Paris

7 Where _____ the helicopter / design / 1936?
  a Britain b Germany c France

8 How _____ over 1,500 people / kill / in Chile and Peru / 1960?
  a by a giant wave b by an earthquake
  c by a war

Student B

Work with a partner. Make questions in the past simple passive tense to ask your partner.

Listen to your partner's questions and choose one of the answers. How well did you do?

Now read out your questions and ask your partner to choose one of the answers, a, b or c. Circle your partner's answers. Then check with the answers below. Add up your partner's score. How well did your partner do?

Answers
1 1120 2 Italy 3 1710 4 Mexico 5 1592 6 about 20,000,000 7 1903 8 1889

General Knowledge quiz

1 When _____ the first playing cards / use / China?
  a 1550 b 1435 c 1120

2 Where _____ reading glasses (spectacles) / invent?
  a France b Italy c England

3 When _____ St Paul's Cathedral / complete / London?
  a 1810 b 1710 c 1610

4 From where _____ chocolate / bring / to Spain / 1520?
  a India b Mexico c Peru

5 When _____ ruined city of Pompeii / discover?
  a 1392 b 1492 c 1592

6 How many people _____ kill / by 'Spanish flu' ('La Grippe') / 1918?
  a about 3,000,000 b about 10,000,000
  c about 20,000,000

7 When _____ the first aeroplane / fly / by the Wright brothers?
  a 1913 b 1903 c 1920

8 When _____ the Eiffel Tower in Paris / complete?
  a 1889 b 1902 c 1906

PHOTOCOPIABLE © Cambridge University Press 2010 Resources Unit 7 161

Grammar practice 7

1 Complete the questions. Use the past simple passive form of the verbs.

1 Where __was__ the robber __caught__? (catch)
2 Where _____ the last Olympics _____? (hold)
3 Where _____ the money _____? (find)
4 When _____ the painting _____? (steal)
5 How many people _____ in the accident? (injure)
6 When _____ that photo _____? (take)
7 Where _____ the shipwreck _____? (discover)
8 When _____ those houses _____? (complete)
9 How many houses _____ in the storm? (damage)

2 Complete the sentences. Use the present or past simple passive form of the verbs.

1 Fiat cars __are built__ (build) in Italy.
2 The Statue of Liberty _____ (give) to the Americans by the French.
3 Gold _____ (discover) in California.
4 *Harry Potter and the Chamber of Secrets* _____ (film) in Oxford.
5 Our school exams _____ (hold) in June every year.
6 The competition winner _____ (give) a prize of €100.
7 A lot of rice _____ (grow) in China.
8 These houses _____ (build) in 1900.
9 A lot of fruit _____ (export) from Spain every day.

3 Right (✓) or wrong (✗)? Correct the wrong sentences.

1 The treasure was discover in 1957. ✗
   The treasure was discovered in 1957.
2 This book was published in 2001. ☐
3 *Hamlet* was wrote by William Shakespeare. ☐

4 The World Cup final was watched by millions of people all over the world. ☐
5 My dad's car was stealed last week. ☐
6 The ceiling in the Sistine Chapel was painted by Michelangelo. ☐
7 Nothing was destroying in the earthquake. ☐
8 *The Two Towers* film was directed by Peter Jackson. ☐
9 John F Kennedy was shooted by Lee Harvey Oswald. ☐

4 Complete the text with *a*, *an* or *the*.

Last year we went to Corsica for our summer holiday. We stayed in ⁽¹⁾ __a__ villa near the beach. When we arrived it was difficult to find ⁽²⁾ _____ villa because it was dark. We drove for two hours and finally we found it. We went inside. ⁽³⁾ _____ villa had three bedrooms, ⁽⁴⁾ _____ living room, ⁽⁵⁾ _____ kitchen, ⁽⁶⁾ _____ bathroom and ⁽⁷⁾ _____ swimming pool. It was small but very comfortable. My mum was happy too because ⁽⁸⁾ _____ kitchen was small and she decided not to cook there. We went to ⁽⁹⁾ _____ different restaurant every night! ⁽¹⁰⁾ _____ swimming pool was great because the weather was so hot.

Communication activity 8

A
A large caravan ideal for living in permanently or for holidays. It has a kitchen, no bathroom, a living room and space for three people to sleep.

1
Sam is 28 and wants to buy her first house or flat. She works in the town centre and likes to cycle to work every day. She doesn't mind what kind of house it is but she prefers small houses.

2
Vic and Sara are a young couple with a baby who is six months old. They live in a one-bedroom flat at the moment. They would like a bigger house and plan to have more children. They would like to have a big garden.

B
A flat in a new block. It has one bedroom, a bathroom, a kitchen and a living room. It has fantastic views over the city of Oxford. It is near local shops and a direct bus route into the town centre. The flat is on the 13th floor and there are no lifts.

C
This detached house is in a quiet road near the centre of town. It has five bedrooms, three bathrooms, a large garden, a big kitchen with a modern electric oven, a living room and a dining room.

3
Andy and Clare are a couple who want to escape from city life. They would like to move to the countryside and don't mind what kind of house they move to. They want to be far away from people and local facilities.

4
Mark and Antonia are a couple who enjoy travelling and would like to buy somewhere for their holidays. They have camped a lot in the past and would like to spend a year travelling around Europe.

D
A lovely semi-detached house on the outskirts of Cambridge. It has three bedrooms, a bathroom, a small kitchen, living room and dining room. It has a big garden and there are a lot of local facilities nearby, e.g. shops, schools and parks.

E
A beautiful cottage in the heart of the English countryside with views of fields and mountains from every window. It has two bedrooms, one bathroom downstairs, a large kitchen and a living room. The nearest town is ten kilometres away and there are no local shops.

5
Anna and Jon are a young couple who got married last year. They live in a one-bedroom flat but would like to buy a bigger house. They don't want a house with a lot of rooms but two or three bedrooms would be fine.

6
Maria Abbott has four children and her husband works in the town centre. They have no car. They live in a two-bedroom house at the moment and would like somewhere bigger. If possible, they would like all the children to have their own bedroom.

F
A small terraced house in a busy part of Ardenbright. The house has two bedrooms. It is in a popular street with families and young children and there are lots of local facilities nearby. There is a swimming pool, a park, a supermarket with a large car park and a library.

Grammar practice 8

1 Complete the sentences with *too much*, *too many* or *not enough*.

1 What shall we do? There *aren't enough* chairs for everyone.
2 I've got _____ homework this week.
3 There are _____ people here today.
4 It's dark! There's _____ light in here.
5 There are _____ cars in my town and _____ pollution.
6 Let's finish this tomorrow. There's _____ time today.
7 I think I've eaten _____ cakes!
8 If there's _____ food, you can take some home.
9 There are _____ stairs in our house for my grandmother.

2 Right (✓) or wrong (✗)? Correct the wrong sentences.

1 There are too much tourists in my town in the summer. ✗
   There are too many tourists in my town in the summer.
2 There's too much pollution nowadays. ☐
3 There are too much cars on the roads today. ☐
4 This website is terrible. There's not enough information on it. ☐
5 Sorry, that's too many pasta for me. ☐
6 I can't see the singer. There are too many people in front of me. ☐
7 There's too many time to do my homework. ☐
8 Yuk! There's too many sugar in this tea! ☐
9 There are not enough books for everyone. ☐

3 *Will* or *going to*? Circle the correct verbs.

1 A: Have you washed the car yet?
   B: No, sorry. I *'ll do* / *'m going to do* it now.
2 A: What are you doing this summer?
   B: We *'re going to stay* / *'ll stay* with my cousin in New York.
3 A: The phone's ringing.
   B: OK. I *'ll answer* / *'m going to answer* it.
4 Don't use that knife! You *'ll cut* / *'re going to cut* yourself.
5 A: Why do you want a bigger house?
   B: Because we *'re going to have* / *'ll have* another baby in the summer.
6 A: Your dad's car is very old, isn't it?
   B: Yes, he *'s going to buy* / *'ll buy* a new one.
7 A: Can I take your order now?
   B: Yes. I *'ll have* / *'m going to have* the soup and the chicken, please.
8 A: It's so hot in here, I can't breathe.
   B: OK. I *'ll open* / *'m going to open* a window.
9 A: What are you doing this weekend?
   B: We *'re going to see* / *'ll see* that new Brad Pitt film.

4 Match the statements with the responses.

1 It's raining now.   a It's going to rain later.
2 What are you doing tonight? b We're going to Peru.
3 It's freezing in here.   c We'll go out later.
4 We haven't got any milk.   d I'll close the window.
5 Look at those dark clouds! e It'll bite you.
6 The phone's ringing!   f OK. I'll answer it.
7 I haven't done enough work for the exam. g We'll go to the supermarket.
8 Don't go near that dog!   h I'm going to the cinema with Mike.
9 What are you doing this summer? i I'm going to fail.

Communication activity 9

What do you have to remember in Britain? Work with a partner. Read the quiz questions and circle *must*, *mustn't* or *have to* if you think the rule is true and *don't have to* if you think the rule is false. Then ask your teacher for the answers. How well did you do?

1. You *mustn't / don't have to* forget to wear a seat belt when you travel in a car.
2. You *must / don't have to* learn to play cricket before you travel there.
3. You *mustn't / don't have to* drive on the right.
4. You *mustn't / don't have to* wear a hat when you arrive at Heathrow airport.
5. You *have to / don't have to* drink tea every day between 4.00pm and 5.00pm.
6. You *must / don't have to* remember to say 'thank you' to someone when they give you something.
7. You *mustn't / don't have to* stand in a queue at a bus stop.
8. You *have to / don't have to* buy a dog if you live in a house with a garden.
9. You *mustn't / don't have to* buy stamps in a post office.
10. You *have to / don't have to* stay at school until you are 18.
11. You *have to / don't have to* be 16 before you can get married.
12. You *have to / don't have to* be 18 before you can vote.

Now write similar questions about the customs and laws in your country and ask your partner if they can work out the answers.

Answers

1. mustn't
2. don't have to
3. mustn't
4. don't have to
5. don't have to
6. must (it's considered rude if you don't say 'please' or 'thank you')
7. don't have to (but it's more polite if you do this)
8. don't have to
9. don't have to (lots of newsagents and supermarkets sell stamps nowadays)
10. don't have to (students can leave school when they are 16)
11. have to
12. have to

Grammar practice 9

1 Complete the dialogues with *some of them*, *none of them* or *all of them*.

1 A: Which shirt should I choose?
   B: It's difficult. I like ___all of them___ !
2 A: What were your exams like?
   B: OK, but _____ were very hard.
3 A: Did you check those websites I mentioned?
   B: Yes, but _____ were very helpful.
4 A: Why don't you ring your friends?
   B: I can't. _____ have gone out.
5 A: Have you tried on all of those shoes?
   B: Yes, and _____ fit me. Let's try somewhere else.
6 A: Why haven't you finished all your homework questions yet?
   B: Well, I don't understand _____ .
7 A: Have you got any CDs by Coldplay?
   B: Yes, I've got _____ !
8 A: Do you like these jackets?
   B: No. _____ are the right colour.
9 A: Do you know all the words to the song?
   B: No, I know the first two lines but _____ are very difficult to hear.

2 Circle the correct words.

1 Here's *nothing* / *something* to eat.
2 I've been *everywhere* / *nowhere* in Europe. I think I'll go to Asia on holiday next year.
3 There's *everyone* / *no one* in.
4 I've read all the Harry Potter books and I love *all of them* / *none of them*.
5 I can't believe it! *Somewhere* / *Everywhere* you go, you meet someone you know!
6 I need to do more research. I know *nothing* / *everything* about the Aztecs.
7 There's *everyone* / *someone* at the door.
8 *No one* / *Someone* ever goes to visit my grandmother at the weekends.
9 I'm sorry. There's *somewhere* / *nowhere* near here where you can buy a stamp.

3 Right (✓) or wrong (✗)? Correct the wrong sentences.

1 There's something to do round here. It's so boring.   ✗
   There's nothing to do round here. It's so boring.
2 I can remember everything the teacher said today. I'll help you with your homework. ☐
3 Do you like my watch? No one gave it to me for a birthday present. ☐
4 Would you like a cake? Some of them are chocolate and some of them are apple. ☐
5 There are no rooms in the local hotels this weekend. Nowhere is full. ☐
6 I want to speak to no one in the sports department, please. ☐
7 Where is that letter? I've looked everywhere for it. ☐
8 I think no one should see the new Johnny Depp film. It's brilliant! ☐
9 I was so upset. Someone remembered my birthday this year. ☐

4 Complete the sentences with *must*, *mustn't* or *don't have to*.

1 If you're ill, you ___must___ see a doctor.
2 It's my sister's birthday this week. I _____ forget to buy her a present.
3 I _____ get up early during the holidays. I can stay in bed all day!
4 Sssh! You _____ be quiet.
5 We're having a party on Saturday. We _____ go to the supermarket.
6 You can go to the party but you _____ be home by 10.30pm.
7 Great! We _____ do any homework this weekend.
8 In the UK, children _____ start school until they are five.
9 You _____ talk during exams.

UNIT 9
RESOURCES

166   PHOTOCOPIABLE   © Cambridge University Press 2010   Resources Unit 9

Communication activity 10

Student A

Read texts 1 and 2. In your notebooks, complete the sentences with the present perfect simple or the present perfect continuous form of the verbs in brackets. Read your completed texts to student B who will check your answers. Then listen to student B and use texts 3 and 4 to check their answers.

1 He ª(be) a photographer and a soldier and he ᵇ(work) in department stores in Milan. He ᶜ(design) clothes since the 1970s. His famous designer jeans ᵈ(sell) well in countries all over the world. Who is he?

2 He ᵉ(sing) since he was five years old when he joined the Modena opera chorus. He ᶠ(be) a Maths teacher. He has a great voice and he ᵍ(win) a lot of prizes for his singing and ʰ(travel) all over the world. Who is he?

3 She **has been singing, dancing and acting** since the late 1970s. She **has lived** in the USA and Great Britain. She **has had** a famous first husband. She **has been married** to her second husband, a British film director famous for films like *Lock, Stock and Two Smoking Barrels*, since 2000. Who is she?
(Madonna)

4 She **has been writing** novels since 1997 and she **has written** famous books for children about a boy wizard and his friends. Her books **have sold** in countries all over the world. She **has worked** in Portugal and England and now lives in Scotland. She has two children. Who is she?
(J.K. Rowling)

Student B

Read texts 1 and 2. In your notebooks, complete the sentences with the present perfect simple or the present perfect continuous form of the verbs in brackets. Then listen to student A's answers and use texts 3 and 4 to check their answers. Now read your completed texts 1 and 2 to student A and they will check your answers.

1 She ª(sing, dance, act) since the late 1970s. She ᵇ(live) in the USA and Great Britain. She ᶜ(have) a famous first husband. She ᵈ(be marry) to her second husband, a British film director famous for films like *Lock, Stock and Two Smoking Barrels*, since 2000. Who is she?

2 She ᵉ(write) novels since 1997 and she ᶠ(write) famous books for children about a boy wizard and his friends. Her books ᵍ(sell) in countries all over the world. She ʰ(work) in Portugal and England and now lives in Scotland. She has two children. Who is she?

3 He **has been** a photographer and a soldier and he **has worked** in department stores in Milan. He **has been designing** clothes since the 1970s. His famous designer jeans **have sold** well in countries all over the world. Who is he? *(Giorgio Armani)*

4 He **has been singing** since he was five years old when he joined the Modena opera chorus. He **has been** a Maths teacher. He has a great voice and he **has won** a lot of prizes for his singing and **has travelled** all over the world. Who is he?
(Luciano Pavarotti)

PHOTOCOPIABLE   © Cambridge University Press 2010   **Resources Unit 10**

Grammar practice 10

1 Complete the sentences. Use the present perfect continuous form of the verbs.

1 I _'ve been sitting_ (sit) here for three hours!
2 We .... (not cook) all morning. We .... (only cook) for an hour.
3 How long .... (you/wait) to see the doctor?
4 She .... (not learn) French for very long.
5 They .... (travel) for six months.
6 How long .... (they/come) to Madrid on holiday?
7 My sister .... (talk) on the phone for hours!
8 She must be tired. She .... (swim) all morning.
9 He .... (not work) in Zurich for very long.

2 Present perfect continuous or present perfect simple? Complete the sentences with the correct form of the verbs.

1 I _'ve been doing_ (do) my homework for three hours.
2 A: .... (you/post) the letter? B: Yes, I have.
3 Hurry up! They .... (wait) for us since six o'clock.
4 .... (you/hear) Madonna's new single yet?
5 I .... (search) the Internet all morning.
6 We .... (watch) all the videos we have. What can we do now?
7 How long .... (your brother/ tidy) his bedroom?
8 .... (you/ever see) a UFO?
9 She .... (practise) that piece for three hours and she still can't play it!

3 Right (✓) or wrong (✗)? Correct the wrong sentences.

1 I've read a book all morning.   ✗
   I've been reading a book all morning.

2 Mum! Jack has fallen out of the tree. ☐
3 My parents have been being married for 30 years. ☐
4 What have you been doing all morning? ☐
5 You've been breaking your leg three times. ☐
6 They've just arrived. Shall we eat? ☐
7 I've been having my new computer for three months. ☐
8 Your brother's been watching that DVD twice already. ☐
9 My dad's lost his job. ☐

4 Present perfect continuous or present perfect simple? Circle the correct word.

1 I've *worked* / (*been working*) all morning and I still haven't finished.
2 We've *known* / *been knowing* each other for two years.
3 What have you *done* / *been doing*? I've *talked* / *been talking* on my mobile all morning.
4 Has she *found* / *been finding* a new flat yet?
5 We've *listened* / *been listening* to music all morning. Let's do something else now.
6 I've *visited* / *been visiting* my grandmother twice this week.
7 Have you *finished* / *been finishing* that book I gave you for your birthday?
8 How long have they *had* / *been having* their new house?
9 I've *studied* / *been studying* all night and I still don't know anything!

UNIT 10 RESOURCES

168   PHOTOCOPIABLE   © Cambridge University Press 2010   Resources Unit 10

Communication activity 11

Student A

Give student B clues to help them complete their missing words. Then listen to student B and complete your missing words.

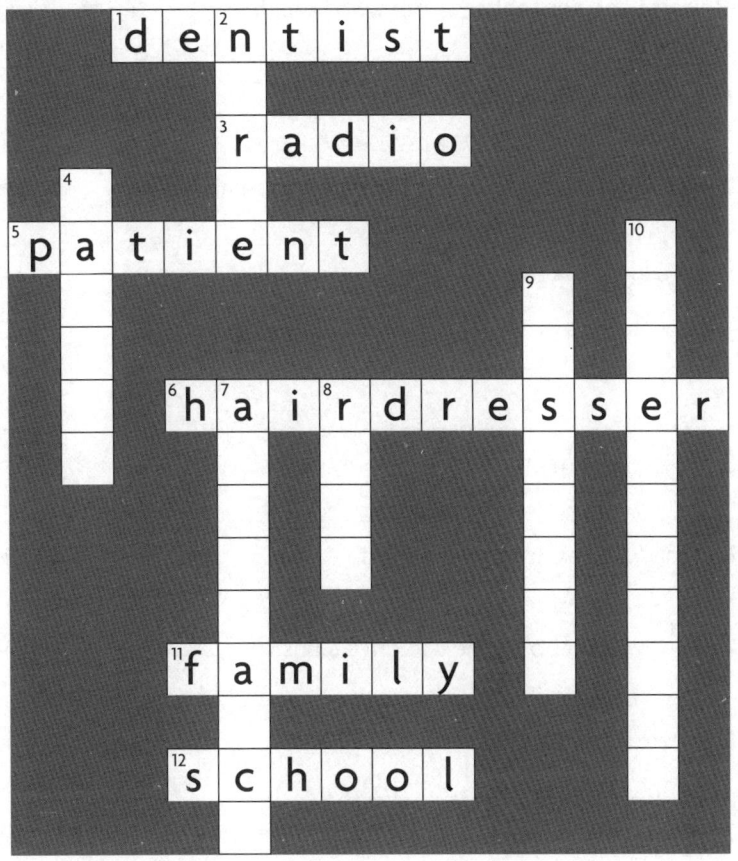

Student B

Give student A clues to help them complete their missing words. Then listen to student A and complete your missing words.

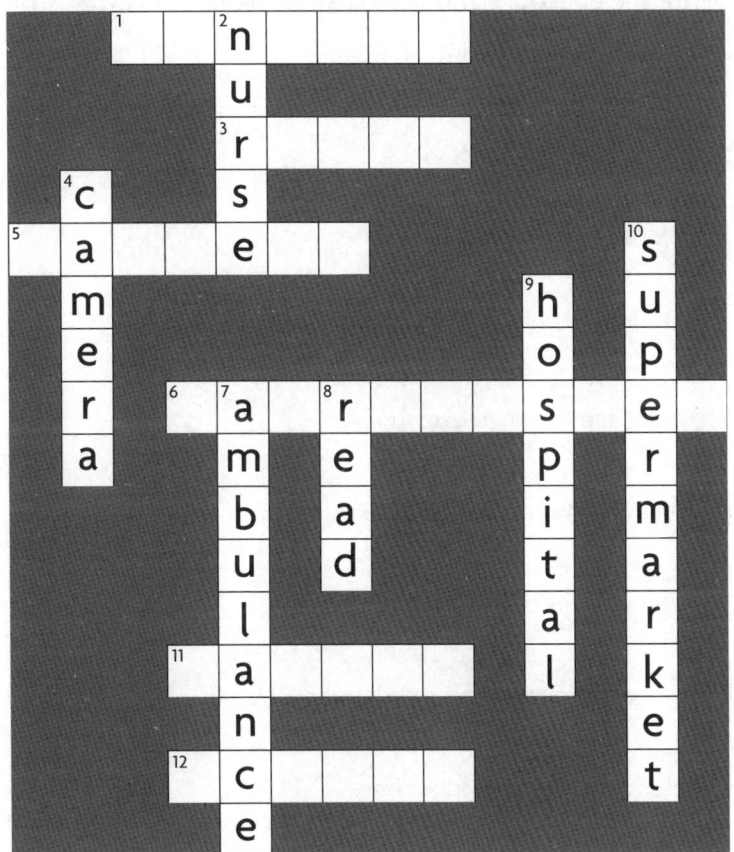

Grammar practice 11

1 Rewrite the sentences using *who, which* or *where*.

1 I know a man. He can run very fast.
   I know a man who can run very fast.
2 I've got a pair of trousers. They are too small.
3 The hotel we stayed at had a big gym.
4 Pippa has a friend. She is a singer.
5 Please give me the pen. It's on my desk.
6 I read a book. It was very good.
7 I know somebody. She can drive a bus.
8 There's the man! He stole €10,000.
9 The city Jane lives in is called Cambridge.

2 Write the questions and then answer them.

1 Peter used to read a lot.
   Did Peter use to read a lot? Yes, he did.
2 Peter didn't use to have long hair.
3 Peter used to want to be a writer.
4 Peter didn't use to eat very much.
5 Peter used to talk to everybody.
6 Peter used to play with his friends.
7 Peter didn't use to like travelling by car.
8 Peter used to stay at his grandmother's house.
9 Peter didn't use to drink coffee.

3 Right (✓) or wrong (✗)? Correct the wrong sentences.

1 I use to love skiing.   ✗
   I used to love skiing.
2 Did you used to play football?
3 She always used to wear black clothes.
4 We used to lived in Liverpool.
5 They didn't used to like going to the gym.
6 Did she use to have lots of friends?
7 Did you use to watched Star Wars?
8 My sister use to smoke.
9 Danny and Eddie didn't used to sing.

4 Complete the sentences. Use *use to* or *didn't use to*.

1 People / not live so long
   People didn't use to live so long.
2 Medicine / not be as good
3 She / get stomach ache every weekend
4 Vinny / get a cold every winter
5 My parents / not go shopping very often
6 People / not use computers
7 He / not work so hard
8 Karen's eyes / hurt when reading
9 The doctor / not live there

Communication activity 12

Student A

Complete this questionnaire for your partner. Write the question and the answer choices for each situation. Can you predict your partner's answers?

Example: If you forgot to do your homework, would you copy a friend's homework, or would you tell the teacher the truth?

Then ask your partner your questions and read the answer choices. Circle the answers your partner chooses. Were your predictions correct? Add up the score at the end and read the analysis below to your partner.

1 If / you / forget / to do / your homework:
   A: you / copy / a friend's homework?
   B: you / tell / the teacher the truth?

2 If / you / borrow / your friend's / camera / and it / break:
   A: you / buy / a new camera without saying anything?
   B: you / tell him or her / immediately?

3 If / you / see / your sister's boyfriend / with another girl:
   A: you / tell / your sister?
   B: you / say / nothing?

4 If / you / find / a wallet with money / in the street:
   A: you / keep / the money?
   B: you / hand / it / to the police?

5 If / you / research / project online:
   A: you / tell / your teacher / use all your own ideas?
   B: you / tell / your teacher?

6 If / someone / you / not like very much / ask / you / on a date:
   A: you / lie and say / you / busy?
   B: you / laugh and say / 'No way!'?

Student B: What do your answers mean?
Mostly As: You don't mind being a little bit dishonest if you think it will help you not to get into trouble.
Mostly Bs: You don't always tell the truth, but you try to, most of the time. If you think you are going to cause someone unhappiness, you sometimes lie. You try to be honest – even if it means you will get into trouble sometimes.

Student B

Complete this questionnaire for your partner. Write the question and the answer choices for each situation. Can you predict your partner's answers?

Example: If you missed the last bus or train home in the afternoon, would you phone your parents, or would you walk home alone?

Then ask your partner your questions and read the answer choices. Circle the answers your partner chooses. Were your predictions correct? Add up the score at the end and read the analysis below to your partner.

1 If / you / miss / the last bus or train home in the afternoon:
   A: you / phone / your parents?
   B: you / walk / home / alone?

2 If / you / not wake up / in time for school / tomorrow:
   A: you / stay / at home all day?
   B: you / go / to school / late?

3 If / you see / someone / cheating / in an exam:
   A: you / tell / them / you know / what happened / after the exam?
   B: tell / the teacher / immediately?

4 If / someone / ask you to try a dangerous sport:
   A: you / say / 'Not without training!'
   B: you / feel excited and say / 'Let's go!'?

5 If / you / see / a dog / fall / into a lake:
   A: you / not be worried / because / dogs / can / swim?
   B: you / try to rescue / the dog?

6 If / someone / in a chatroom / ask / for your phone number:
   A: stop / using the chatroom / warn your friends to be careful?
   A: you / give it / immediately?

Student A: What do your answers mean?
Mostly As: You don't take unnecessary risks. You won't do something if you think it will hurt someone.
Mostly Bs: You are a risk-taker. You like adventure and aren't afraid of what might happen. However, sometimes you should be more careful not to take risks that may put you in dangerous situations.

Grammar practice 12

1 Complete the sentences. Use the verbs in the correct form to make the second conditional.

1 If / I knew / good doctor / I go to him
   If I knew a good doctor, I would go to him.

2 I / play tennis every day / if / I / could

3 If / I / go to bed early / I / not be so tired

4 You / take good photos / if / you / have a good camera

5 I / phone you / if / I / have a mobile phone

6 Lucy / let you drive / if / you / ask her

7 If / I / be rich / I / go on holiday now!

8 I / pass my exams / if / I / study

9 He / see you / if / you / turn the light on

2 Write the questions.

1 They would write a book, if they had time.
   Would they write a book if they had time?

2 If Mary could swim, she'd go every day.

3 If she knew the secret, she'd tell you.

4 I wouldn't tell him if I were you.

5 If you came tomorrow, I'd have more time.

6 I'd die if she didn't love me!

7 If I didn't have so much homework, I'd go.

8 He wouldn't be cold if he had a jacket.

9 If Sam could, he'd fix the computer.

3 Right (✓) or wrong (✗)? Correct the wrong sentences.

1 If he drank enough water, he isn't be thirsty. ✗
   If he drank enough water, he wouldn't be thirsty.

2 If he used the computer, he'd finish sooner. ☐

3 If he shouted, she won't know he was there. ☐

4 Will you buy them if they had your size? ☐

5 If she couldn't sing, she wouldn't be so rich. ☐

6 Would you be pleased if Ireland won? ☐

7 He wouldn't have a party if it isn't Saturday. ☐

8 If you save your work, you wouldn't lose it. ☐

9 Would you danced if they weren't there? ☐

4 Complete the sentences. Use the verbs in the correct form to make the second conditional.

1 If I ___had___ some bread, I ___would make___ a sandwich. (have/make)

2 If Tom _____ to live in America, he _____ his accent. (go/change)

3 He _____ if he _____ a dishwasher. (not wash up/have)

4 _____ they _____ tonight if it _____? (travel/rain)

5 Tanya _____ an aspirin if she _____ a headache. (take/have)

6 _____ Gregory _____ if he _____ the lottery? (work/win)

7 The dog _____ his bone if he _____ it all the time. (eat/not lose)

8 If John _____ too much, he _____ fat. (eat/be)

9 If you _____ the book, you _____ the answers. (read/know)

Communication activity 13

1 When I arrived at the café,

2 When she got to the airport, she realised

3 When he got home, he realised

4 When she arrived at school, she realised

5 When we got home,

6 John didn't recognise her because

7 They arrived late at the cinema and

8 When I switched on the TV,

PHOTOCOPIABLE   © Cambridge University Press 2010   Resources Unit 13

173

Grammar practice 13

1 Complete the sentences. Use the past perfect form of the verbs.

1. The army __had fought__ (fight) and won.
2. The photographer _____ (take) enough photos, so he left the wedding.
3. The farmer _____ (feed) the sheep by the time the sun went down.
4. The footballer _____ (score) a goal before he broke his leg.
5. The explorer _____ (reach) the North Pole by the time his supplies ran out.
6. The driver _____ (stop) at the red light when he answered his mobile phone.
7. The journalist _____ (write) an article before her computer crashed.
8. The cyclist _____ (win) the tour and he was exhausted, but happy.
9. The professor _____ (teach) her students all she knew.

2 Write the questions.

1. She'd met him before.
   Had she met him before?
2. Katie had never believed in aliens, until she saw one.
   _____
3. She had never travelled to India before.
   _____
4. Jack had taken photos before they arrived.
   _____
5. Joe had walked for ten kilometres.
   _____
6. When Sue arrived, Anna had already left.
   _____
7. He had died before the doctor arrived.
   _____
8. When I arrived, the train still hadn't left.
   _____
9. She hadn't finished her homework by 11pm.
   _____

3 Complete the sentences. Use the past simple or past perfect form of the verbs.

1. By the time we __got__ to the party, it __had finished__ . (get/finish)
2. They _____ a lot of Chinese before they _____ to live in China. (learn/go)
3. Sophie _____ the cinema when she _____ younger. (not enjoy/be)
4. The farmer _____ the eggs before it _____ dark. (collect/get)
5. By the time the footballer _____ the goal, the other team _____ ! (reach/score)
6. By the time he _____ six, he _____ all of the books in the series. (be/read)
7. When I _____ home, they _____ the dinner. (get/make)
8. He _____ to do it on time, but he _____ by Tuesday! (promise/not finish)
9. David _____ the meeting as he _____ it in his diary. (forget/not write)

4 Right (✓) or wrong (✗)? Correct the wrong sentences.

1. Had John invited Paul to his party before he knew the truth? ✓
2. The cat had grown while they are away. ☐
   _____
3. Susie had spent hours looking for her glasses when he said they were on her head! ☐
   _____
4. That scientist made the important discovery before anyone else had thought it possible. ☐
   _____
5. Had Charles go to America before? ☐
   _____
6. Sarah hadn't been in London all day. ☐
   _____
7. Mike had been at work since six o'clock in the morning. ☐
   _____
8. Had she already left when you will phone? ☐
   _____
9. Derek has taken him home when I called. ☐
   _____

UNIT 13 — RESOURCES

Communication activity 14

FINISH

15 If he'd studied hotel management, …

14 If we'd booked our holiday earlier, …

13 If I hadn't lost my wallet, …

9 If the weather had been sunny last weekend, …

10 If the team had played better, …

11 If the train had arrived on time, …

12 If he'd had a better education, …

8 They would have passed their exams…

7 If the climber had had better equipment, …

6 If I'd known it was your birthday, …

5 He wouldn't have crashed his car if…

4 If he hadn't spent all his money, …

3 If she'd done her homework, …

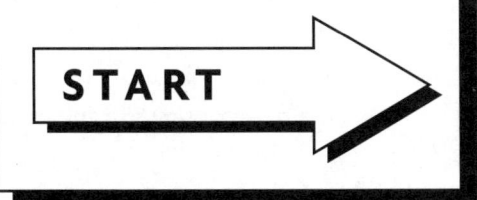

1 If they'd had more information, …

2 If they'd seen the ladder, …

Grammar practice 14

1 Put the direct speech into reported speech.

1 'I'm going on holiday,' said John.
   John said that he was going on holiday.

2 'It's my birthday,' Mary told us.

3 'We have to go to our English class,' said David.

4 'You should drink lots of water,' said Tom.

5 'You can go when you've finished,' Dad said.

6 'A black cat crossed my path today,' said Harry.

7 'You're always so lucky,' complained my sister.

8 'I made her a star,' the director told them.

2 Write the direct questions in reported speech.

1 'What is the weather like?' she asked.
   She asked me what the weather was like.

2 'Are we going to the cinema?' she asked him.

3 'What time are we leaving?' asked Tom.

4 'When did you go to Africa?' he asked me.

5 'When do they go to bed?' Helen asked her.

6 'What's for dinner, Dad?' the children asked.

7 'Are you always so lucky?' he asked her.

8 'Where did he take you on your first date?' Ana asked her.

9 'Where have you been?' she asked me.

3 Right (✓) or wrong (✗)? Correct the wrong sentences.

1 If we had gone to the zoo, we would have seen the elephants. ✓

2 If Clive had played, they would have won. ☐

3 If we have gone by car, we would have arrived earlier. ☐

4 If we had borrow the money, we would have bought the house. ☐

5 She wouldn't have got to sleep if the music had been loud. ☐

6 He wouldn't pass if he hadn't studied. ☐

7 The clothes wouldn't have been clean if he hadn't used the washing machine. ☐

8 We wouldn't gone if he had been ill. ☐

9 If he has felt cold, he would have worn a jumper. ☐

4 What would have happened if things had been different? Write the sentences.

1 James ate too much food so he was sick.
   If James hadn't eaten too much food, he wouldn't have been sick.

2 Sheila lost her keys so she couldn't get in.

3 Paul saw a shooting star so he made a wish.

4 Billy didn't study so he failed the exam.

5 Sam went out and his camera was stolen.

6 She wasn't in the play so she didn't get a prize.

7 He broke a mirror so he had seven years' bad luck.

8 The director saw him and made him a star.

9 John was late and there was no dinner left.